This is the book for our times! Alex's personal experience as a teacher, mother, and astrologer is woven together beautifully. I was touched by her caring attitude toward the delicacy of the role of teacher, and educator – and parent! A much needed book in an increasingly complicated world for young people coming of age. All teachers (and parents and students) will learn a lot from reading *Growing Pains*.

Erin Sullivan, author USA

As a teacher, I use astrology, at times, to help me understand at-risk students. Trenoweth's book *Growing Pains* is an extremely helpful resource in explaining how planetary birth (natal) Saturn and Jupiter placements help determine how a child learns and relates to others in the classroom. Whether you interact with young people in personal or professional contexts, I think you'll find her insights to be both fascinating and useful. Highly recommended.

Lori Hoyt, practising teacher in the USA

Every parent wants the best for their child, especially when it comes to their education. *Growing Pains* is an indispensable resource for understanding your child's unique template for learning. This book offers an objective perspective, along with insightful guidance and practical tips to help you naviagate your child's journey through school.

Cassandra Tyndall, astrologer and mother, Australia

Alex Trenoweth does that rare thing few astrologers find a way to do: take real astrology out into the world of laypeople and show them how to benefit from its insights. This book can help adolescents themselves, teachers and parents understand one of the most important and powerful pairs of cycles in astrology and discover the wealth they have to offer. Alex draws on her experience as a teacher and astrologer to show how the cycles can be used to grasp and get the best of critical developmental cycles and presents them in a way that brings out the richness and depth of astrology in her inimitable style. I am so pleased this book is out in a new edition: unlike the latest theory on adolescent development, its value to parents and students will never go out of style.

Rod Suskin, astrologer, South Africa

How I wish that this wonderful book had been around 36 years ago when I became step-mother to a 13 year old! Not only would I have learnt so, so much from this excellent work by an experienced, thoughtful, caring teacher and very fine astrologer, but I am confident that I would have bought copies for his friend's parents and often exasperated teachers. As it is, I have already gifted this to local teachers and plan to buy a copy for another mother today. This work is a valuable addition to any astrological library but to parents and teachers it should be seen as one of the finest works on understanding the adolescent and working through those *Growing Pains*.

Christeen Skinner, Cityscopes London Ltd. UK

As someone who taught high school for thirty years, but who knows little about astrology, I can say I found many things that Alex Trenoweth presented had classroom implications and applications. Alex uses astrology in the classroom for a better understanding of individual students as well as transits that correlate to age and grade-level periods of intellectual and emotional development. Her ideas that relate to the Jupiter and Saturn transits can have practical applications in curriculum development.

Some of what she conveys has already been learned by practical experience by many teachers. For example, if anybody asked me what are the most difficult ages to teach, I'd say 14 or 15. Astrologically, this would be the period of their Saturn opposition wherein a sense of independence is combined with a "healthy" opposition to authority. We teachers would blame it on puberty, which is also true, but also fail to see it as a rite of passage or coming of age in the educational sense.

Perhaps her most practical tip for a teacher might be to simply make a class list of students by their birth dates (oldest to youngest). In the high school classroom, I've noticed the difference between the older and younger students in the class both in behavior and ability. In the lower grades, the difference is even more pronounced.

Finally, when you get down to it, education is our nation's number one problem. If we are to have citizens who are both productive and responsible more resources are needed to provide students and educators with more options and not more standardized testing. They're the ones that will be left to solve problems left by previous generations.

Alan Bronstein, teacher, USA

Sensitive, kind and caring teacher and author of *Growing Pains*, Alex Trenoweth has identified herself with troubled adolescents. Her in-depth study of astrology, with psychological input, coupled with an intense urge to search for solutions to help such adolescents, have been brought together in this marvelous book.

Alex has paved a mid-path between a highly technical approach and a total ignorance about the synchronicity between cosmic planetary motions.

Using the planets of Jupiter and Saturn, she demonstrates the waxing and waning of periods of growth and expansion with periods of trials and tribulations.

Studying the cosmic cycles of these two major planets would be extremely rewarding for parents, teachers and guides as well as for the adolescents as themselves. It is a must-read for anyone who works with children—or for adults who still have the child within.

Shankar Nash Kapoor, Justice (retired) Delhi High Court, India

If every parent and every teacher read this book it would be a better world. Kids have suffered educationally, not because teachers don't care, but because a lack of understanding of their inbuilt dissimilarities and associated specific needs is not conducive to the flowering of their potential. This book, written by a teacher and astrologer, will put this right. Not only does it offer insightful and humorous descriptions of character, and methods of getting the best out of that character, it also offers descriptions of famous personalities that come with handsome portrait drawings, and these descriptions allow you to see how the character traits you learn about manifest in the real world. I love this book.

Chrissy Philp, UK

Astrology is an invaluable tool to understand individual and whole year groups of school pupils. Alex Trenoweth's *Growing Pains* draws on her pioneering work in the classroom. It is recommended reading for teachers, parents and, indeed anyone who wishes go beyond projecting their own expectations, and instead relate to children and adolescents as they are.

Roy Gillett B.Ed [Hons Ldn], UK

Concerned parents are going to find this book helpful, as regards guiding and encouraging their teenage children, and what kind of encouragement is likely to prove effective. The different zodiac signs lend 'colour' to the working of these two spheres. Its author Ms Trenoweth is a mother, schoolteacher and professional astrologer so is able to explain these things out of real experience. There are cheerful books giving tips about bringing up teenagers, however this one gives that much-needed help in terms of the different zodiac signs of Jupiter and Saturn. Plus, modern readers will not fail to appreciate use of a celeb bio-pic for each one of these, to help build up the picture.

For any teacher who believes character-building is more important than exam results, this has to be an important book. By using celebs in this way, Trenoweth focuses on the concept of success, to show how people have used their God-given talents to make something of their lives. In today's schools, encouraging pupils is far from easy and the twelvefold pattern here described indicates how this should be done. As a head-of-year in a modern Academy she has put these findings into practice, in a way that made sense to her schoolteacher colleagues.

Astrological Journal of Great Britain

Growing Pains is a really inspired and useful way of using the Jupiter and Saturn cycles to help kids, parent and teachers through the stormy waters of adolescence.

Anne Whitaker, UK

Alex Trenoweth delights us by creating a bridge between astrology and education that informs the readers of the cycles of Jupiter and Saturn in the growing process of adolescents on their way to adulthood. Undoubtedly, this book is a unique combination of Alex's experience as teacher and astrologer. A must-read!

Ana Andrade, Peru

Alex has highlighted this area of astrology to the great benefit of parents who care to listen. What she has to say is perceptive and wise. Her pupils would have been nurtured so well by her understanding of 'where they were coming from'. I commend you to Alex, her books, and what she has to say.

Hedley Spargo, teacher, UK

Teenagers!!!
Part child, part adult, sometimes full monster!!! At least they appear so. The sad truth is they appear that way, simply because we adults have forgotten what our experiences of the world were when we were that age; or we simply have no understanding of how their minds work. That will all change when you read this wonderful book by Alex Trenoweth. Her experience as both a high school teacher and an astrologer has made not only an understanding of these years easily available, but she offers wonderful insights as to how to make your relationship with your teenager more meaningful. If you want to help your teen make the most of these changes s/he is experiencing, then this book is a must, whether you are a teacher or a parent.

Chris Turner, Australia

GROWING

PAINS

Astrology in Adolescence

Alex Trenoweth

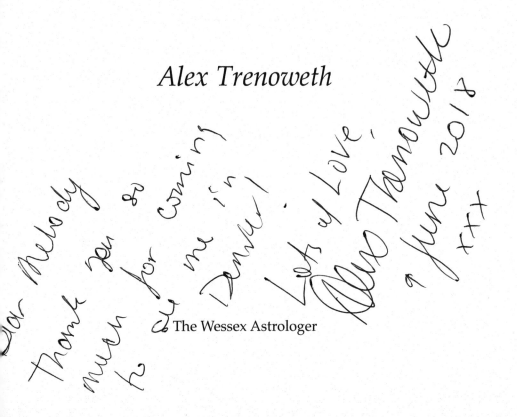

The Wessex Astrologer

Dear Melody
Thank you so
much for coming
to see me in
Denver!
Lots of Love,
Alex Trenoweth
9 June 2018
xxx

Published in 2017 by
The Wessex Astrologer Ltd
4A Woodside Road
Bournemouth
BH5 2AZ
www.wessexastrologer.com

Previously published by My Spirit Books 2013
9781908810243 Paperback
9781908810250 Kindle
9781908810267 Ebook

Cover Design by Jonathan Taylor

A catalogue record for this book is available at The British Library

ISBN 9781910531228

Dedication

For my family.

For my teachers and pupils.

For Rachel Ward, the best boss in the world.

For Nick, my hero.

Contents

Foreword

"Give me the child and I will give you the man", as the well-known Jesuit motto has it. Although we may not agree with the original intent of the phrase, which was indoctrination, it still contains a truth everyone recognises: that what we learn, and how we learn, when young will shape our behaviour in later life.

Astrologers, of course, go even further back than the child, preferring to work from the moment of birth. But in recent years astrology has perhaps concentrated too much on that moment, projecting it forward onto the adult to delineate the character of the individual without stopping to look at what happens in between, during childhood and adolescence.

This book is a welcome step towards rectifying that error, by recognising that the astrology of the individual is not just the snapshot of a moment but an ongoing process, created by the unfolding cycles of the planets. It focuses on those moments when the cycles of the outer planets first make themselves felt, during the teenage years.

There is an old joke among both teachers and parents that whoever decided that children should sit public examinations at the same time as going through puberty was a genuine sadist, but the astrology of adolescence can add an extra layer to that by superimposing the cycles of Jupiter and Saturn, one to boost growth and the other to restrict it.

A guide to these troublesome years using the insightful vocabulary of astrology would be hugely useful for everyone, but to my knowledge has never been available — until now. Here, at last, is the answer to every parent's questions about how their child actually thinks — and every teacher's conviction that some year groups really are horrible, while others are sweet and eager to learn. It's to do with the signs that Jupiter and Saturn were in. Best of all, with a list of Jupiter-Saturn conjunctions in the appendix, it becomes easy to see how those cycles continue for the rest of our lives. Understanding the child, therefore, lets us understand the adult, too.

Bernard Eccles,
Past President of the Astrological Lodge of London

Introduction

As a teacher of adolescents, I wanted to use my skills and knowledge as an astrologer to enhance my career and yet at the same time be accessible to my colleagues as well as the parents of my pupils. I also wanted to challenge my history pupils to embrace the cyclic patterns of events by using the thematic approach of astrology. Although my astrology colleagues help people from all walks of life and almost all ages, they tend to avoid adolescents, who need the most guidance. And so this book is for adolescents, the people who love and care for them and anyone who is curious about how to get the most out of life. I've used celebrity examples, not because I think celebrity is a measure of success but because beneath every Hollywood fairytale, there is a person who has been 'lucky and has worked hard enough to achieve success. This book can help you to work with your natural talents and time your own cycles of growth and development for satisfaction and accomplishment.

Astrologically, Jupiter and Saturn are the planets associated with opportunity and discipline. The placement of Jupiter in the birth chart indicates where and how we are confident and, therefore, where we are likely to take risks. By contrast, the placement of Saturn indicates where and how we fear making mistakes. In the human life cycle, Jupiter is activated first followed by Saturn. The effect is that new opportunities introduced into our lives are followed by a period of honing and developing the skills we have learned.

Usually your Jupiter and Saturn sign will be different to your Sun sign and will take a little time and effort to locate in charts. This is because their cycles around the earth (from our point of view) take far longer than that of the Sun. To find where Jupiter and Saturn are in your chart, it is easiest to start with the year of your birth, referring to the tables at the back of the book, and at the beginning of each chapter.

For example, if you were born in 1990, you would find that Jupiter was in the sign of Cancer from January to August 1990 and in Leo from August 1990 to September 1991. If you then add your date of birth, say for example 2 April, 1990, you would then know Jupiter was in the sign of Cancer at your birth. It works in exactly the same way for finding the sign of Saturn. Once you have worked out the signs of Jupiter and Saturn, it is important to remember that these planets don't stop moving. They continue to revolve and make connections known as transits.

Connections between planets are described as aspects. The conjunction aspect is when planets are close together in the zodiac. The opposition aspect is when planets are in opposite signs in the zodiac. A square is when they are at 90° angles to each other and a trine is when they are at 120° angles to each other.

The planets don't always move in a forward motion from our point of view. Sometimes they appear to move backwards in a motion known as retrograde.

Jupiter and Saturn working together

Imagine laying brick or stone work. We all know bricks and stones are useful for building anything from walls to castles. But there is a skill to laying these materials and it is not as easy as throwing a bit of cement or mortar around and slamming them together. Bricklayers/stonemasons use tools such as levellers to ensure the bricks are even, and they understand the quality of the materials they are using. They know that certain types of bricks and/or mortar are not suitable for a very wet climate whilst others wouldn't suit a very hot one.

In the laying of bricks metaphor, Jupiter represents the bricks and stones and Saturn represents the mortar. Jupiter is used to expand; Saturn is used to hold the bricks together. In the learning process, if the quality of the bricks (Jupiter) is understood, then the suitability of the mortar (Saturn) can be adjusted to ensure a long-lasting finished product. Admire the beauty of cathedrals which have stood for hundreds of years.

Like brickwork, learning is a step by step process. The first time we do anything seldom results in a perfect product. Repeated practice and an understanding of consequences are the keys to improving. A child's first Jupiter opposition at the age of six and the return at about the age of twelve, as well as the first Saturn square at seven and the opposition at about the age of fourteen and a half, are crucial stages of learning. In learning, as in brickwork, the foundation is often the key to ensuring how well a structure will hold up. As parents and teachers, we can help children to understand how they learn. We can help with the process of learning if we understand the material with which we are working. We can look on our children's work and can see if their foundations are wobbly. We can correct and encourage without dictating. In fact, we all have a natural way of doing this via our own Jupiter and Saturn. We, as mature and experienced adults, are continuing to build our fortresses and cathedrals.

The global castle

Although this book is written to be used as a guide to help individuals tap into their learning processes, it is worth bearing in mind that Jupiter and Saturn play a collective role for the whole world. From the point of view of ancient celestial observers, the orbits of Jupiter and Saturn took the most time to complete a cycle (12 and 30 years respectively). Their orbits provided a method of measuring time over a number of years rather than days (the orbit of the sun) or months (the orbit of the moon). Approximately every twenty years, Jupiter and Saturn meet in the sky in an alignment that eventually became known as a Great Conjunction (when these planets are near to the same degree in the same sign).

Great Conjunctions were noted for heralding important events or the birth of important people. For example, it has been theorised that the Star of Bethlehem was a great conjunction.

Although visually less spectacular than solar or lunar eclipses, Great Conjunctions caught the imagination of later astronomers such as Tycho Brahe and Johannes Kepler, who indicated such conjunctions were auspicious. Galileo, who, building on the work of Brahe and Kepler, eventually helped to convince a disbelieving world that the earth revolved around the Sun, was born during a Great Conjunction. Shakespeare, whose work is littered with astrological references, was also born during a Great Conjunction.

The Great Conjunction, fascinating in itself, is a part of measuring even longer periods of time. Early observers of this cycle noted that successive Great Conjunctions took place about 120° later in the zodiac in a sign of the same element.* From any given starting point, every third great conjunction would occur about 9° ahead of its starting point. This time frame of 60 years was known as a trigon. The period of time it takes for Great Conjunctions entering a new element to entering the next element is a period of about 200 years.

After about 800–960 years, Great Conjunctions begin a new cycle and return to similar degrees. Appendix 2 shows a full cycle of Great Conjunctions from the years 1007–2199. Continued research on this cycle will be addressed in future publications.

Recently, the shift changed from conjunctions occurring in earth signs to those occurring in air signs. In 1981, for the first time in centuries, the conjunction took place in Libra, edging the world into a whole new element (although in May 2000 a single conjunction took place in the earth sign Taurus). The Jupiter/Saturn conjunction in Libra coincided with our global focus on the lifestyles of the rich and famous as depicted in TV shows such as *Dallas* or *Dynasty*. Furthermore, the focus was on how the rich played, not on how hard they worked or the price they paid to get there. When the next Jupiter/Saturn conjunction occurred once again in earth signs in 2000 we, as a collective, were able to giggle at the eighties and see it for what it was — a vain attempt to portray life as we might like to think it could be if we only had the right friends and moved in the right social circles. The next Jupiter/Saturn conjunction will occur in the sign of Aquarius in 2020, perhaps launching our understanding of technology into the stratosphere. In schools, technology is changing so quickly that teachers are beginning to acknowledge they are training pupils for jobs that don't even exist yet.

Our current educational system is based on factory-model schools from the 19th century, which are no longer appropriate for the needs of today's students. Astrology can be enormously beneficial in streamlining resources - keeping within budgetary constraints - so that the education we offer our children is more focused on their individual needs rather than our guesswork or what the latest thinking is. It also can help parents and teachers become more effective authority figures. The following pages give an indication of how this might be achieved.

---

* Each sign of the zodiac is associated with an element:
Fire: Aries, Leo and Sagittarius   Air: Gemini, Libra and Aquarius
Earth: Taurus, Virgo and Capricorn   Water: Cancer, Scorpio and Pisces

JUPITER

In the birth chart, the sign Jupiter occupies remains fixed, but from our point of view Jupiter continues to move through the zodiac and will continue on his journey even after a person has passed on to the next life.

Jupiter takes just over eleven years to complete one journey through the zodiac. The motion of Jupiter at birth (whether it has just gone into direct motion, is about to go into retrograde motion once, twice or three times or whether it has been in direct motion for some time) can affect exactly when it returns to its exact position at time of birth. So the time of its return to its exact natal position may differ slightly for individuals.

Jupiter completes its first cycle at about the same time young adolescents start secondary school. They go to a bigger school with older children, meet other pupils from different religions and who speak different languages. They are taught a wide variety of new subjects and are expected to move to different classrooms to be taught by a variety of teachers. This is in sharp contrast to their experiences in primary school, and as a result their perceptions of the world change.

They begin to eat more and start to grow at a faster rate, the growth rate becoming more pronounced as girls experience a growth spurt before boys. Suddenly, and maybe for the only time in their lives, girls are bigger than boys. Within a year, the boys will catch up and surpass the girls in height and weight.

To return to any point, say a place you have visited a few times before, gives you the opportunity to evaluate what changes have been made and what changes should be made for the next visit. For pupils experiencing their first Jupiter return, an evaluation is made of their learning process. In the first twelve years of their lives, they have learned how to communicate verbally and through written language, but they lack finesse and control. Very few pupils at this stage of their education would be able to complete a research essay. They have learned to walk and run, but they still have the potential to learn how to travel faster and more efficiently. They literally stand on this return point and instinctively know that there is so much more to come. So they make a good run at Life, the Great Adventure. There's so much to see and do, so many new people to meet, so much fun to be had. They are enthusiastic and boisterous because they are excited about what's in store for them. They believe that life is going to be wonderful because they have faith in Goodness and automatically assume they will be protected. So they take ridiculous chances, as if life were lived on a gigantic bouncy castle, exponentially taking more and more chances until they finally find their limits.

They need parents, teachers and other significant adults to provide boundaries without crushing their spirits. If they are crushed, they cannot take advantage of their re-evaluated learning process. They need us, as authority figures to say, "Jump around all you like but if you're going to insist on backflips, then we need to make a few rules about safety."

Mythologically, Jupiter was the god of gods. He was thunder and lightning, the judge of law and order who wasn't afraid to strike down wrongdoers with his bolts of lightning Because he was a sky god, his perspective of viewing things from on high supposedly gave him unquestioned omniscience. Jupiter is often associated with religion and higher philosophies. He was also well known for his lack of fidelity and his wonderful acting skills: he has appeared as a swan, a shower of gold, a bull and a shivering little bird at the window sill of an exceptionally beautiful goddess who later became his long suffering wife Hera (she took the poor little bird to her breast and Jupiter returned to human form). Therefore, Jupiter in astrology represents the ability to take advantage of a situation and milk it for all its worth, without putting in the expected effort.

Pupils at the start of their Jupiter returns possess some of the characteristics of the mythical Jupiter. Whilst they may not actually wield lightning bolts, they are quick to point out injustices through play fighting. They have an abundance of energy that wears everyone else out. They can only see their own morality because they haven't yet learned that others might have a different sense of right and wrong. And like the mythological Jupiter, they are curious about sex, an interest that intensifies as the hormones kick in.

Pupils experiencing their Jupiter returns are learning about the world around them. They have specific ways of learning, and this section will help you to help them make the most of their abilities.

The following sections describe the learning processes for Jupiter in each of the zodiac signs and provide a celebrity example. Typically, celebrities are successful people and it can be useful to see how Jupiter and Saturn manifest at times of success.

Jupiter in Aries

7 June 1927	–	11 September 1927
24 January 1928	–	4 June 1928
12 May 1939	–	30 October 1939
20 December 1939	–	15 May 1940
22 April 1951	–	28 April 1952
5 April 1963	–	12 April 1964
19 March 1975	–	26 March 1976
2 March 1987	–	8 March 1988
14 February 1999	–	28 June 1999
24 October 1999	–	14 February 2000
7 June 2010	–	9 September 2010
22 January 2011	–	4 June 2011
11 May 2022	–	28 October 2022
20 December 2022	–	16 May 2023

The racehorse

Imagine being at the starting gates at the biggest race of your life. On either side of you, as far as you can see, are other snorting horses just as eager to prove their speed as much as you are. The starting pistol explodes.

And they're off. For learners with Jupiter in Aries, every lesson represents a race. It doesn't matter to them if they haven't practised the objective beforehand. To them, every other pupil in the classroom is a competitor and they will do anything to avoid coming last. If failure appears imminent, they will either drop out entirely in shame, or they will resort to cheating like mad dogs. Fighting and jostling to gain a place in the dinner queue is not uncommon: these learners will resort to aggression if they think they are not fast enough. And they'll be seriously annoyed with their teacher if they think you neglected to do something to help them prepare.

These learners are always ready to learn. They are not patient. When learning to read, they were probably frustrated by the primary school teacher's insistence on learning to read aloud slowly and clearly, and writing neatly. To them, it's all about getting to the finishing line. Books are quickly read through but comprehension questions will be ignored. Art subjects may have felt like an unwelcome distraction, and any attempt to buddy them up with someone else is likely to be extremely difficult – unless it involves a race to see who can finish first.

Jupiter in Aries children need to see how their progress measures up to someone else's so they can surpass them. For these reasons, in a class of Jupiter in Aries children, careless spelling mistakes, sloppy handwriting and attention to minute detail will be a problem – unless they have something to measure themselves against. Very often, they will hone one skill in which they become unbeatable.

Teachers of Jupiter in Aries children will be more successful if they break learning into chunks as often as they can, and allow the pupils to compete against each other. The trick is to allow them to use speed to perfect fine skills. For example, in writing, instead of giving them a long passage to copy, give them only their weakest letter to concentrate on. Help them to keep track of their progress in making a perfectly-formed cursive capital 'W' by seeing how many they can do in thirty seconds, comparing the results with those of the rest of the class and then re-testing. Keep tasks short, simple and quick. Eventually, these learners will need to apply patience to their tasks. They'll need to think about the importance of pacing themselves, planning ahead and saving their strength for the really important races. Girls with Jupiter in Aries are more likely to learn these skills with greater accuracy. Once the boys see they have been outdone by the girls, and are clear about how they can work more efficiently without compromising accuracy, they should catch up.

By the time they reach secondary school, they will need to re-learn these lessons. In a bigger school with more children, it will be back to the drawing board in order to teach them that attempting to outdo each other with speed produces sloppy, inaccurate work that is unpleasant to look at and difficult to mark. Secondary school teachers will also greatly benefit by employing shorter assessments for learning tasks. For example, learning a word for the day and seeing how many different sentences the word can be used in and then giving them a task that practically begs them to use their new word. For maths, mental arithmetic competitions using basic functions help them to secure rote mastery of numbers and their patterns. This will prevent accumulated errors based on simple mistakes.

Pastorally, issues may arise around self-esteem, feelings of inadequacy or a drop-out attitude that have their roots in never coming in first place. All pupils have strengths and weaknesses and, for the child with low self-esteem, allowing them to compete against their peers in a subject they're good at will normally allow you, the teacher, to determine where basic skills are lacking. Slowly building their status amongst their peers will be especially crucial when they are around the age of fifteen.

If you're a teacher with Jupiter in Aries, you may unconsciously compete with both colleagues and pupils. One day you will lose. Use this experience to remember how it feels and help your pupils to avoid it. Also, remember that not every race is the biggest race of your life, and this extends to expecting your pupils to rise too quickly to your expectations. And resist boasting about how quickly your class is progressing in the staff room. It irritates your colleagues.

Fine-tuning the role of Jupiter

Jupiter in Aries is ruled by Mars, the planet of action, energy and initiative. To get a more specific idea of how a person with Jupiter in Aries grows, look at the sign Mars occupies.

Mars in Aries – This is high energy indeed! It may seem that these children are born ready to learn. The words "slow down" will have no effect whatsoever on them. Hobbies and interests are taken up and abandoned with lightning speed. Teachers should keep lessons at a fast pace and change activities quickly. Parents may find these children exhausting and may be tempted to opt for nursery equipment that keeps them contained. Just remember that all children need to be free to explore, but make sure safety is always a priority.

Mars in Taurus – These children may tend to dawdle and luxuriate in the finer things of life, but they need to be reminded of the importance of education. They like to collect nice things and may be very slow to accept change. For teachers, this is a highly kinaesthetic group. They like to touch and count things or make things prettier. Parents may find these children are hard to keep satisfied: they like top quality stuff and they can be incredibly persistent until sated.

Mars in Gemini – These children can talk the hind legs off a donkey when they are ready to learn (and they are always ready!). Naturally curious about the world, they will drive you crazy with questions, and once they learn to read they will zip through books before you've even had a chance to build the bookshelves to accommodate their growing library. For teachers, lessons must be varied and objectives clear. These pupils can lose focus very easily. For parents, a changing routine that keeps them guessing about what will happen next is the key to keeping them happy.

Mars in Cancer – These children tend to cling to the familiar, especially the primary care giver, so starting school can often be the first taste they have of being away from home. They like things that remind them of the past, and usually find moving home phenomenally traumatising. For teachers, it can be difficult to get these children to take to new topics and therefore clear links between topics are essential. For parents, a slow and prolonged introduction to changes in routine or environment is necessary to prevent avoidable distress.

Mars in Leo – These children like to be centre stage in learning, and they will only learn if they think you are watching. They usually love dramatic performances, so dressing up and play acting can breathe new life into even the most boring or tedious lessons. For teachers, constant feedback on progress is essential. For parents, it is important that only the right behaviour is rewarded with attention so that the young thespians don't get the idea that tantrums are the only way to get your attention.

Mars in Virgo – These children are concerned with order and cleanliness. They like rucksacks with compartments and enjoy planning their routines far in advance. They don't want to get their hands dirty or engage in behaviour that might make them ill. For teachers, these pupils are the ones who produce perfect essays, grammatically pure with few spelling mistakes. The problem is that this often reduces the volume of work they produce. For parents, the key word for these children is 'efficiency'. They have a discerning eye and high standards that can mean they avoid traditional childhood activities.

Mars in Libra – These children are social learners who often can't bear independent study. They are polite to a fault because they believe they can be friends with anyone, no matter how many warnings you give them about talking to strangers. For teachers, group activities come naturally to this group but they must be trained for exam conditions too. Good luck in trying to impose silence! For parents, there should be few problems in encouraging social outings but, as in the advice for teachers, they need to develop independent skills too.

Mars in Scorpio – These children are usually secret learners who surprise everyone with just how much attention they had been paying all along. They like games of mystery or activities that frighten them (just a bit). For teachers, research projects usually come easily to these learners and they will loathe meaningless tasks. For parents, these children have a very healthy interest in anything you think they shouldn't know about, so it is important to create an atmosphere where all subjects can be discussed in a polite forum.

Mars in Sagittarius – These children love adventure and thrive on activities which pose an element of risk. Quests, treasure hunts and anything that allows their *bon vivant* to show itself will appeal to them. For teachers, lessons based on foreign or religious studies and battles for freedom will keep them interested. For parents, the reckless abandon with which these children play can seem a little disconcerting. Always teach – and help maintain – safety precautions.

Mars in Capricorn – These children tend to have a mature attitude towards learning. One can almost imagine them smoking a pipe whilst wearing slippers and a robe. They may watch other children playing and then go back to reading their newspapers. For teachers, games based around business studies will keep the attention of these pupils, but generally speaking they like the formal atmosphere of school. Parents may find that they are the ones being ordered about, so firm boundaries are usually called for when dealing with these children.

Mars in Aquarius – These children like high tech games and stories of fighting for equality. They also like whacky ideas and out-there concepts such as conspiracy theories, UFO accounts and crop circle news. For teachers, ICT activities are appreciated, but often the humble biro is not. Try shaking up the normal routine of a lesson by offering the plenary first and ending with the starter. For parents, the passions of these children can be difficult to predict. Expecting to expect the unexpected while acting surprised usually keeps these children happy.

Mars in Pisces – These children understand and have compassion for all living creatures. The death of a butterfly will have these learners composing poems or requiems. For teachers, an understanding and heartfelt compassion for every pupil is a must: this group will know who your favourites are. For parents, encouraging their artistic talents but not allowing them to become lost in it is the key to keeping these children happy.

Case study – Stacy Ferguson

Fergie (of The Black Eyed Peas)
27 March 1975 13:24 PT
Hacienda Heights, California, USA 34°N00'25" 11°W57'49"
Rodden rating: AA; Collector: Taglilatelo
Jupiter in Aries; Mars in Aquarius; Saturn in Cancer; Moon in Libra
One Jupiter return (March 1987)
Three Saturn oppositions: (March 1989, June 1989, December 1989)
Time between first Jupiter return and last Saturn opposition:
approximately 2 years, 9 months
First Saturn return: September and November 2001 and May 2004

Stacy Ferguson was a straight-A pupil, a girl scout, a spelling bee champion and a cheerleader who began her performing career as the voice of Sally in the *Peanuts* cartoon as transiting Jupiter was square to its natal position in 1984. She joined the band Wild Orchid in 1991 as transiting Jupiter opposed her natal Mars. As transiting Jupiter opposed its natal position, as well as making a series of three oppositions to her Sun's natal position, she went on a sex and drugs spree: "I have had lesbian experiences in the past. I won't say how many men I've had sex with, but I am a very sexual person." [1]

She developed a crystal methamphetamine addiction during this time and continued to use the drug after she left the group under a Jupiter square in 2001. During this time, The Black Eyed Peas were recording *Elephunk*, a project they did not finish until "Fergie" joined the group.

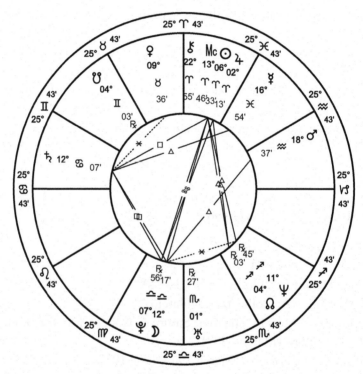

Stacy Ferguson – 27 March 1975

Their album was released as transiting Saturn was square to her Sun. At her first Saturn return, The Black Eyed Peas embarked on a world tour. When Fergie's first solo album was released in September 2006, both Jupiter and Saturn made contacts by transit to her natal Pluto. This great unleashing of power led to five top singles and several music awards. Jupiter was square natal Saturn and opposite natal Pluto.

Jupiter in Taurus

5 June 1928	–	12 June 1929
16 May 1940	–	26 May 1941
28 April 1952	–	9 May 1953
12 April 1964	–	22 April 1965
27 March 1976	–	23 August 1976
16 October 1976	–	3 April 1977
9 March 1988	–	21 June 1988
31December 1988	–	11 March 1989
29 June 1999	–	23 October 1999
15 February 2000	–	30 June 2000
5 June 2011	–	11 June 2012

Bulls on amphetamines

Imagine a herd of over excited bulls charging towards you. You'd get out of the way pretty quickly wouldn't you? Bulls are big, heavy animals that are normally isolated from their females, and every other animal, because their sheer strength, impatience and inability to consider the consequences means someone or something will be irreparably damaged. On the flipside, bulls are generally fairly hard to antagonise, and left to their own devices would pretty much hang around in a field, chewing their cud rather than get all hot and bothered chasing something around. We all know the expression "like waving a red flag at a bull", implying that it takes something special to get the bull's attention, but once you have it you had better be able to get out of the way.

For learners with Jupiter in Taurus, unless what is being offered entices them, you as the teacher will not get anywhere. These pupils will seem to be able to happily watch you get in a lather during a lesson and then seem to deliberately choose not to engage with you. It looks like they are lazy learners who need to be whipped into shape.

As primary school learners, pupils with Jupiter in Taurus probably learned that reading offered them a sort of control over their teachers. Reading made their teacher react in some way: perhaps compliments were showered upon them or rewards given. Eventually, however, once the Jupiter in Taurus child got the basics of reading and the compliments and rewards stopped, they were in danger of losing interest in reading. They read for pleasure or to use the skill to find the answer they want, but when it comes to putting them through their paces because you want them to, they can't be bothered. At this point, things can go two ways: either the teacher gives up, lets them have their way and allows them to coast through the lessons, or the teacher gets all the bangs and whistles out with ideas they got from the *Times Educational Supplement*.

They get the red rag out. Some may resort to subtle, psychological mind games to get Jupiter in Taurus learners moving, others use what could be construed as just plain dirty tricks in the form of bribes. This works, of course. The Jupiter in Taurus learners shift, but what do they really learn? They learn they can be easily manipulated, are too easy to rankle, and when they reflect on their experience, they learn how not to let that happen again. In other words, they become even more stubborn. There are ways of easing this process without causing too much resentment. Although Jupiter in Taurus learners may not verbalise it (because it is such an intrinsic part of their makeup), they are body conscious: they know their bodies work by the natural process of eating, digesting and eliminating. Having masticated the lesson, pupils need time to digest the information and then time to eliminate the things they don't need. And let's face it, in a classroom of thirty pupils, a lot of rubbish can go on and teachers have to accept that not everything that happens is directly relevant to every child. Drop some information into their brains, check back in a few days to see whether it has taken root, then add to their thinking in ways that allow them to discover how much they've learned. For example, use projects they can add to bit by bit to be displayed and admired later, binders that can be filled with new pages for a class project, or photographs that record new experiences or graphs that demonstrate progress. Once they can see their potential for growth, this group will expand and develop their knowledge independently and in their own time. They are also more likely to retain and absorb what they need. Just because they are quiet, doesn't mean that learning isn't taking place.

For younger Jupiter in Taurus pupils, merits and demerits allow them to indulge in their favourite pastime: collecting things. If they don't start their tasks within a certain time, they get demerits that count against the merits they have previously collected. Let them play banker with their rewards by balancing the merits and demerits and then allow them to "purchase" their rewards from catalogues. Get the parents on side by showing them the things their child would like if they do what they are asked. From playing at trading, Jupiter in Taurus learners can see how give and take applies in the real world, but in the process they can also learn about human interchange. By the time they are adults, these learners will have digested the concept of the Law of Reciprocation, which generally means things come and go and one does not have to hold onto things in the fear of losing them. They learn that avarice is pretty pointless and that philanthropy is a pretty amazing concept they'd like to try.

For secondary school learners, a new school represents a new luxury. They will arrive in September already stimulated and excited, but they need to be kept in this state by other teachers. Knowledge needs to be perceived as its own reward, and competitions that lead to new experiences allow this knowledge to continue expanding and will keep these learners moving and prevent them from stagnation. Allow them to regularly show their classmates what they have learned, or even give them opportunities to teach you once in a while. As they digest new information, they need the chance to let it out to make room for more.

Pastorally, eating problems on either end of the spectrum could pose challenges around the age of fifteen because they feel alienated from their bodies and wish to employ unnatural methods (such as starving or binging) to control their growth. Obviously, these issues need to be carefully supervised, as even seasoned professionals are perplexed by them.

If you're a teacher with Jupiter in Taurus, it's easy for you to get in a rut with the same lesson plans and the same activities. It may be difficult for you to try new methods and techniques. Technology may really irritate you, but look at it from the point of view that such a small machine can hold more information. Go on, you know you can't resist adding things to your collection.

Fine-tuning the role of Jupiter

Jupiter in Taurus is ruled by Venus, the planet of love, beauty and harmony. To get a more specific idea of how a person with Jupiter in Taurus grows, look to the sign Venus occupies.

Note *Venus rules the signs of both Taurus and Libra. The main difference between Taurus and Libra is that in Taurus there is an emphasis on natural beauty whereas the emphasis in Libra is on artistically enhancing the natural to make it even more beautiful (as in the case of romantic love when two individuals combine to create a new relationship).*

Venus in Aries – These learners generally have a lusty attitude towards learning, but they can be content to let someone else do all the work. They like to be teased or antagonised into learning. Teachers will be familiar with the skill of target questioning, which will keep even the most reluctant learner on their toes. Parents usually find these children are very good at getting what they want, but they quickly lose interest once they actually have it.

Venus in Taurus – These learners like to learn by building on knowledge which has already been acquired. They need to understand how lessons will benefit them in the future (i.e. make them rich). Teachers can help them by ensuring justification for the lesson's importance and showing them how the lesson will progress in advance. Parents will usually find that these children are fascinated with nature and how things grow.

Venus in Gemini – These learners love to learn and they appreciate variety. They will simply wander off somewhere else if the scenery becomes too familiar. Teachers usually find that these pupils respond well to rotating work stations where activities change frequently. Parents usually discover that these children have very good knowledge of the local area, and simple encouragement to collect information on the near environs keeps them entertained.

Venus in Cancer – These learners like to develop a good sense of history. They like to think things never change, so they develop roots in the area in which they live. Teachers can usually keep them learning if the basic routine is steady and the teaching displays are never completely changed but are allowed to evolve and develop (as opposed to tearing them off the wall every Christmas or Easter). Parents generally find that these children need extra encouragement in moving away from the familiar. In new situations, it usually helps if the child is allowed to have one reminder of home to bring into school with them.

Venus in Leo – These learners like to take great pride in having their work admired. Display their achievements and reward them as publicly as possible. Teachers usually find that any opportunity to show off brings out the best in these learners. Parents usually become concerned with these children's tendency to boss or dominate others with the sheer force of their personality. In situations such as these, it is important to always catch these children being good so that bad habits are not given undue attention.

Venus in Virgo – These learners like routine and organisation. They tend to eschew activities that get them dirty and usually actively find ways to be helpful to you. Teachers often find these pupils are fussy about their equipment and will keep it neat and in good working order. Parents usually find that these children can be quite fussy and discriminating. As they know what they like, it is usually better to work within their limitations than to fight a losing battle.

Venus in Libra – These learners enjoy socialising so much that they can forget what school is about – learning. Minute social changes, or worse, impolite nuances, can be so distracting to these pupils that not even the basic lesson gets accomplished. Teachers should encourage independent learning, but will discover more work gets done if these learners are allowed to work in pairs. Parents will often discover the social adeptness of these children is utterly charming – until they become old enough to date (which will always be too soon).

Venus in Scorpio – These learners will make it abundantly clear what they like and what they don't. Generally speaking, they relish topics that are considered out of bounds in a regular lesson. If others aren't squirming with embarrassment, these pupils aren't happy. Teachers usually discover that these pupils are quite happy with independent research (although boundaries need to be firmly established and maintained). Parents usually discover that these children love and hate so passionately that they ultimately get their hearts broken. Fear not, it's all part of the growing process for them.

Venus in Sagittarius – These learners like to know that they are in for an adventure but they often need a little convincing that it is worth the effort. They understand the meaning of a long journey and will happily go along with anything, providing that there is an explanation of what is in it for them. Teachers can help them by plotting their progress against long term goals. Parents will often be alarmed at the risks they take, but usually these children are safety conscious and will have considered the long term implications of their goals.

Venus in Capricorn – These learners like tradition and are usually so highly distrustful of new teaching techniques that they will balk at any attempts to modernise lessons. They are old-fashioned paper and pencil pupils. Teachers usually discover that these pupils take learning seriously, hand their homework in on time and submit solid, yet unadventurous, work. Parents may find it frustrating to have a child who doesn't like to go outside and play with other children.

Venus in Aquarius – These learners like cultivating their reputation for being weird. They like their Mr Spock attitude and actively go about doing everything as back to front as they can. Teachers usually find that these pupils are brilliant with high tech gadgets but will struggle to get them to hold a book the right way up. Parents wonder what kind of karma they have acquired to be responsible for a child who is so popular and yet so strange.

Venus in Pisces – These learners like to get lost in their work. They will stare at the same page for hours, or start humming to themselves, louder and louder, as they colour in their pictures. Teachers usually discover these pupils hiding out of sight in the cloakroom or somewhere else dark; such is their need to remove themselves from the harshness of the classroom. Both parents and teachers know that these children need direction, not harsh discipline.

Case study – Robert Downey Jr.

4 April 1965, 13:10 EST
New York 40°N42'51" 074°W00'29"
Rodden rating: A; Collector: March
Jupiter in Taurus, Venus in Aries, Saturn in Pisces, Neptune in Scorpio
First Jupiter return: July November 1976, March 1977
First Saturn opposition: November 1978, February and July 1979
Time between first Jupiter return and last Saturn opposition: 3 years
First Saturn return: February 1995

Robert was a child actor who appeared in several of his father's films, most notably the surrealist *Greaser's Palace* in 1972 at his first Saturn square. His parents divorced at his first Saturn opposition. His first lead role was in *The Pick Up Artist* in 1987, as Saturn opposed his North Node. During this time, he also portrayed the drug-addicted rich boy in *Less Than Zero*, a role he came to call 'The Ghost of Christmas Future' because his real life became an exaggerated reflection of the character he played.[2] During the filming of his Oscar nominated performance in *Chaplin*, transiting Jupiter came into conjunction with his natal Mars, Uranus and Pluto and opposed his natal Saturn three times. However, by his first Saturn return in 1994, Saturn had made transits by opposition to the same planets three times and shortly afterwards Jupiter did the same by square three times. Robert had an extremely productive film career, but Saturn conjunct his natal Chiron saw the first of his drug arrests.

In 2000, transiting Jupiter and Saturn were both in the sign of Taurus and transited Robert's Moon by conjunction and Neptune by opposition during his time on *Ally McBeal*. He was unceremoniously sacked from the show and lost his leading part in *America's Sweethearts*.

Later that summer, transiting Saturn was conjunct his natal Jupiter three times during the worst of his troubles with the law in July 2001 and he pleaded no contest to charges against him. Instead of being jailed as everyone expected, he was sent to drug rehabilitation.

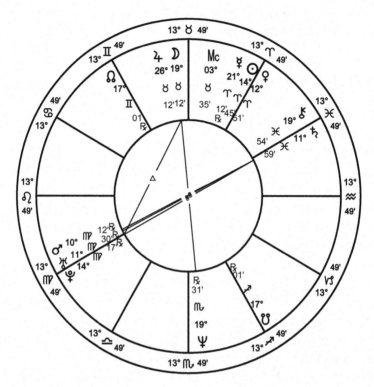

Robert Downey Jr. — 4 April 1965

In August 2001, just after his wife left him (with their son) and as Jupiter made minor aspects to his Moon and Neptune, a contrite Robert was filmed in the Elton John video *I Want Love*.

Saturn opposed itself and was conjunct Mars in 2008 as he filmed his next blockbuster film, appropriately enough called *Iron Man*. Jupiter made transits to the same planets in 2010 when he filmed *Iron Man II*.

Transiting Jupiter was conjunct his natal Saturn just before the release of *Iron Man II* and square the same point just before the release of *Iron Man III* in 2013. He has been clean for nearly half of a Saturn cycle and at time of writing (2017), has a full schedule of top roles scheduled for the next couple of years.

Jupiter in Gemini

13 June 1929	–	26 June 1930
27 May 1941	–	10 June 1942
9 May 1953	–	24 May 1954
23 April 1965	–	21 September 1965
17 November 1965	–	5 May 1966
24 August 1976	–	16 October 1976
3 April 1977	–	20 August 1977
31 December 1977	–	11 April 1978
22 June 1988	–	30 November 1988
12 March 1989	–	30 July 1989
1 July 2000	–	13 July 2001
12 June 2012	–	26 June 2013

The enormous library

Imagine entering a library that holds a copy of every single book or magazine printed. What would you choose to read first? Second?

To Jupiter in Gemini learners, the enormous library is both heaven and hell. It is heaven because they know that books are the key to getting on in this world. Viewed this way, books hold all the information people need to know to be successful, respected and, most importantly, knowledgeable. To these learners, knowledge is God – and they see God as a harsh judge of those who don't read. The enormous library becomes a hell of feeling obligated to read every book in preparation for the Big Book Review that God will ask them to write one day.

Welcome to the Jupiter in Gemini classroom of super-speedy learners – or ones that are completely terrified that they will never measure up.

These pupils will take to the rote learning of letters and sounds like proverbial ducks to water. The teacher could be lulled into a sense of false achievement. The learners know the letters, can imitate the sounds that represent them and they know the order they are supposed to follow. They probably also asked to be shown letters in Greek or Japanese. The problem can be that these learners won't take the leap of faith needed to put the sounds of letters together to form words. They memorise long passages of familiar books and even know when to turn the page. Because they are such natural mimics, the teachers think they are okay to move onto bigger, more complicated books. So down come the thicker books with far more complicated passages and fewer pictures and out comes independent reading time where pupils are expected to sit for longer periods of time 'reading'. Looking at jumbles of letters that seem to make no coherent sense is only fun for a few minutes. Soon the group start doing what they like to do best: chatting.

So the teacher comes down on them quite hard. They are punished for not being able to read and the learners get the distinct impression that reading is all important, God-like even. By a miraculous process, many of the pupils suddenly get it and are reading fluently, quietly and with voracity. For them the heavenly chorus of "hallelujah!" sounds. The class quickly polarises into those who can read and those who can't, with those who can't read being forced to kneel at the altar of knowledge until they see the light and convert.

Thus converted, these learners discover a world full of books to be read, subjects to study and lessons to learn. They may be voracious readers but teachers need to ensure that their pupils learn to pace themselves.

They can't wait to get to secondary school to meet new people, new teachers and new subjects. They know that reading can take them places, and they eagerly consume books, ask for more, and the dutiful teachers keep giving them what they want because they are so happy to see such devotion to knowledge. When the pupils reach about the age of fifteen, their teachers suddenly realise that they are unable to analyse texts or apply precision to their science experiments, or they start to make careless mistakes in their maths work. It becomes apparent that these learners have spent their educational lives accumulating knowledge, but they lack the skills to sort out the valuables they need to do well in their exams. It's like emptying out their metaphorical rucksacks only to find they don't have a clue where they're going, where they've been or where they are at the moment. But they have exams to take, so teachers suddenly start cramming higher skills down their unwilling necks.

Of course, some will just get on with it and see these skills as further additions to their rucksacks, but others will have learned not to take exams so seriously. Because these pupils are so versatile, either extreme is likely to allow them to find employment. However, unless they are able to keep learning, these learners will just blow from job to job like tumbleweed in a ghost town.

Teachers with Jupiter in Gemini often fall into the category of Jacks of all trades, masters of none. They teach maths one year, ICT the next and then move to English. They make a genuine effort to get to know their colleagues and are extremely adept at finding out what they are good at and what they can offer to pupils. As masters of networking, they are invaluable assets to their pupils but their feet are itching and they may periodically feel the need that knowledge exists somewhere else other than where they are at that moment. It's time to move on. Again.

Fine-tuning the role of Jupiter

Jupiter in Gemini is ruled by Mercury, the planet of communication and travel. To get a more specific idea of how a person with Jupiter in Gemini grows, look to the sign Mercury occupies.

Mercury in Aries – These children normally speak their mind impulsively and without a thought for others. Their barbed tongues also endow them with a certain straight-to-the-point eloquence. Witty, but not usually charming, these pupils will have to be taught to be aware of the feelings of others. Hot-headed exchanges in the playground are to be expected.

Mercury in Taurus – These children enjoy talking so much that their speech is boiled down to carefully chosen words and phonetic nuances. Sometimes these pupils will even decide there is nothing important to say, and will therefore remain quiet until called upon. Teachers may find these pupils enjoy singing, and more tedious lessons will be learned if they have a chance to exercise their vocal chords in more unconventional ways. Parents may be alarmed that these children would rather not talk but would, instead, prefer to quietly watch the world go by. Don't worry; they will grow out of it.

Mercury in Gemini – These pupils see the world as one big opportunity to learn, and they will seize every chance they get to add to their vast library of knowledge. Although they come across as knowing something about everything, they can lack depth in their knowledge and very often bore too easily. With their short attention spans, they need help showing commitment to their studies. Parents are usually impressed with their child's eagerness to speak, but soon wish for a bit of peace and quiet.

Mercury in Cancer – These learners are creatures of habit and memory and tend to avoid unfamiliar territory if at all possible. They have learned that the unfamiliar is where the hurt is. Because they take everything to heart, they have a difficult time in sorting fact from opinion. Teachers can guide them to select reliable sources of information and to be remorseless when disregarding useless information. Parents can encourage an interest in local interests and offset major changes by allowing their child to bring in a little reminder from home when inevitable changes arise.

Mercury in Leo – These learners never tire of being admired for their quick wit, passion and eloquence. Unfortunately they seldom give others a chance to speak. For teachers, circle time can become a three-ringed circus with pupils all vying for attention as if no-one had ever noticed them before. They must be taught to take their turn. Parents usually find it irresistible to let little Johnny recite poetry in the style of Lawrence Olivier, but must remember that resentment can build up.

Mercury in Virgo – These learners learn by consuming a mental diet of the finest organic ingredients. Detesting the trivial, they soon earn a reputation for being hard-nosed critics. With their discerning minds, these learners are almost always the teachers' pets and very often these pupils attract resentment from others. Parents of these children may often worry about their bookish ways but rejoice in their ability to master the most complex ideas.

Mercury in Libra – These learners do not seem to learn if left to their own devices. They need another person to not only keep them company but to compare themselves to. Sensitive to the needs of others, they are quick to balance out any inequalities and will smoothly hammer out differences amongst their other friends. Teachers despair over their inability to maintain silent conditions in exams. Parents of these children worry over their lack of academic progress, but soon discover their true talents reside outside of books.

Mercury in Scorpio – These learners seem to be able to look straight through the insignificant stuff and head directly to the jugular vein of knowledge. Their acidic remarks in class often make their teachers think their personal papers have been snooped through. Sometimes these pupils can be difficult to like and they need to understand how they hurt other people. Parents of these children wonder what they get up to in their bedrooms, behind closed doors. If in doubt, check it out.

Mercury in Sagittarius – These learners don't so much talk as preach. Although they seem to possess a curious mind, they can sometimes seem to lack discretion in their choice of conversation. Someone always gets offended and does exactly what these learners like best: engage in a hot debate. Teachers need to continually encourage these pupils to justify their opinions with facts rather than hot air. Parents of these children will often become worried over their child's intrepid search for truth that usually leads them to a foreign country. Or a black eye.

Mercury in Capricorn – These learners understand the importance of earning an education. They sneer at experimentation and eagerly embrace the tried and trusted. Teachers worry because they are often pedestrian-like in their quest for knowledge. However, they always learn at a steady rate and often just need a bit more confidence so that they can bring their ideas out into the open. Parents often marvel at the zest these children show for household chores and responsibilities.

Mercury in Aquarius – These learners like to do things differently from the rest of the class and they will do anything to avoid the conventional way of doing things. They do most of their learning outside of the classroom but will occasionally deign to demonstrate their knowledge if the teacher sits down with everyone else. Teachers worry that their obsessions with the strange and unnatural will prevent them from getting into Oxbridge. Parents just worry.

Mercury in Pisces – These learners need to be at one with the learning process. This is usually accomplished through learning by osmosis (placing a book under their pillow and dreaming of exam success). Teachers very often feel more like alarm clocks than educators and are frequently disturbed by these pupils' blind acceptance of all facts presented to them – even those that seem on opposite ends of the spectrum. Parents worry that their child expresses themself better through art and music rather than through words and numbers.

Case study – Oprah Winfrey

29 January 1954, 4:30 CST
Kosciusko, Mississippi 38°N03'27" 089°W35'15"
Rodden rating: A; Collector: Rodden
Jupiter in Gemini, Mercury in Aquarius
Saturn in Scorpio, Pluto in Leo
First Jupiter return: July 1965
First Saturn Opposition: April 1970
Time between first Jupiter return and last Saturn opposition: 4 years, 10 months
First Saturn return: November 1983
Second Saturn return: December 2012, April and September 2013
Fourth Jupiter return: April 2013

Allegedly, Oprah could read at the age of three, at the time of her first Jupiter square, and she was nicknamed "The Preacher" at Sunday school for her ability to recite Bible verses. Such is the eagerness of Jupiter in Gemini to acquire information and regurgitate it on demand. Oprah had been sexually abused from the age of nine, when Saturn made a series of conjunctions to natal Mercury. This aspect demands silence, so it is astrologically unsurprising she kept this a secret until 1986 when Jupiter transited the same point. Transits from Jupiter and Saturn to this point feature in many aspects of her life. When Jupiter transited Mercury by opposition in 1967, she ran away from home, became pregnant and gave birth to a son who died in infancy. In 1971, at the end of an intense affair, transiting Saturn was square to her natal Mercury.

Shortly after the death of her son, her academic prowess was

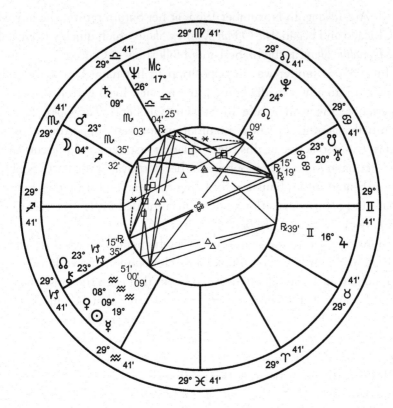

Oprah Winfrey – 29 January 1954

discovered and she was sent to an affluent high school. Tired of having her impoverished background rubbed in her face, she began to steal money from her mother. She was then sent to live with her father, changed to a school where she regularly made the honour roll, was voted most popular girl, was part of the debate team and eventually won a full scholarship to Tennessee State University for her oratory skills. At seventeen, when Jupiter was conjunct her natal Neptune, she won the Miss Black Tennessee beauty competition.

In 1976, Jupiter was square her natal IC in Sagittarius, and later opposite Saturn in Scorpio, as she began work as a news anchor in Tennessee – she was the first black person to do this as well as the youngest anchor the channel had ever had. In 1978, Saturn was in the middle of a series of three conjunctions to natal Pluto and three squares to Mars, and Jupiter was conjunct Uranus as she worked on a show called

People Are Talking. In November 1983, at her Saturn return, she moved to Chicago and began *The Oprah Winfrey Show* which quickly trounced *The Donahue Show* as the highest-rated talk show in Chicago.

In 1985, as Jupiter was in opposition to her natal Uranus, Oprah launched into a new media branch: the movies. Even with little acting experience, she won a role in Steven Spielberg's *The Color Purple*, eventually gaining an Oscar nomination for best supporting actress. Saturn was also active at this time, squaring first her natal Mercury and later her natal Mars, so appropriate for her portrayal of the feisty Sophia who is beaten into submission for being too loud and strong. A Jupiter square and Saturn opposition to her Sun coincided with voice over roles in *Charlotte's Web* and *The Bee Movie* in 2006.

Transiting Saturn was semi-square Oprah's natal Mercury three times in 1996 when she began her Book Club. Her opinion and endorsements had such an effect on sales of featured books that even the most obscure tomes became instant best sellers. It was a force that became known as the 'Oprah Effect'. She discovered further power in her words when she nearly sank the American beef industry with her comments on mad cow disease. Her bacon was nearly cooked when she was taken to court by Texas cattlemen who were furious that their businesses had been so badly damaged. During the time of the trial (she was eventually found not liable) Jupiter had made a series of three conjunctions to Mercury, the last of these in February 1998. Shortly afterwards, Jupiter and Saturn began making a series of transits in tandem to several of her natal planets.

Although she has always been generous, following the lesson learned from her first-hand experience of the Oprah Effect, she began using her influence to persuade others to give to good causes. Oprah's Angel Network raised $80,000,000 in the Jupiter cycle of its existence. As of 2007 it is estimated she has given away $303,000,000 of her personal fortune and she has become the first black person to be listed as one of the top fifty philanthropists in the USA.[3]

Jupiter in Cancer

27 June 1930	–	17 July 1931
11 June 1942	–	30 June 1943
25 May 1954	–	13 June 1955
21 September 1965	–	17 November 1965
5 May 1966	–	27 September 1966
16 January 1967	–	23 June 1967
20 August 1977	–	30 December 1977
12 April 1978	–	5 September 1978
1 March 1979	–	20 April 1979
31 July 1989	–	18 August 1990
14 July 2001	–	1 August 2002
26 June 2013	–	16 July 2014

The home you never want to leave

Imagine being a guest in a grand home. It's a beautiful place with a huge back garden, a swimming pool and Jacuzzi, a library, a three car garage, a cinema room and a massive kitchen. Your every need is met by the best hostess you have ever known...

The problem with this kind of home is that the occupiers quickly discover that they feel swallowed up. It's not uncomfortable but it's so filled with children and animals and family members that no-one ever wants to leave. As Jupiter in Cancer learners know, if you can't share your good fortune with the people you love, it just isn't a home.

In the classroom, Jupiter in Cancer learners look at their peers and teachers as if they are a sort of extended family. They already understand and value the importance of nurturing and caring, developing and growing, but they completely over-react at the first inkling of someone else's suffering. Whilst it is wonderful they look after children with special needs, or a classmate who has been hurt in games, it can be maddening to the teacher that in their eagerness to help they have missed the point of the lesson. In fact, Jupiter in Cancer learners will be so distracted by ensuring that their neighbour can read the letters, and emotionally supporting them through the process of learning, that they will overlook their own needs. And so the teacher comes down hard on them. Like gardeners, the teachers try to toughen them up by uprooting them to a different seat or putting them in a different classroom. At home, discipline may mean the pupil is isolated from people they love until a task is mastered. Whatever the scenario, Jupiter in Cancer learners are left with the distinct feeling that they should have done something more to help or support their classmates. These learners may think, "If only I tried a little harder, I could have really made a difference to so and so." They feel guilty and come to resent the authority figures who demanded that they focus on their own needs rather than those of others. But they learn to be tougher and less caring – at least on the surface. They also come to hate authority figures who block their instinctive need to nourish others. And so it can be a challenge to educate them.

In primary school, Jupiter in Cancer pupils should be allowed to indulge in their belief that being concerned about the welfare of others truly is the cornerstone of a better society. Teaching Jupiter in Cancer learners to care about reading because it leads to being in a better position to help others can motivate them. Reading about how they can help an orphanage can inspire them to become astute and persuasive writers. Because they care about you, their teacher, they will do anything to make you happy (and they always know when you aren't, even though you take pains to hide it), but isn't it better to channel and direct their caring souls to doing something to make the world a caring society? When these learners enter the world of logic and reason, they will find their own ways of making the transition more comfortable. They instinctively understand what others need and, if you annoy them, they have ways of making you very unhappy indeed. Be gentle with them, because they have very long memories.

By the time they reach secondary school, Jupiter in Cancer learners are ready to discover what tools they can acquire to help them to be the helpers of humanity they want to be. Whether they come to view the school as a torture chamber or a sort of hospital where they can get better is largely down to their own perceptions of their experiences – don't let them blame the teachers. By the time they reach the age of fifteen, these learners will find it a challenge to work independently. They need to be with others to admire the other person, thus boosting their confidence, or to be admired so they can benefit from the same boost. Of course, exams are a solitary activity, but knowing they have helped someone else through the process gives them the confidence to concentrate on what they need.

If you are a teacher with Jupiter in Cancer, you probably entered the profession because you wanted to help your pupils become better people by teaching them that home and family are the heart and soul of the world. Unfortunately, you have probably been (or perceive you have been) subjected to the heartlessness of a dog-eat-dog world and wish to accommodate its short-comings by over-indulging everyone you meet. 'Discipline' is a dirty word to you, but sooner or later you will understand that sometimes it is necessary to be cruel to be kind.

Fine-tuning the role of Jupiter

Jupiter in Cancer is ruled by the Moon. If using a noon chart, you need to bear in mind that the speed of the Moon's movement during any day is about fourteen degrees. Therefore, a chart set for noon might not accurately signify which sign the Moon is in. If the Moon at noon is in the early degrees of a sign, there is a possibility that the Moon at the time of birth might be in the previous sign. Similarly, if it is in late degrees, it may be in the next sign.

Moon in Aries – These learners continuously feel the urge to keep moving onto the next lesson before the current lesson has been mastered. They become frustrated when pressed for details, or if asked to show how they arrived at their answer. Teachers need to try to teach them patience and precision, especially those in the early years. Parents of these children should encourage hobbies that involve a commitment of some sort, such as looking after animals or doing a regular chore.

Moon in Taurus – These children continuously feel the urge to remain static. They not only dislike change, but they also engage in delaying tactics to avoid moving forwards, often slowing the progress of other pupils. Teachers need to use slick transitions to the next lessons, and clear closures to the previous ones, to persuade these stubborn learners to move forward. Parents may find they have overly fussy eaters on their hands, and it may help if the basic ingredients for a favourite dish are shown to be used for a different dish.

Moon in Gemini – These children continuously feel the urge to try different things. They are smorgasbord learners who will try anything, but usually only once. Teachers will be challenged to keep them occupied but these pupils will usually have good ideas themselves for keeping lessons fresh and exciting. Parents will probably spend lots of money on books and short-lived hobbies.

Moon in Cancer – These learners remember everything and use their memories to suit their moods. Emotionally complex, they will plunge into Shakespeare one lesson and then bitterly complain about him the next. Teachers will be challenged by the moodiness of these pupils, but can help them to gain valuable insight into their emotions by getting them to analyse what they are feeling. Parents usually discover that these children find it difficult to let go of the past and need support developing new habits as they grow older.

Moon in Leo – These learners compulsively seek the limelight. Even sitting quietly is a performance worthy of an Oscar and teachers may feel continual competition in leading the class. It is often a good idea to let these learners have their moment and move on. Parents may be ground down by sibling rivalry and accusations of favouritism. These children are over-sensitive to any indicators of lack of attention, so making a point of giving them what they crave can help calm the household.

Moon in Virgo – These learners can't help but put things in order. They compartmentalise everything they learn. For teachers, it helps if the skills required for the lesson are announced at the start of the lesson. Parents will usually find these children appreciate a clear routine for getting messy then clearing up afterwards. These children won't usually engage in activities that will get them dirty unless they know they can wash their hands afterwards.

Moon in Libra – These learners need to be with other people. Sharing and demonstrating good manners is second nature to them. Teachers will find they work better in pairs and then will find they cannot work on their own for exams. These pupils must be taught how to work independently. Parents usually discover that these children, even the boys, prefer the Disney versions of fairy tales.

Moon in Scorpio – These learners compulsively search to find out how things work. This includes human psychology and the links between people. Teachers can usually direct their curious questions into research, but the research needs to be well guided. Parents may find that no matter how well they have brought these children up, as adults, they come to regard themselves as survivors, as if they had lived in some sort of hell rather than had a very ordinary childhood.

Moon in Sagittarius – These learners compulsively seek adventure. They boldly ask relative strangers about politics and religion and proceed to give their own opinions. Teachers usually have very eager learners but their enthusiasm needs firm boundaries and clear health and safety rules. Parents typically come to expect that these children will move abroad, convert to a strange religion or embrace an odd philosophy – if only for a short while.

Moon in Capricorn – These learners need to have solid routines, clear objectives and an understanding of the value of learning. Teachers usually find these learners will do anything for merits but will not take risks. They play everything safe and build their knowledge carefully from one lesson to the next. Parents may find it tempting to give additional responsibilities to these children because they so badly want to prove how well they could manage, but what they really crave is respect from others.

Moon in Aquarius – These learners compulsively seek opportunities to rebel. They like to think they are unique, one of a kind. Teachers may come to regard them as freedom fighters, because they behave as if every lesson were intended to imprison them. Let them practise their rhetoric and then help them (and the rest of the class) analyse what they said and its effect on others. Parents will have to accept that they simply cannot know what to expect next.

Moon in Pisces – These learners compulsively seek opportunities to become lost. They know if they just stopped to look at their maps and timetables, they would know exactly where they should be. But it's so much more fun for them to test their psychic powers. Teachers despair of their blank expressions but are elated by their skills in poetry and music. Parents usually recognise their tender little feelings and go to great lengths to protect them – thus relieving their progeny of the need to get a grip on the harshness of life.

Case study – Steve Jobs

24 February 1955, 19:15 PST
San Francisco, California, 37°N46'30" 122°W25'06"
Rodden rating: AA; Collector: Rodden
Jupiter in Cancer; Moon in Aries
Saturn in Scorpio, Pluto in Leo
First Jupiter return: August 1966
Saturn opposition: July and October 1970 and April 1971
Time between first Jupiter return and last Saturn opposition: 4 years, 9 months
First Saturn return: November 1984

In late 1968 and early 1969, transiting Jupiter was opposing Steve's Moon when he was hired to work for the Hewlett-Packard company by Hewlett Packard himself. Not bad progress for a lad who had not yet reached his first Saturn opposition. Natally, Steve had Jupiter conjunct Uranus, so his talent for high technology was greatly magnified. This conjunction's placement in the sensitive sign of Cancer enabled him to remove the remoteness of Uranus, giving him the ability to make high technology appealing to the average person and not just to geeks.

By the time of his first Saturn opposition, he had met Steve Wozniak and the two would eventually establish Apple Computers Incorporated. During his final year of high school, Jupiter made three conjunctions to his South Node whilst also squaring his natal Moon. He enrolled in college later that year, but instinctively knew that further education wasn't for him, so only attended free classes for which he received no

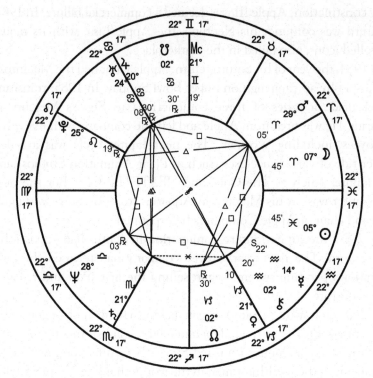

Steve Jobs – 24 February 1955

credits or certification. There is one extremely fortunate outcome: a class on calligraphy inspired him to ensure Mac had multiple typefaces and proportionally-spaced fonts. In 1974, after a series of three conjunctions of Saturn to his South Node, he got a job with Atari, a popular manufacturer of home video games. As Jupiter made a series of three conjunctions to his descendant in Pisces, Steve travelled to India to search for enlightenment. By the time Jupiter had opposed his Neptune the following year, he had returned to California as a Buddhist, shaved his head and begun to wear traditional Indian clothing.

Jupiter opposed Saturn a few months later in July of 1976, when Steve and Wozniak created the Apple I home computer. In August 1977, as Jupiter was conjunct his South Node, Apple became Apple Computers Incorporated and the first widely-used home computer was released. Transiting Saturn was conjunct Pluto the following year when his daughter Lisa was born. During 1981-81, the Saturn/Jupiter conjunction in Libra opposed Steve's natal Moon on four separate occasions. Due to faulty construction, Apple III was deemed a commercial failure. In 1983, as Saturn was conjunct his Neptune, the Apple Lisa, with its mouse controlled icons, also failed in the marketplace.

In 1984, the year of his Saturn return, Apple launched the Macintosh with a splashy ad campaign on Super Bowl Sunday. In 1985, transiting Jupiter made a series of three conjunctions to Steve's Mercury in Aquarius. He was fired from Apple and left the company with five other employees, including Wozniak. The next Jupiter cycle was a roller-coaster ride of varied successes (such as Pixar Animation Studios) and semi-failures (such as The Cube and NEXTSTEP OS). But the next time Jupiter was on his Mercury in Aquarius in 1997, Steve was made CEO and chair of Apple Computers Incorporated.

By 2000, the Jupiter/Saturn conjunction in Taurus had opposed his natal Saturn. The next year, Steve's company had released the next generation operating system, begun selling the first iPod and released iTunes software.

In 2004, as transiting Saturn began making a number of aspects to his natal planets, Steve was treated for a rare but curable form of pancreatic cancer. In 2006, as Jupiter transited Steve's Saturn by conjunction, he became one of the wealthiest men in the world, thanks to Disney buying Pixar for $7.4 billion. Pixar had been started by Steve as Jupiter passed over his ascendant in Pisces and then sold as Jupiter had squared and Saturn opposed his natal Mercury by transit. In 2010, Saturn was in opposition and Jupiter was in conjunction with his natal Moon, the year Apple sold fifteen million iPads.

Jupiter in Leo

17 July 1931	–	11 August 1932
1 July 1943	–	26 July 1944
14 June 1955	–	17 November 1955
19 January 1956	–	7 July 1956
27 September 1966	–	16 January 1967
24 June 1967	–	19 October 1967
28 January 1968	–	15 June 1968
6 September 1978	–	1 March 1979
20 April 1979	–	29 September 1979
19 August 1990	–	12 September 1991
2 August 2002	–	27 August 2003
16 July 2014	–	11 August 2015

The ultimate king of the jungle

Imagine living in a castle where everyone thinks they are the REAL king (or queen). Even the servants and pets have the idea they are somehow above everyone else. Who's the best person to ask for help when you really need it?

Jupiter in Leo learners usually have the idea that they know better than everyone else – whether or not they actually disclose this or keep it to themselves. If you're their teacher, you'll be treated like their hired help. Let this idea persist and you'll be running around for them, retrieving pens, crayons, extra paper and hairspray so they look good for school photos.

These learners will not like situations where they might be presented in the worst light, but give them the opportunity to shine in the spotlight and you'll never get them off the stage. In group work, the competition to be king of the classroom is high. Take advantage of this, but be prepared for the tears of the losers. This group will need to learn the value of sharing, equality and working together.

Jupiter in Leo learners usually struggle to accept new concepts and ideas. Using dramatic teaching devices to explain lessons (letting these pupils do some acting) is the key to their generous hearts. Letting them role play allows them to explore their ample creativity and displaying their work should give them a huge sense of pride. This group of learners will thrive on competition that lets them show off their new skills.

As secondary school approaches, the game of king of the castle intensifies. They may all feel the impending end of the reign. Some may start experimenting with new ways of gaining attention. Guide them to show off their academic skills and reinforce benevolent behaviour.

The first few weeks of secondary school for these learners are likely to be a headache for the teachers because of the jostling to be the boss of the year. It's a newer, bigger kingdom and the spoils of war are far greater. This group like taking risks, so teachers should be prepared for ostentatious displays of egoism. To counteract this tendency, encourage their equally showy displays of generosity and altruistic spirit. Give them a chance to show how chivalrous they can be by letting them lead charity events and provide ample opportunities for them to show off their dramatic flair.

At about the age of fifteen, these learners suddenly go quiet. Human interactions become a fascination to them. Some may take on research projects in the quest for academic glory and some may become fascinated with life and death processes. Of course, they do outgrow this and discover that further joys in the world come through travel or religious studies.

If you are a teacher with Jupiter in Leo, it might be hard for you to step back and allow your pupils to learn independently. You like to think that under your guidance, they have learned everything they know. Be honest with yourself and remember all the things you learned without the help of a teacher butting into every little thing you got up to.

Fine-tuning the role of Jupiter

Like everything else with Leo, finding the ruler of Jupiter is not difficult: it is their sun sign and is obvious from just the date of their birth.

Sun in Aries – These children creatively find ways to express themselves when learning. Their work stands out as their own and often there is some sort of hallmark making their product easy to identify. Teachers usually find they are sunny, pleasant and enthusiastic pupils – until they're asked to sit down. Parents usually wish someone would just turn out the light so they can get some sleep.

Sun in Taurus – These pupils are adept at creating beauty and comfort wherever they are. They can turn even the most austere surroundings into an art gallery. Teachers will normally find difficulty in getting them away from the easel to sit behind a desk, but will be won over by their beautiful handwriting. Parents will usually worry over this child's obsession with money and material comforts.

Sun in Gemini – These children are adept at communicating creatively with anyone. They can adjust their manner, tone of voice and choice of words to suit any occasion. With their being seldom lost for words, teachers usually can't get them to be quiet for long – unless they are allowed to write. Parents find they are worn out from chasing them around and will benefit from having lots of people around to share the load.

Sun in Cancer – These children learn best when they feel secure. Disliking unfamiliar people or places, these pupils need to feel protected and looked after, or they need to feel they are the ones offering comfort and security. Teachers usually find these pupils need reassurance that all is well, and they need to give this or risk having these pupils withdraw from learning activities. Parents usually discover these children have a talent for genealogy and local history.

Sun in Leo – These children learn best when they are at the centre of attention – whether for good behaviour or bad. It is important they understand from an early age that only good behaviour is rewarded with attention. Teachers typically find these pupils hold court in group work situations, and their antics can influence other pupils in a positive or negative way. Both parents and teachers need to guide these pupils into sharing centre stage.

Sun in Virgo – These pupils learn best when they are allowed to express their creativity through precision. They require learning tools to help them do this: clear lesson objectives, equipment in good working order and a clean working environment. If teachers don't meet these requirements, then these pupils become the teacher's pet by sharpening pencils, cleaning the board and organising the cupboards. Parents need to set aside times to be messy with clear assurances that all mess will be put to right afterwards.

Sun in Libra – These pupils learn best by being given opportunities to engage with others. Unfortunately, the current examination system does not make allowances for this, and these learners greatly benefit from being taught independent skills. However, teachers can ease the swallowing of this bitter pill by providing lots of individual study offset by group activities such as peer assessment. Parents usually don't worry about these children until they start dating – clear, non-negotiable rules are required, but avoid making judgments.

Sun in Scorpio – These pupils learn best by being in control of their learning. Track their progress and show them how their efforts pay off. Teachers are usually taken aback by these pupils' ability to find weaknesses in others (and hiding weaknesses in themselves). In the right circumstances, these pupils can obsess over seemingly innocuous points. Parents usually find that these children are of the 'all or nothing' variety, and discover it can help to allow them to explore (within reason) their own instincts.

Sun in Sagittarius – These pupils learn best when allowed to explore their creativity. They will find inspiration in adventures, faraway lands, and people who hold unusual philosophical views. Teachers will typically not have problems with getting these pupils to learn, but they may seem to lack the ability to set realistic goals and targets. Parents usually discover, after several trips to A & E, that safety precautions are necessary to keep these children safely corralled.

Sun in Capricorn – These pupils learn best when allowed to exercise their creativity in a step by step process. Give them a blank canvas and they will leave it blank and go back to their Lego constructions. Teachers usually find these pupils use a pecking order of their own design and see to it that they are at the top end of the scale. Parents should encourage these children to acknowledge their sensitive sides.

Sun in Aquarius – These pupils learn best when allowed to experiment. Yes, they will make a lot of noise and create a lot of mess, but they almost always see mistakes as a chance to improve. Teachers usually find these learners do not conform to situations where there is only one leader. Everything must be taken in turns. Parents usually worry about their child's eccentric tastes.

Sun in Pisces – These pupils learn best by being allowed to explore alternative outcomes to known situations. They like "what if ?" questions and the further removed from reality, the better. Teachers often feel that keeping these pupils on track is a challenge. Parents typically need to give these children clear directions, otherwise they become lost.

Case study – Pamela Anderson

1 July 1967, 4:08 EDT
Ladysmith, Canada 48°N58' 123°W49'
Rodden rating: A; Collector: Rodden
Jupiter in Leo, Sun in Cancer
Saturn in Aries, Mars in Leo
First Jupiter return: October 1978, January and June 1979
First Saturn opposition: October 1981
Time between first Jupiter return and last Saturn opposition: 3 years
First Saturn return: April 1997

During the summer of 1989, as Jupiter in Gemini transited her ascendant, Pamela was minding her own business at a football game when a bored cameraman broadcast her image onto the giant screens.[4] There really can be no better astrological significations for the start of the career of a woman who made her name by showing off her, um, huge twins. Fortunately the combination of Jupiter's influence and the sign of Leo make for a personality with a good sense of humour.

By October of that year, she had appeared on the cover of *Playboy* magazine. By February 1990, she was featured as playmate of the month as Saturn opposed her natal Mercury. Her career with *Playboy* spans three decades and she has appeared on more *Playboy* covers than anyone else. Later that year, Jupiter was square to Saturn, then conjunct Mercury and, perhaps most tellingly, square to her Moon when she decided she needed to artificially enhance her already ample bosom. In 1992, transiting Jupiter was conjunct her Uranus/Pluto conjunction when she won the role in *Baywatch* that would make her a household name.

Jupiter was square her natal Sun and conjunct her natal Neptune in Scorpio when the notorious sex tapes featuring Pamela with her husband Tommy Lee were leaked. Jupiter was again square her natal Sun and conjunct her natal Neptune in Scorpio when *Borat* (the movie made repeated references to Pamela and also contained a mock kidnapping of her) was released in 2006, the same year it was announced she would receive a star on Canada's Walk of Fame and she announced she would marry rocker Kid Rock. Interestingly, both marriages took place during similar patterns of Jupiter transits.

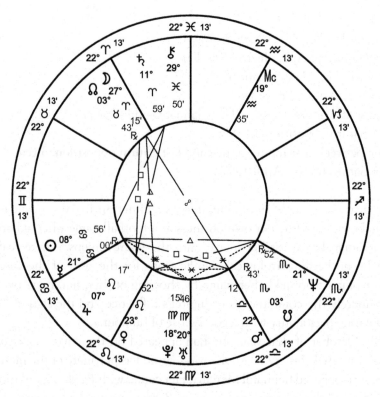

Pamela Anderson – 1 July 1967

Jupiter in Virgo

27 August 1920	–	25 September 1921
12 August 1932	–	10 September 1933
27 July 1944	–	25 August 1945
17 November 1955	–	18 January 1956
8 July 1956	–	13 December 1956
20 February 1957	–	7 August 1957
20 October 1967	–	27 January 1968
16 June 1968	–	15 November 1968
31 March 1969	–	15 July 1969
30 September 1979	–	27 October 1980
13 September 1991	–	10 October 1992
28 August 2003	–	25 September 2004
12 August 2015	–	9 September 2016

The French polisher

Imagine having the task of buffing a large floor space to an incredible shine. It's a huge job and can only be done by hand – and there's no-one to help you. Far from rushing through the job, you relish in the perfection of technique to achieve the very best standards. You're not bothered that progress is slow. After all, you know it will all be worth it...in the end.

It's a bit of an understatement to say that Jupiter in Virgo pupils like things to be perfect. They're the kind of pupils who painstakingly choose exactly the right materials for going back to school. The pencils they use will not only be perfectly sharpened, but the material they are made from will also be ecologically sound. The lead will have been researched and then chosen for its durability. They won't let others share their crayons for fear of wearing them down unevenly or, worse, contaminating the implements with germs. Pens must not blot and the paper they write on must not be dented or smudged. Jupiter in Virgo pupils will drive their teachers crazy as they tidy their workspaces and carefully organise their shelves. There's always a long queue to wash hands before lunch and the complaint box for the canteen is always full. Jupiter in Virgo pupils can't be pleased so it's better to give up before you even try.

Okay, that last bit was an exaggeration but it's not too far from the truth of the perils Jupiter in Virgo pupils face. For in their search for perfection, their progress is often so slow that their teachers give up on them – even if these pupils do have their noses in books most of the time (when they're not disinfecting everything, that is). They hate to be rushed and will hide their work and take a punishment for doing nothing rather than submit work that is less than perfect. Very often these pupils will have their own intricate systems which may seem chaotic to the teacher but is in fact in an order they understand. Don't mess with their stuff, and one day they will bowl you over with what they have learned. A far greater threat is that Jupiter in Virgo pupils frighten people with their well-meaning but harsh criticisms. Peer assessments often precipitate World War Three – with the teachers. Group work means that germs will be shared, so teachers will have to keep industrial containers of anti-bacterial gel nearby just to encourage Jupiter in Virgo pupils to sit closer together. However, these pupils are very good at independent study. Their research is thorough if they are shown how to do it right. Their work is immaculate both grammatically and in its presentation. They are quiet but deep thinkers who laboriously choose the best words to suit the purpose of the given assignments.

By the time these pupils reach their first Jupiter return and enter secondary school, they will have had a chance to re-organise themselves. They know themselves better and they can't wait to have a chance at 'real' study. They'll be disappointed if there isn't enough homework and devastated if they lose their diaries. Locker room chaos after PE will cause them to have a nervous breakdown. They will have some sort of routine for preparing for the next day that is best left alone for them to figure out how to make it better – even if they are the type of Jupiter in Virgo who seems to thrive on disorder. These pupils will normally follow the rules, but by the time they are fifteen this tendency will change enormously. Given a little freedom, they crave more, and suddenly it's a philosophical battle to get them to do their ties up properly or wear their hair in a less time-consuming style. They may change their religion or become fascinated on some faraway cause in the Far East.

If you are a teacher with Jupiter in Virgo, you will have developed your own systems of organising yourself and your pupils which may or may not be admired by other teachers. You probably avoid the canteen or, conversely, consume so much junk food that you require your own postcode. You like extremes and secretly wish everyone would make up their minds to be as fastidious (or not) as you. However, somehow you always get the task of organising the no-nonsense staff dos and many colleagues will swear by your ability to pull together a fabulous party without breaking a sweat – but this only means you are adept at hiding your stress. In turn, this means you suffer headaches, bouts of flu and other maladies far more than others. You become known as the pharmaceuticals hoarder and everyone will know you have every type of cold remedy known to man carefully alphabetised in your cupboard. You love Ofsted and secretly smile as you watch your colleagues fret and work themselves into forced early retirements.

Fine-tuning the role of Jupiter

Mercury rules Virgo as well as Gemini. However, in Gemini, Mercury's ability to change and adapt is more apparent. In Virgo, Mercury's preference for precision and its connection to health matters is clearer.

Mercury in Aries – These pupils quite literally learn by using their heads. Like Vulcans, they are orderly, methodical and adept at removing human emotion from any situation. Teachers will be thrilled by their precise mathematical calculations, but their pupil's search for the formula in artistic endeavours will leave them cold. Parents are usually alarmed by the number of head injuries these children receive.

Mercury in Taurus – These pupils learn by touching things and talking things through. Typically, these pupils resist new ideas and prefer to chew over previous lessons. Teachers struggle to get these pupils to experiment with new ideas and concepts. Parents are usually convinced they are raising a future member of the Conservative party.

Mercury in Gemini – These pupils learn by using precise language. They typically have extensive vocabularies with lots of big words such as those found in medical dictionaries. Teachers usually discover (eventually) that these pupils are excellent mimics rather than original researchers. Parents think they are raising parrots rather than children.

Mercury in Cancer – These pupils learn by using their gut instincts. If something doesn't feel right, they won't go with it. Teachers usually find these pupils have a nose for reliable resources and can spot anachronisms with ease. These pupils are naturals when it comes to history. Parents just think they need to get out a bit more.

Mercury in Leo – These pupils learn by using their natural abilities to gain attention. If the spotlight isn't on them, giving them the incentive to show what they can do, they lose interest. Teachers usually discover instant feedback keeps them inspired. Parents are often worn down with their demands for attention.

Mercury in Virgo – These pupils learn by using methodical thought processes to analyse information. Natural learners, they usually favour mathematics and sciences or any activity which allows them to employ precision. Parents usually think they have hypochondriacs on their hands.

Mercury in Libra – These pupils learn by measuring differences. They are usually able to get people to work together by pairing strengths and weaknesses. Teachers often appreciate their manners, but despair at their inability to make firm decisions for themselves. Parents often trust these children to plan parties and other special occasions.

Mercury in Scorpio – These pupils learn by using their personal power to get people to do things they would not ordinarily do. Some people might call this a hypnotic hold over others; others might attribute it to considerable psychic powers. Teachers would call it the inherent ability to get out of homework. Parents would agree with the teachers.

Mercury in Sagittarius – These pupils learn by using their fearless sense of adventure to explore strange new worlds and philosophies. Teachers appreciate their enthusiasm for learning but secretly wish they would stop breaking things. Parents, fed up with being preached at all the time, just wish for a bit of peace and quiet.

Mercury in Capricorn – These pupils learn by using their talents for building firm and lasting foundations. They understand step one thoroughly before they progress onto step two. Teachers are sometimes maddened by their slow progress but impressed by how well they remember and use previous lessons. Parents think they live with miniature Bob the Builders.

Mercury in Aquarius – These pupils learn best by using their ability to embrace experimentation. There's really nothing they won't try – except the tried and trusted method of doing things. Teachers are often puzzled by these students' boredom in the classroom and should try stepping aside and letting them teach every now and again. Parents have come to accept that 'predictable' is a word not found in their vocabulary.

Mercury in Pisces – These pupils learn best by using their ability to tune into the moods of others. They have the uncanny talent of understanding artists' or writers' intentions. Teachers know the trick to getting these pupils to do a task they don't want to do is to make them feel guilty. Parents try to use this technique to get them to clean their room, but it usually doesn't work and they end up doing it themselves.

Case study – Tom Hanks

9 July 1956, 11:17 PDT
Concord, California 37°N58'41" 122°W01'48"
Rodden rating: AA; Collector: Rodden
Jupiter in Virgo, Mercury in Cancer
Saturn in Scorpio, Pluto in Leo
First Jupiter return: October 1967, Feb, June 1968
First Saturn opposition: May 1971
Time between first Jupiter return and last Saturn opposition: 3 years, 7 months
First Saturn return: January 1985, April and October 1985
Second Saturn return: November 2014
Fifth Jupiter return: August 2015

Tom's parents had split and re-married different people and produced several half-siblings before his first Jupiter opposition. In a *Rolling Stone* interview he said that he was an evangelical Christian and his perception of his teenage years is that he was disliked by both fellow pupils and teachers, but he would yell out funny captions for film strips. He knew acting was for him and he spent his time watching plays alone, eventually winning his first accolade in 1978 (the year transiting Saturn was conjunct his natal Jupiter) playing a villain in *The Two Gentlemen of Verona*.[5] After this, he moved to New York and starred in low budget films and eventually in the television comedy, *Bosom Buddies*.

Although the television series didn't last, the impression Tom made on his audiences did. In 1982, as Jupiter made a series of three conjunctions to his natal north node, Tom made a guest appearance in *Happy Days* and caught the eye of Ron Howard who was casting for

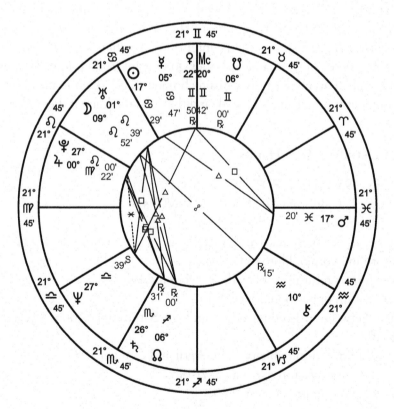

Tom Hanks – 9 July 1956

Splash. In 1984, just before his Saturn return (three hits between January and October 1985), Tom had starred in this box office hit as well as the successful *Bachelor Party*.

Shortly following his Saturn return, transiting Saturn was conjunct his North Node as he proved he could play a serious role. *Nothing in Common* (1986) was a turning point in his career. As transiting Jupiter opposed natal Saturn, Tom portrayed a boy who wished to be a man and became fully mature overnight. *Big* established Tom as a major Hollywood talent. The transits for this time are so appropriate, they are pure poetry.

Unfortunately, the next couple of years saw Tom lose his way slightly as he starred in a couple of duds. *The 'Burbs* (1989), *Joe Versus the Volcano* (1990) and *The Bonfire of the Vanities* (1990) did nothing for his career. The only saving grace at this time was the Disney film *Turner and Hooch*. Saturn had opposed his natal Mercury from December 1988, and only Jupiter's transit to the same position saw his career pull out of its nosedive.

The start of his third Jupiter return towards the end of 1991 saw him filming what would become the start of his climb back to the top of his game. *A League of Their Own* led to *Sleepless in Seattle* and then *Philadelphia*, the film for which he won Best Actor at the 1993 Academy Awards. During filming, and as the film was released, transiting Saturn squared its natal position and opposed Pluto's position. For the role as a gay lawyer who contracted AIDS (at a time when the AIDS scare was at its highest as Pluto was in Scorpio), Tom had lost two and a half stone (thirty-five pounds) and thinned his hair to play a dying man suing his firm for discrimination.

During the following year, 1994, transiting Saturn opposed natal Jupiter and Tom starred in *Forrest Gump* as a man who witnessed, and even influenced, some of the major events of the latter half of the twentieth century. Tom won his second Academy Award for Best Actor and became only the second actor to achieve the accolade (interestingly, Tom and Spencer Tracy, the other actor, were the same age when they achieved this). After a series of three Jupiter conjunctions to his North Node, Tom then starred in *Apollo 13* and was the voice of Woody in *Toy Story*.

Transiting Jupiter squared natal Saturn and opposed natal Pluto as he worked on *Saving Private Ryan*, a film for which he eventually won his fourth nomination for the Academy Award's Best Actor (he had five nominations with two wins). It was described at the awards ceremony as the finest war movie ever made. He went on to other successes in the same time period: *You've Got Mail* and *Castaway* (his fifth nomination for Best Actor at the Academy Awards).

In 2001, as transiting Jupiter was conjunct his natal Mercury in Cancer (Jupiter would make a series of three hits, the last in March 2002), Tom starred in *The Road to Perdition*, which was about a father and son who take revenge on the mobsters who killed the other members of their family. The film is striking for its lack of dialogue and concentration on emotion and imagery – influences that might be expected for planets in the sensitive sign of Cancer. He followed this role with *Catch Me If You Can* as a federal agent pursuing a con artist. In mythology, the gods Mercury and Jupiter were known for their trickery and ability to shape shift. These were the planets active during this time. In that same year, Tom assisted his wife (Rita Wilson) in producing *My Big Fat Greek Wedding*, a surprise runaway hit. In June 2002, he became the youngest recipient (at the age of forty-five) of the American Film Institute's Lifetime Achievement Award.

As transiting Jupiter conjoined his natal Neptune in 2001, Tom worked on his role as a professor of religious iconology and symbology who escapes a murder charge with the help of a cryptologist in *The Da Vinci Code*. The religious themes and allusion to mysterious symbols share common ground with Neptune. When transiting Saturn made a series of three conjunctions to his natal Saturn in 2009, it was announced Tom would again play the role in *Angels and Demons* – and be paid the highest salary ever paid to an actor. Overall, he has been in seventeen films that have grossed over $100 million worldwide. *Toy Story 3* is one of his highest grossing films, and was released as transiting Jupiter was square natal Saturn and opposite natal Pluto.

Jupiter in Libra

26 September 1921	–	26 October 1922
11 September 1933	–	10 October 1934
25 August 1945	–	25 September 1946
14 December 1956	–	19 February 1957
8 August 1957	–	13 January 1958
20 March 1958	–	6 September 1958
16 November 1968	–	30 March 1969
15 July 1969	–	16 December 1969
2 May1970	–	15 August 1970
27 October 1980	–	27 November 1981
11 October 1992	–	10 November 1993
25 September 2004	–	26 October 2005
10 September 2016	–	9 October 2017

The matchmaker

Imagine that you are a perfectly content singleton who is not in any hurry to become shackled to one person for the rest of your life. You eat what and when you like, you watch the programmes you want on television and channel surf at will. You can be as messy as you like – or as neat as you like without worrying someone is going to come along and try to change your perfectly ordered world as deemed by your own good self. There's a knock at your door and it's your colleague from school.

"Sorry," she says, "I was just passing by and I thought you might like Robert."

From behind the hedges stands the man of your dreams...

The Jupiter in Libra child is usually fascinated with relationships of all sorts. They are the kind of kid who will tell you they are in a serious relationship when they are only five years old. They'll be the one sobbing their heart out at break because their dreamboat had floated from the dock and is drifting towards another object of affection. They can recount the rows, punch ups and every vicious exchange of words of any soap, but reading just doesn't make sense unless there is someone else they can share their knowledge with. By the time they are six, they start to understand that certain letters go with others to forms groups of words. Put this way, reading appeals to them.

In the classroom, this usually well-mannered pupil is deeply unhappy if they have to sit with someone they don't like and will see no problem in acting as if that person has leprosy, the black plague or the galloping Ebola virus. They will wave their hands under their noses to disperse the smell, spray perfume/deodorant and generally behave as if they had never learned the most basic of human manners: tolerance. Seat them next to someone they like and you have a different problem entirely. Smart girls suddenly act as if their brains have leaked from their skulls and oozed between the floorboards. The grubbiest, sweatiest of boys starts to preen and flutter his eyelashes.

These pupils are social beasts and they really will learn better with strategic pairing. Left to work on their own, these pupils will start doodling the names of their future betrothed in the margins complete with love hearts in a variety of pastel shades. Reward them every now and again by letting them choose who they work with, but make sure you point out the differences in work output should they become distracted. These pupils will moon at each other for an entire lesson if you let them. Secondary school offers Jupiter in Libra pupils a chance to see what else is on offer. Relationships again become a focus and whilst it is true all pupils, regardless of their Jupiter sign, enjoy a good row, these pupils will not settle until every detail is revealed. Don't turn your back on them otherwise when you check the floor after the lesson it will be littered with notes. This group tends to dislike competitive PE sports but thrives in the artistic subjects and humanities.

School dances are an inevitable part of student life, and the hoo-ha over the event can seem extreme. There will be much fussing over who will go with whom and what will be worn that will go on for weeks. The actual event is likely to indulge their sweet tooth, making their manic mating ritual behaviour from the sugar-high top quality entertainment in itself. It's worth volunteering to be a chaperone just to watch them strut. At the age of fifteen, these pupils begin settling down and taking their studies seriously. Boys will realise that an education is the key to a good job and increases the likelihood of marrying successfully. Girls may need good female role models and guidance so they can explore their options rather than settling for something (or someone) that will not make them happy in the long run.

If you are a teacher with Jupiter in Libra, manners are of the utmost importance. You understand social eloquence is the key to a happy life filled with joyous people who actually enjoy being together. Organising the staff Christmas party (or any other social event) gives you deep, personal satisfaction. If you teach fine arts, your concerts, art exhibitions and welcome-to-the-staff occasions will never be forgotten for their highbrow feel and sense of belonging you bring to those attending. Of course, what you're really hoping for is an invitation to the next wedding...

Fine-tuning the role of Jupiter

Jupiter in Libra is ruled by Venus, the planet of love, beauty and harmony. To get a more specific idea of how a person with Jupiter in Libra grows, look to the sign Venus occupies.

Venus in Aries – These learners like to work independently if there is an opportunity to share progress afterwards. There is often a strong need for social approval. Teachers usually notice that these pupils find it difficult to make decisions because they so easily adapt to both sides of an argument – and they don't want to make themselves look ugly by being angry. Parents can assist by helping them to set targets that appeal to their needs as opposed to making someone else happy.

Venus in Taurus – These learners take pride in their classroom so artistic displays usually grab their attention. They will show others around the classroom – often using a guiding hand – as if they are personally responsible for the beautiful surroundings. Teachers are usually successful if they use learning techniques that cater to kinaesthetic learning, especially activities such as nature walks or short hikes. Parents usually find that these children are interested in investments or activities that promote stability.

Venus in Gemini – These pupils simply love to socialise, and most of their conversation is about the next party. They are bright and keen learners, but are not quiet for long. These are the kind of pupils that plan the school prom when they should be studying for exams. Teachers usually discover a little begging helps. Parents know withholding their allowance until the results are in helps them to keep focused.

Venus in Cancer – These learners love to prepare for their family's future. Even from a young age, they have a good understanding of relationships on all different levels. Teachers usually find they have a knack for history and topics that have a practical focus. Parents get the idea that from a fairly early age these children fear – and can often predict – changes in the family structure.

Venus in Leo – These children like to learn by being the centre of attention. Usually there is something striking about their hair or its bold style. If teachers can get them to put the styling gel away, they typically discover a zest for acting or drama-based learning. There are often huge strides in learning – but only if everyone's watching. Parents often realise they have a thespian on their hands from birth.

Venus in Virgo – These children like to learn by making clear choices about the people they work with. It can be very difficult to persuade them to work with someone they have taken a dislike to. Teachers, of course, try to mix up the class but these learners can be fairly rude if forced to socialise with someone who they see as uncouth. Parents usually have to tolerate long litanies about the perfect social stature.

Venus in Libra – These children like to learn by socialising with their polar opposites. Girls are fascinated with boys and vice versa. Although there is usually no problem with getting these pupils to mix, teachers are typically challenged to get them quiet. Parents start despairing about the dating game when these children are young.

Venus in Scorpio – These children like to learn by de-coding the mysteries of a lesson – which is often why they are learning in the first place. They are fascinated by danger or situations which may seem unsafe. These pupils understand power games on all sorts of different levels. Teachers can help them by giving them the tools to understand themselves.

Parents can help them by being upfront about the consequences of risk-taking.

Venus in Sagittarius – These learners love anything that enhances the speed at which they can grow, but they need to compare their progress with that of others. They often have more than one full-on project on the go and they often fantasise about some adventure or another. Or they convert to Buddhism one day only to take to Judaism the next. Teachers usually discover that they will do anything to get out of lessons, so firm consequences for poor behaviour must be crystal clear – more so than for other pupils. Parents may find these children continually engage in horseplay and so give up on any attempts to keep priceless antiques around.

Venus in Capricorn – These children like to learn by exploring traditional roles in society. Their lips curl in distaste when discussing major advances in civilisation. Teachers typically find these pupils make clear progress step by step but will occasionally make the odd leap for the right reward (for example the opportunity to run for student council). Parents often think their child is a chip off the old block.

Venus in Aquarius – These children like to learn by exploring the unusual or the downright strange. They are naturally rebellious and like to experiment. Teachers generally resort to giving them an instruction to do the exact opposite of what they're supposed to do. Parents become used to things exploding in the basement.

Venus in Pisces – These pupils like to learn by submerging themselves in information. To anyone else, they look lost. To themselves, they are tuning in to their environment. Teachers usually find these pupils cannot use words to describe what they have learned but can express themselves through symbols or artistic means (music or poetry, for example). Parents are usually worried about a lack of ambition but come to realise the child himself understands what he is doing.

Case study – Madonna

16 August 1958 7:05 EST
Bay City, Michigan 43°N35'40" 83°W53'20"
Rodden rating: DD (conflicting/unverified); Collector: Rodden
Jupiter in Libra, Venus in Leo
Saturn in Sagittarius, Jupiter in Libra
First Jupiter return: November 1969, June and July 1970
First Saturn opposition: August 1972, November 1972 and May 1973
Time between first Jupiter return and last Saturn opposition: 3 years, 7
months

During 1963 Saturn was conjunct Madonna's Chiron three times. Both
Saturn and Chiron are associated with pain and loss, creating a veritable
sore point in the native's life. In this year, Madonna lost her beloved
mother to breast cancer. In the months before her mother's death,

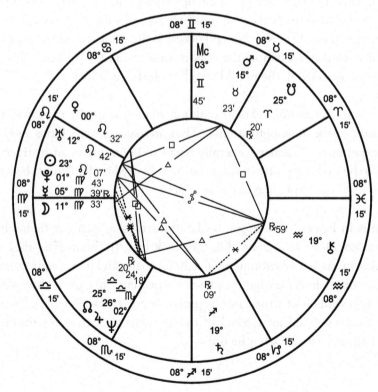

Madonna – 16 August 1958

Madonna had noticed her mother's personality had changed from the attentive homemaker she was, although she did not understand the reason. Her mother, unable to explain her dire medical condition, would often begin to cry when questioned, at which point Madonna would respond by wrapping her arms around her mother tenderly. Later she recalled that she felt stronger than her mother during this time.

Madonna later reflected more poignantly: "We were all wounded in one way or another by [her death], and then we spent the rest of our lives reacting to it or dealing with it or trying to turn it into something else. The anguish of losing my mom left me with a certain kind of loneliness and an incredible longing for something. If I hadn't had that emptiness, I wouldn't have been so driven. Her death had a lot to do with me saying – after I got over my heartache – I'm going to be really strong if I can't have my mother. I'm going to take care of myself."[6] It's a beautifully reflective statement of Saturn conjunct Chiron.

Madonna was a straight A pupil and a cheerleader, but she also had the reputation for being rebellious: she would do cartwheels and hang upside-down on monkey bars to show her underwear to the boys. Even at a young age, Madonna knew how to get attention. Eventually, she persuaded her father to let her take ballet lessons and she won a dance scholarship to the University of Michigan.

In 1977, as Jupiter was conjunct her MC and opposed to her natal Saturn, she decided to move to New York to try her luck as a dancer. "It was the first time I'd ever taken a plane, the first time I'd ever gotten a taxi cab. I came here with $35 in my pocket. It was the bravest thing I'd ever done."[7]

Later, as Jupiter was conjunct her natal Venus, she was sexually assaulted in an alleyway. Around this time, she had also posed in the nude – for very little money – and the photos would come back to haunt her.

By 1979, transiting Saturn had made a series of conjunctions to her stellium of planets and ascendant in Virgo. Within a few months, transiting Jupiter made the same connections by conjunction three times. During this time, she had met and fallen in love with Dan Gilroy and become a part of the band *Breakfast Club*. By 1982, she had left the group and enlisted the help of a different boyfriend, Jellybean Benetiz, to release her first album, *Madonna*, which came out in October 1982 as Saturn was exactly conjunct her natal Jupiter.

By late 1983, transiting Jupiter was conjunct her natal Saturn. In 1984, Saturn was in opposition to her natal Mars in Taurus and she had successfully convinced young girls that fishnet stockings, Capri trousers, rosaries, and see through, lacy tops were the height of fashion. 'Like a Virgin' (so appropriate for someone with a stellium in Virgo!), released that year, made her a global superstar on a par with Michael Jackson. Her performance at the first MTV awards, where she appeared on stage atop a giant wedding cake, wearing a wedding dress and bridal veil, adorned with her characteristic 'Boy Toy' belt buckle and rolling around on the floor in a mock display of sexual ecstasy, took place as Saturn made its last in a series of three conjunctions to her natal Mars in Taurus.

In 1985, as transiting Jupiter was square her natal Mars, she appeared in her first film *Desperately Seeking Susan* and went on her first world tour with the Beastie Boys. Transiting Jupiter also opposed her natal Venus and squared her Mars when *Playboy* and *Penthouse* published photos of her taken earlier in her career. In August that year, she married Sean Penn and her third album, released in 1986 as Jupiter made a series of oppositions to her stellium in Virgo, was inspired by him.

In 1987 Jupiter opposed itself and Madonna embarked on the Who's That Girl tour and by December she had divorced Penn. In 1989, as Jupiter was in the middle of three conjunctions to her natal MC, she made a deal with Pepsi to promote its products. Having always pushed her luck with her use of rosaries and other religious symbols, she completely overstepped the mark by choosing this campaign to debut her single 'Like a Prayer'. The symbols of stigmatas, burning crosses and Madonna's fantasies of making love to a black saint were a little too much and, after condemnation from the Vatican, Pepsi cancelled the sponsorship arrangement. Not all was lost, however, as she got to keep the $5 million retainer fee.

Between Jupiter's conjunction with Venus in August 1990 and Saturn's final opposition to Venus in February 1991, Madonna appeared in *Dick Tracy*, had a relationship with legendary lothario Warren Beatty (shortly after they split, he married the actress Annette Bening and had four children with her) and began her Blond Ambition tour. *Rolling Stone* called it an "elaborately choreographed, sexually provocative extravaganza".[8] The Pope told everyone to avoid it.[9] (The laser disc version of the tour would win her a Grammy in 1992). She also released

In Bed with Madonna, a chronicle of her tour, as Jupiter made a series of conjunctions with her stellium in Virgo. The other active transit during this time was Jupiter's series of three conjunctions with natal Uranus in Leo that began in November 1990 and ended in June 1991. It was the era of her press-baiting antics.

As Saturn squared her natal Mars, Madonna began production of her book *Sex*, which featured adult-themed photographs of her that attracted negative publicity; she also released her album *Erotica*. Perhaps it was because the book and the album coincided, or maybe it was because the CD wrappers for the single resembled a condom packet, or because her next tour (The Girlie Show World Tour) featured her as a dominatrix, or that she appeared in the box-office flop *Body of Evidence* or that she asked David Letterman to sniff her underwear. Whatever it was, by the time Saturn opposed her natal Sun in 1993, everyone reckoned they had seen enough of Madonna and her career was finished. Or so they thought.

By the time Saturn made oppositions to her stellium in Virgo and Jupiter squared her natal Sun in 1994, Madonna got the message. Her next album *Bedtime Stories* was far more subdued. By 1995, as Jupiter squared her stellium in Virgo, Madonna won the title part of *Evita*, a role for which she won several awards. In October 1996, she gave birth to her first child, Lourdes, as both Saturn and Jupiter made minor aspects to her natal planets by transit.

The following year in 1997, as Jupiter made contacts by conjunction with her natal Chiron (the same planet Saturn had made conjunctions with when her mother died), Madonna moved her religious beliefs from Catholicism to Kabbalah. During the release of the subsequent album *Ray of Light*, both Saturn and Jupiter again formed heavy transits to her stellium in Virgo. The album is far more thoughtful and introspective than her previous work and eventually won four Grammies and was honoured as one of Rolling Stones' 500 greatest albums of all time.

Saturn's conjunction with natal Mars in 1999 saw the release of 'Beautiful Stranger' for the film *The Spy Who Shagged Me*, which won her another Grammy. In 2003, Jupiter made another series of conjunctions with her stellium in Virgo. This time, she open-mouth kissed Britney Spears and Christina Aguilera on live TV, thus resuming her press-baiting antics, on astrological cue one complete Jupiter cycle on from her *Erotica* era, as transiting Jupiter was again on natal Uranus by conjunction.

Saturn's opposition to her Chiron, from September 2006 – the very combination of planets that were active when her mother died – was the beginning of Madonna's quest to adapt David, a Malawian child.

In April 2008, *Hard Candy* was released as transiting Saturn was conjunct within a degree of Madonna's natal Pluto and would pass over her natal Mercury and Moon as well. Late in 2008, she also announced her divorce settlement with Guy Ritchie.

In 2011-12, transiting Jupiter opposed her natal Neptune three times. During this transit, she directed her second feature film *W.E.* (about the affair between King Edward VIII and Wallis Simpson) which was panned by critics but had won her a Golden Globe for her musical contribution to the soundtrack, 'Masterpiece'.

In late 2011, transiting Saturn in conjunction with her natal Jupiter joined the mix of potent energy, and anyone who had any doubt about who the real 'Queen of Pop' was were duly corrected as Madonna took centre stage at the Super Bowl XLVI half-time show in February 2012. In a set that took 1500 crew members to assemble in seven minutes for a twelve minute show and that utilized the staging talent of Cirque du Soleil as well as a fine ensemble of contributing performers, Madonna's performance became the most watched half-time show in history (a record later broken by other performers) and set the bar for future sports shows. She was not paid for her performance but as we shall see, to the Material Girl, money isn't everything.

Just in time for the final transiting Saturn conjunction with her natal Jupiter and in the wake of her Super Bowl performance, Madonna released *MDNA*, her twelfth studio album, in March 2012. All the publicity from the Super Bowl funneled straight into record sales and *MDNA* received the largest number of pre-booked sales from iTunes shortly after its release.

Despite her incredible successes, Saturn in Sagittarius ultimately searches for The Truth as understood by the native, and for her second Saturn return in late 2016, Madonna adopted twin four-year-old sisters from Malawi and moved away from the limelight to raise them.

Jupiter in Scorpio

27 October 1922	–	24 November 1923
11 October 1934	–	9 November 1935
25 September 1946	–	24 October 1947
13 January 1958	–	20 March 1958
6 September 1958	–	10 February 1959
25 April 1959	–	5 October 1959
17 December 1969	–	1 May 1970
15 August 1970	–	14 January 1971
5 June 1971	–	11 September 1971
28 November 1981	–	26 December 1982
11 November 1993	–	9 December 1994
27 October 2005	–	24 November 2006
10 October 2017	–	8 November 2018

Dracula in algebra lessons

Imagine having to sit next to the Count himself in lessons. He doesn't say much and yet you know exactly what he is thinking. His piercing stare looks straight into your soul and you know he is enjoying your discomfort. And then there's the smell...

Okay, not all Jupiter in Scorpio learners smell bad, but you still can't help thinking they have seen things you never have and never will. It can make reading seem rather pointless – which is exactly what they want you to think. These pupils have a very good grasp of human psychology from an early age and will have no problem in using it to their advantage if it means they don't have to learn what you want them to learn. By the age of six, the very last thing they will want to do is sit on a carpet because you want them to learn letters and phonics. So you have to get them to see the advantage of reading and writing by making them want to learn. Show them some graphic novels or books about horror movies. Convince them that knowledge is power early and they will begin to understand that the more they learn, the more they need to learn about the world and how it works.

In the classroom, they are stubborn learners who are extremely reluctant to do as you want them to do. Threats of punishment are unlikely to make them flinch, so pretend to ignore them and let them see how much fun they are missing out on. At the age of six, the progress of these pupils can seem to grind to a halt. This age is an extremely crucial one for learning to read and write but the more attention you give them, the more they enjoy the position of power they have over you. They understand they can stress you, their parents and their fellow classmates with their needs. So they do it. True neurological cases aside, these pupils will get hungry for knowledge again eventually and they will be suddenly cured of whatever stalling technique they were using. Whilst it is important for them to progress, it is also important to let these pupils discover that they are the ones in charge of their own achievements.

As these pupils mature, they don't become less heavy going. They easily tune into what makes you uncomfortable: they snigger behind your back and trigger off every insecurity or unpleasant memory you have ever had. They curl their lips in a sneer that reminds you of that episode in the playground thirty years ago. Their apparent control over you is every reason for you to encourage them to be independent learners who take responsibility for their own learning. You can be nothing more than a guide through the dark corridors. Hold your light high and resist the urge to pull them back from the brink of danger. These pupils need to ride on the edge and you will probably never hear of how many risks they actually took. To them, dicing with death (either literally or metaphorically) is the fastest way to meet God.

Secondary school offers these pupils a chance to become involved in every drama going on. Scratch the surface of some commotion, and you're likely to find they have been involved somehow. For the next drama, you'll have to scratch even deeper because they are learning the art of evasion. Eventually, you'll find no trace of their involvement because they've set someone else up to be the fall guy. On the flip side, there will inevitably be pupils who are terrified of their own power. They are frightened of change because they have learned that where there is gain, there is a loss attached. Someone they love dies and they inherit money, they meet the love of their life but endure years of abuse (both given and received), or they indulge in their occult fantasies only to be sucked into the abyss. They love mysteries, 'unsolvable' puzzles and, pointed in the right direction, they love to research.

If you are a teacher with Jupiter in Scorpio, chances are you enjoy putting on your Vincent Price accent and scaring the hell out of your pupils. Your taste in literature is scandalous and parents are terrified to complain for fear you will put some sort of hex on them if they do. You've probably bedded the head teacher, the secretary and maybe their partners as well. If the school is lucky, you're the one teaching sex education because you understand the art of the calculated risk, and your photos of herpes infections, dying AIDS patients and real or pretend accounts of bordellos are the most effective ways of ensuring that your pupils always use a condom. Your descriptive monologues of the aftermaths of motorcycle accidents, the results of drink-driving and terrifying visions of the afterlife are enough to keep even the most adventurous, careless and lucky pupils on the well-worn, safe path.

Fine-tuning the role of Jupiter

Jupiter in Scorpio is traditionally ruled by the planet Mars and co-ruled by Pluto (either or both planets can be used). For the interpretation, the element of power and control is added to the traditional Mars drive. As Scorpio is co-ruled by the god of the underworld, there can be an element of evasiveness in these pupils. What follows may seem harsh, but these guys need to be handled with a firm, informed hand (as do all the Jupiter in water signs). A good sense of humour is important too.

Mars/Pluto in Aries – These children learn by exercising self-control. They get what they want by understanding themselves and their limitations. Teachers usually find these children work very well on their own but become sulky and disagreeable in pairs or in groups. Parents understand that the quieter they are, the more they need to pay attention.

Mars/Pluto in Taurus – These children learn by controlling their working environment. They sneakily adjust the heating or air conditioning and take an abnormal interest in school acquisitions. Teachers typically find that these pupils are adept at acquiring useful materials for the classroom (and don't ask how or why). Parents usually benefit from their ability to spot a bargain.

Mars/Pluto in Gemini – These children learn by keeping everyone on their toes. They are nervous and fidgety and want everyone else to be too. Teachers usually find fidget toys to keep restless hands occupied can help to keep them focused. They need short, sharp learning objectives and plenty of breaks. Parents should offer a wide range of activities for them – otherwise they find things that will keep their parents busy.

Mars/Pluto in Cancer – These children like to learn by manipulating the emotional context of lessons. They cry out in exaggerated pain or laugh hysterically at inappropriate times. Teachers soon recognise diversion techniques and learn to ignore these outbursts. They can usually pull them back on task by putting a fear of failure into them. Parents can help them by not allowing themselves to be open to emotional blackmail of any sort.

Mars/Pluto in Leo – These children learn by creating drama, sometimes of a sexual nature, to draw attention to themselves. Precocious, they are adept at turning the most innocent gesture into something much more sinister. Teachers, who usually take pride in having seen everything, get a little nervous around these pupils but cannot fault their research skills. Parents will often wonder where they went wrong – and that's when these children know they have Mum and Dad wrapped around their scheming little fingers.

Mars/Pluto in Virgo – These children learn by exploring the dark side of life without getting themselves dirty in the process. Keen observers and brilliant interviewers, these pupils have the knack of teasing information out of whatever they are studying. Teachers know they are brilliant analysts with the ability to focus on what is relevant and important. Parents are often concerned by how hard these children work and should encourage them to check it's worth it on a frequent basis.

Mars/Pluto in Libra – These children learn by controlling the people they work and play with. They understand human psychology and are adept at making themselves appear faultless. Teachers can keep them engaged by continually changing the seating plan but eventually realise this is like giving Jesse James the keys to the bank. Both teachers and parents can help these children learn by helping them to get what they want by asking politely rather than by resorting to psychological warfare.

Mars/Pluto in Scorpio – These children learn by tuning into the undercurrents of social situations. They seem to understand that humans are motivated by three things: power, money and sex. Teachers can help them learn by teaching them survival skills in the classroom. Of course, learning isn't a matter of life or death but these pupils need to believe that to keep them engaged. Parents can worry these children know too much about things they shouldn't know about. There's probably not a whole lot they can do about this.

Mars/Pluto in Sagittarius – These children learn by taking risks and putting themselves in life or death situations because they allow them to form their own philosophies about bigger questions. Teachers and parents can help these learners by giving them the tools to simulate outcomes: what would happen if they didn't pass their exams, what would happen if they didn't clean their room? These pupils need to understand the end to understand the means.

Mars/Pluto in Capricorn – These children learn by using their social status to garner special attention from the teacher. "Don't you know who my father is?" they might ask the teacher. "My father will see to it you are struck off the teaching register." Although usually quite hard working, these pupils seem to be under the impression such threats actually endear themselves to their teachers. Parents are usually goaded into investigating lacklustre marks and very poor home/school relations can ensue. All problems with authority figures should be handled fairly by both sides.

Mars/Pluto in Aquarius – These children learn by using their skills in experimentation. They will resist rules, and the more that are put into place, the more they will see them as things to be broken. Although teachers cannot maintain a laissez-faire style classroom all the time, they can occasionally step back and let the pupils do some teaching. Parents may often feel as if they're not needed because the child appears so independent. This is a ruse. The term 'quietly available' applies.

Mars/Pluto in Pisces – These children learn by pretending to be more lost than they really are. Typically, they have too much self-control to become completely lost but this doesn't prevent them from trying to get you to do their work for them. Teachers typically find it can be hard to maintain their focus but explicitly clear instructions and 'what to do if lost' directions can help keep them on form. Parents too can help their child by encouraging them to make clear short term goals.

Case study – Alfred Hitchcock

13 August 1899, 3:15 GMT
Leytonstone, England 51°N30'0 °W10'
Rodden rating: DD (conflicting/unverified); Collector: Rodden
Jupiter in Scorpio, Mars in Libra,
Saturn in Sagittarius, Jupiter in Scorpio
First Jupiter return: November 1910
First Saturn opposition: August 1913, November 1913
Time between first Jupiter return and last Saturn opposition: 3 years
First Saturn return: Feb, May, November 1928
Second Saturn opposition: December 1957
Fifth Jupiter return: September 1958

Alfred described his childhood as lonely and sheltered. Astrologically, his Saturn was in opposition to his Jupiter before his first Jupiter return. Although Saturn in this situation did not inhibit growth (Alfred was obese from early childhood), it does not indicate a happy free-range adolescence. Once, his father sent him to the local police station with a note asking the constable to lock up Alfred as a punishment. His mother would make him stand at the foot of her bed as retribution. Right on astrological cue, his father died during Alfred's first Saturn opposition.

By the time of his second Jupiter return in 1919, Alfred had begun to use these childhood experiences in his published writings. His early writing always had a twist at the end, a hallmark of his later films. The short story "Fedora" was his final short story of this era. Written and published in 1921, it coincided with the Jupiter/Saturn conjunction of that year. Both planets were square his natal Neptune. The description of the main character was said to be an eerily accurate description of his wife – whom he hadn't even met yet. It was also during this time that Alfred became interested in the medium of film.

In 1924, as Jupiter made a series of conjunctions to natal Saturn, Alfred moved to Germany where he was inspired by the Expressionist techniques of filming being used. Just before his Saturn return, as transiting Saturn opposed his natal Mercury, Alfred found his first commercial success with *The Lodger: A Story of the London Fog*. After a series of Jupiter oppositions to his natal Sun, Alfred married his wife Alma. She became known as the 'woman behind the man' in her biography as she was his closest collaborator, but she was always keen to avoid public attention. Alma was born only one day after her husband. Although the angles and the Moons of their charts are different, many astrological factors, most notably Saturn and Jupiter, are identical. She understood Alfred like no-one else.

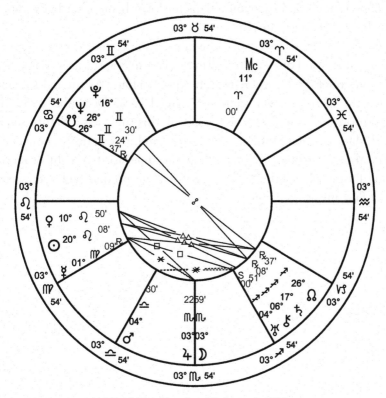

Alfred Hitchcock – 13 August 1899

Alfred's films, such as *North by Northwest, The Birds, Frenzy, Notorious* and, most famously, *Psycho* are known for featuring men who have troubled relationships with their mothers. Natally, he had Jupiter conjunct the Moon in Scorpio, so perhaps it isn't surprising the psychologies of the male leads in his movies had difficulties disentangling themselves from their mothers.

The troubled son theme appears to have started with the film *Notorious*, made just as Jupiter was conjunct Alfred's natal Moon. It features a man whose mother's suspicions about his new bride turn out to be correct. By the end of 1958, as Jupiter in Scorpio was again conjunct his natal Moon, Alfred was working on *North by Northwest*, a story about a man who is ridiculed by his mother because he is paranoid about being pursued by government agents. In *The Birds*, Alfred has a man struggling to cope with rampaging avians and a clingy mother as Jupiter squares his natal Moon in Scorpio, a transit that repeated when he filmed *Frenzy* (whose main character loves his mother but wants to kill all other women) in 1972.

However, *Psycho* is the ultimate mother/son complex movie. During filming at the end of 1959, transiting Jupiter in Sagittarius was opposite Scorpio's ruler, Pluto, in Gemini in Alfred's chart. As the most famous scene, the iconic shower scene, was filmed 17-23 December 1959, the opposition was exact. Also active during this time was a Saturn square natal Mars, co-ruler of the sign of Scorpio, in Libra. Funnily enough, the scene that most upset the censors at the time was the sight of money being flushed down the toilet. Until *Psycho*, no-one had ever seen a toilet flushing at the cinema.

Jupiter in Sagittarius

25 November 1923	–	18 December 1924
10 November 1935	–	2 December 1936
24 October 1947	–	15 November 1948
10 February 1959	–	24 April 1959
5 October 1959	–	1 March 1960
10 June 1960	–	25 October 1960
15 January 1971	–	5 June 1971
11 September 1971	–	6 February 1972
24 July 1972	–	25 September 1972
27 December 1982	–	19 January 1984
10 December 1994	–	3 January 1996
24 November 2006	–	18 December 2007
9 November 2018	–	2 December 2019

Party for centaurs

Imagine the most raucous party you've ever been to. Alcohol flows freely, couples make out in every corner, there's three fights going on simultaneously and the place is a mess. Now times that by ten. Welcome to the party of the centaurs.

Pupils with Jupiter in Sagittarius seize life by the throat, shake it all about, wave it from the flagpole, dunk it into their coffee and then come back for seconds. Or thirds. Their enthusiasm is exhausting, their questions never-ending, their energy ever-flowing. Teach them to read? Chances are they started reading well before you ever met them. Kant, Marx, Derrida, Foucault, Hume, Plato, Camus and Chomsky? They've been on their Kindles since kindergarten. You won't teach these pupils anything. They will teach you.

Or so they like to think.

The trick in handling Jupiter in Sagittarius pupils is to think big. Give them something to chew on so they will stop asking questions for long enough for you to direct them towards an answer. This too is key: let them find their own answers. Reluctant learners simply have not had the right opportunities to thrive. Keep changing the seating arrangements and mix groups often. As they learn, these pupils can be shockingly insensitive. No religion, creed or culture is safe around them. To you, it's blatant crudeness and lack of manners. To them, the knowledge they gain is manna from heaven. Ever optimistic, they often over estimate their own abilities – all the time. There will be tears at assessment time but these very tears soon dry and then they're off again, exploring some strange new world or secretly joining the Hare Krishnas.

As these pupils continue to grow – and they will never stop growing – they become frustrated and impatient with tedious lessons on handwriting (they can probably already out-type you), reading primers (they are probably better read than you) and local geography (they are probably better travelled than you). Even at the age of six. By the age or nine, they are railing against the confines of the classroom walls but always find a route to the freedom they so crave. Getting them to accept responsibility for their own actions is an impossibility – someone else is always at fault.

By the time they reach secondary school, they will have sampled different religions, lifestyles and cultures. But they will thrive on the changes a bigger school can bring. They may drive the older pupils crazy with their boundless energy and be the sources of every teacher's recurrent bout of laryngitis but these pupils know how to milk an opportunity. They will set up a business dealing in contraband items (but get caught), they will try smoking (but get caught), mix vodka with their juice (but get caught), will break every uniform rule several times (but get caught) and fight endlessly (but get caught). The good thing is their naughtiness is so open, so in-your-face that you can't help but laugh at their clumsiness. So laugh. There is just no point in getting stressed out with them. You won't change them. Just make sure to keep a school-wide detention strategy or you will be home late every single night.

Of course these pupils do calm down. Eventually. But only a little bit. By fifteen, their lives (and probably yours) will be utter chaos and everyone wonders if they will ever be ready for exams. And then suddenly, they sort themselves out. They realise they want to do well in their exams because if they don't, they may miss out on their big chance to blow town and hit the road to seek newer, bigger adventures.

If you are a teacher with Jupiter in Sagittarius, chances are you enjoy thinking you're the life of every staff party and every pupil's favourite teacher. It doesn't matter how many times everyone tells you that you can't sing, you're still the first, last and middle of the karaoke queue. You're also the first in line for the buffet, bar, dance floor but the last to call a cab. You may have learned that physical punch-ups aren't much fun, but you still enjoy antagonising everyone. This goes for your pupils as well. You have more complaints for stepping on your pupils' dogmatic (from your point of view) beliefs than all the other teachers put together. The head teacher hates you and has been trying to sack you for ages but can't get anything to stick. There is nowhere you haven't been, no language you are unable to speak and no person living who doesn't want to tear the skin from your pudding. You're obnoxious, not funny, too happy and really, really, really, the rest of the staff would like to enjoy a quiet drink without you. But everyone accepts that just isn't going to happen (and secretly, everyone enjoys how much fun you are!).

Fine-tuning the role of Jupiter

Jupiter in Sagittarius is ruled by Jupiter. Jupiter in this sign is at its most potent.

Case study – Hillary Clinton

26 October 1947, 8:00 CST
Chicago, Illinois 41°N51' 087°W39'
Rodden rating: DD (conflicting/unknown); collector: Rodden
Jupiter in Sagittarius, Jupiter in its dignity
Saturn in Leo, Sun in Scorpio
First Jupiter return: February, April, October 1959
First Saturn Opposition: April 1963, July 1963, January 1964
Time between first Jupiter return and last Saturn opposition: 4 years, 2 months
First Saturn return: August 1977
Second Saturn return: September 2006, February and June 2007
Fifth Jupiter return: November 2006

Hillary's foray into politics began when she was thirteen and canvassing South Side Chicago in 1960 when she found evidence of electoral fraud against Richard Nixon. During this year, transiting Jupiter began a series of three oppositions to Uranus in Gemini. She was a teacher's pet and graduated in the top five per cent of her class. She enrolled in the all girls' college, Wellesley, in 1965 and was the institution's first student commencement speaker in 1969 as Jupiter was conjunct natal Neptune in Libra.

In the summer of 1973, Saturn was conjunct Uranus in Gemini and she had received her Juris Doctor degree and Bill Clinton proposed to

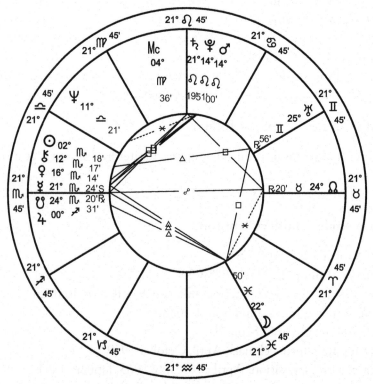

Hillary Clinton – 26 October 1947

her. She demurred because she was concerned she would lose her identity and become over-shadowed by his. Shortly after this, she was a member of the impeachment inquiry staff in Washington during the Watergate scandal. With Saturn opposite her North Node in Capricorn in the summer of 1974, she learned she had failed the District of Columbia bar exam but passed the Arkansas exam. She decided to follow Bill to

Arkansas. In the spring of 1975, Jupiter had opposed her Neptune and shortly after, she agreed to marry Bill.

In October 1978, Jupiter began a series of squares to her natal Sun. During this time, she began gambling in Cattle Futures contracts, a successfully speculative venture that ended when she discovered she was pregnant with her daughter Chelsea as Jupiter was opposite her North Node in July 1979. She had made $100,000 on a $1,000 investment in cattle, but the winnings were to prove a thorn in her side. During this time, she and Bill had also become entangled with the Whitewater Development Corporation.

As Saturn conjoined her Sun in 1983, she was named Arkansas Woman of the Year. In 1992, Bill was made the Democrat candidate for presidency. Saturn in Aquarius made a series of three oppositions to her Mars in Gemini. During this time, it was alleged Bill had had an affair with a nightclub singer. To allay the rumours, they appeared on 60 Minutes together. Bill admitted he had caused pain in his marriage but denied the affair. Although credited for rescuing his campaign, Hillary had caused outrage by seeming to insult women who stay at home baking cookies and hosting tea parties. The appearance drew comparisons to Lady Macbeth.

In 1993, Jupiter was in conjunction with her Neptune when the Clintons took office. Just before the final conjunction, Vince Foster had committed suicide and Hillary had been implicated in removing files on the night of his death. She was also accused of firing White House staff and replacing them with staff from Arkansas, a scandal which became known as Travelgate (perfect for a Jupiter to Neptune transit).

By the end of 1993 Jupiter was conjunct her Sun. Her ambitious (and contentious) healthcare plan had been proposed earlier that year and had met with such opposition that in 1994 she was forced to wear a bullet-proof vest. She was eventually subpoenaed to appear before the federal grand jury over the Whitewater Development Corporation scandal, the first First Lady to have been ordered to do so. She was eventually cleared of any wrongdoing in 2000 as both Jupiter and then Saturn opposed her natal Jupiter.

In 1998 the Lewinsky scandal broke out. Bill Clinton would eventually be impeached and then acquitted later than summer. During this time, Hillary publically defended her husband and eventually decided to stand by him in light of his infidelities. In 2000, transiting Saturn and then Jupiter began a series of oppositions to her Sun in Scorpio in the wake of her husband's relations with Lewinsky, and Hillary and her husband were forced to deal with the astronomical legal bills accrued as a result of the hearings. She eventually admitted in 2014 that they had left the White House in debt, just after transiting Saturn was conjunct her natal Sun.

Hillary's successful bid for State Senate in 2000 took place as Saturn then Jupiter made a series of oppositions to the natal place of Jupiter and Venus in Sagittarius. In 2015, as transiting Saturn was conjunct her natal Jupiter and Venus and as Jupiter in Leo was in a series of three squares to her natal Sun in Scorpio, she announced her candidacy for US presidency. Although she would lose the election, she did become the 5th presidential candidate in history to win the popular vote but yet still lose the election.

Clinton has won many awards, particularly for her work with women, children and health. In Gallup polls, she has been named 'Most Admired Woman' ten times in a row.

Jupiter in Capricorn

18 December 1924	–	6 January 1926
3 December 1936	–	20 December 1937
16 November 1948	–	12 April 1949
28 June 1949	–	30 November 1949
1 March 1960	–	10 June 1960
26 October 1960	–	15 March 1961
13 August 1961	–	3 November 1961
7 February 1972	–	24 July 1972
25 September 1972	–	23 February 1973
20 January 1984	–	6 February 1985
4 January 1996	–	21 January 1997
19 December 2007	–	5 January 2009
3 December 2019	–	19 December 2020

The credit card bill in January

You've spent loads of money you haven't even earned yet, put on excess weight and had to buy new clothes, the house is a mess, the kids are completely comatose on sugar. But you had lots of fun, right? Now it's payback time.

Pupils with Jupiter in Capricorn have a frighteningly realistic view of life. They know there's a time to party and a time to clean up. They will go hell for leather in the playground and then settle down quickly for lessons. And they always have an apple for the teacher. However, it can seem like progress with them is slower than it should be. They are organised, have the right equipment, they've done their homework, they are respectful (sycophantically so) and they don't mess around in lessons. Why aren't they the highest achieving pupils you've ever taught?

Look behind their cheesy grins and you will find pupils who do the bare minimum. They won't extend themselves because something has made them curious or because they are interested in experimentation. If you want them to do well (and if you're a teacher worth your salt, you should!), promise them a reward for going above and beyond the call of duty. You will have to guide them and nudge them in the right direction or be sure to mix them well with their Jupiter in Sagittarius or Aquarius classmates. Shake them up. When discussing religion, prepare yourself for the most dogmatic drivel you have ever heard. Grit your teeth as the pupil with Jupiter in Capricorn insists everyone proves their point of view whilst blindly clinging to their own beliefs – and still claiming to have no loyalties to any one point of view but the right one.

Around the age of six, these pupils become unusually needy and dependent on the family. A family crisis at this age is likely to cause long-lasting trauma even if the pupil seems all right at the time. These children will appreciate the routine of bedtime reading, so therefore it is extremely important for the parents to be on board during the learning to read process. Routine of any sort (be it at home or in the classroom) will provide comfort and security, but too much routine inhibits progressive growth and development. These pupils have the potential to be the ultimate sticks-in-the-mud.

Secondary school provides pupils with a much-needed change of scenery, although Jupiter in Capricorn pupils will see the change as an opportunity to put into practice all the knowledge they have acquired up until that point. They become like the elder statesmen and women of their class. They will be the voice of authority, reason and – if they can lose their 'boring' status – they will hold posts of responsibility that will benefit all they serve. Jupiter in Capricorn pupils, whether they are aware of it or not, are constantly working on their curriculum vitae. They actively search for opportunities to further themselves, and by proxy, fellow pupils. They are usually good judges of character and are adept at knowing who is best able to do which tasks.

When they reach around the age of fifteen, you may get the idea that these pupils really don't need you anymore. They have grown up quickly, are self-sufficient and diligent, and don't need you or anyone else to tell them how serious exams are. They will be ready for work once they complete their studies, normally move up the career ladder quickly, and will generally secure their futures without much prompting from anyone else. They know what they want and will do what they need to get it.

If you are a teacher with Jupiter in Capricorn, you have probably realised that you should have got a little more fresh air when you were the age of your pupils. Even so, you know all that hard work and discipline has paid off now that you are head of the board of governors and own your own school. You don't teach pupils anymore, you teach – sorry, you manage – Ofsted inspectors. All of whom are very scared of you. At the staff parties that you oversee the organisation of, there are no drunken, wild, out of control colleagues. Instead, there are smiling, happy, content workers who bow courteously to you as you enter the room and fetch you lemonade and canapés. You know that they know who pays their salaries. And you are absolutely sure that when you leave the party, everyone else will start to wind down and make their way home so they can be up bright and early the next day just so they can work some more for you.

Fine-tuning the role of Jupiter

Jupiter in Capricorn is ruled by Saturn, the planet of hard work and commitment. The combination of Jupiter and Saturn typically means steady progress. Saturn's position in the zodiac gives an indication as to how a person works towards their goals. Saturn also represents authority figures, so parents and teachers need to be aware of the effects their discipline has on their students' minds.

Saturn in Aries – These pupils learn to work towards self-employment. Typically, they prefer their own company because they fear others will only hold them back. Teachers usually get the clear message that these pupils are not only very hard to please, but are also often disdainful of the lack of discipline imposed on the class. Group work situations usually end with these pupils walking off in disgust and working on their own. Parents usually feel redundant.

Saturn in Taurus – These pupils learn to work either by going all out, or by digging their heels in. They are stubborn learners who find it both difficult to start and difficult to stop what they are doing. They can withstand long periods of isolation and study and often overdo it. Teachers need to harness their practical natures and remind them when it's okay to stop working. Parents often catch them counting their cash.

Saturn in Gemini – These pupils need to work on using their minds efficiently. They doubt their intelligence and so doggedly plod their way through the educational system. Occasionally they give up completely. Teachers usually need to keep assuring them they are doing well even if it seems they are confident in what they are doing. Parents usually find these children don't say much but when they do, their words become solid household law.

Saturn in Cancer – These pupils work on preventing themselves from revealing too much. They are naturally protective of their true selves and take pains to conceal their emotions. Teachers often have problems keeping these pupils engaged because they are too wrapped up in feeling sorry for themselves. They often need to be encouraged to care about their education. Parents may feel emotionally detached from these children and will have to work towards developing a mutually comfortable relationship.

Saturn in Leo – These children work on presenting their best face. They are often terrified of failing – though tempted to show off. They lack self-confidence but resent living in someone's shadow. Teachers can help by giving these pupils roles carrying some responsibility which they always take seriously. Parents should be aware that these children suffer from poor self-esteem and be extra guarded in eroding their fragile egos – even though they seem to exude confidence.

Saturn in Virgo – These children work on finding perfection in learning. Their minds work like highly-tuned machines programmed to discard any problems. They are highly critical of themselves and others and never seem to take a break from their self-imposed duty of finding fault in everything. Teachers usually find they develop scholarly habits and excel in specialised studies. Usually one or both parents are unduly strict.

Saturn in Libra – These children work towards learning to commit themselves to their studies. They learn early on that they can't do everything and therefore must pick and choose what is right for them. This can sometimes take a very long time. However, teachers can usually see that these pupils must commit to something and so can offset their usual vacillation by not giving them choices. Parents wonder if these children will ever get married because their engagements go on for so long.

Saturn in Scorpio – As these children tend to be ambitious, they often think they know better than their authority figures or have plans that will serve their personal targets yet do not fit into the prescribed curriculum. Care must be taken to encourage healthy outside interests without compromising academic requirements. Parents usually encourage these children's ambitions before realising they really don't need encouragement to be ambitious.

Saturn in Sagittarius – These children work towards expanding their horizons. Quite spontaneously, these pupils understand they face insurmountable restrictions and will embark on any means necessary to remove any barriers they may face. Very often, teachers will have to help them overcome religious or moral limitations imposed by their families – limitations to which they will have been blind. Parents will often fear their child will go too far and take extreme steps to stop them going beyond the gated pastures.

Saturn in Capricorn – These children work towards their goals without too much need for guidance. They are naturally at ease with hard work and will resist changes in the status quo. Teachers typically see these pupils are resourceful and practical but not necessarily creative or artistic. Parents of these children may have to be careful of over-emphasising the family's financial standing.

Saturn in Aquarius – These children work towards being free of responsibility. They can convince themselves they are mavericks, but realise that even mavericks have their own code of honour. Teachers discover that these children are so wrapped up in the future that they forget they can find the answers they are looking for in the past: someone else has already done the work. Parents usually come down too hard on these children because they have interpreted a quest for freedom as just another excuse to rebel against authority.

Saturn in Pisces – These children work towards securing their place in a world of chaos. They can see the world in all its unpredictability as a hostile environment waiting to swallow them up. Teachers usually discover that a bit of time out from the craziness of being cooped up in a classroom with thirty other screaming children can be soothing to them. Parents should encourage them to take on responsibility for themselves rather than allowing others to impose their responsibilities on their shoulders.

Case study – Sigourney Weaver

8 October 1949, 18:15 EST
Manhattan Beach, New York, 40°N34'38" 073°W56'51"
Rodden rating: AA; Collector: Rodden
Jupiter in Capricorn, Saturn in Virgo
Saturn in Virgo, Mercury in Libra
First Jupiter return: January and February 1961
First Saturn opposition: April, September 1965 and January 1966
(Jupiter conjunct Saturn, June 1965)
First Saturn return: June 1977
Second Saturn return: September 2008
Fifth Jupiter return: December 2008

Susan Weaver was born into an affluent family of actors and changed her name to Sigourney (a character in *The Great Gatsby*) around the time of her first Saturn opposition. After earning an MA in Fine Arts from Yale University School of Drama in 1974, she acted in a number of minor roles before catching the eye of Woody Allen, who cast her in his Oscar winning movie, *Annie Hall*.

In her first lead role, a post-Saturn return Sigourney starred in *Alien*, which was filmed over fourteen weeks from 5 July to 21 October 1978, the most notable aspect at this time being transiting Jupiter opposing its natal position. The filming may have been quick but the editing process, at twenty weeks, was six weeks longer than the actual filming. Pre-release, Sigourney's transiting Jupiter made a series of squares to her ascendant and was semi-square her Moon. Hard aspects can be

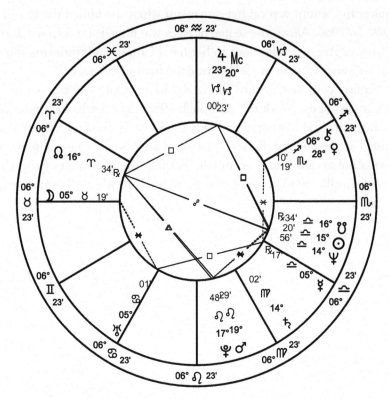

Sigourney Weaver – 8 October 1949

frustrating because there is nothing that can be done to speed up the process. So here we have an actress who wants to be seen (Jupiter square her ascendant) and achieve (Jupiter semi-square Saturn) in a film with the tag: "In space, no-one can hear you scream". Hard aspects, if you can wait, do tend to reward you for your patience. *Alien* was well received (eventually), won several awards and spawned several sequels. Sigourney was also nominated for a Best Actress Oscar, becoming one of the very few women to have done so in the science-fiction genre.

In 1981, Saturn and Jupiter in Libra made a series of three sets of aspects to her Mars, Uranus and Mercury and then conjoined her Sun and Neptune before each opposed her North Node. During this time, she filmed *The Year of Living Dangerously*.

Appropriately enough, in 1983, as transiting Jupiter in Scorpio was on her Venus, she filmed *Ghostbusters*, released in June 1984. Transiting

Jupiter in Gemini was on her ascendant when she filmed the sequel in 1989. In 1986, *Aliens*, the sequel of *Alien* was filmed and released during a series of three conjunctions to her natal Chiron and transiting Jupiter was conjunct Chiron in 1992 during the final instalment.

Saturn conjunct a native's natal Moon usually signals a time of seriousness or even sadness. Although 1988 was a particularly busy year for her, with the filming of two movies (*Working Girl* and *Gorillas in the Mist: The Story of Dian Fossey*), Sigourney took on the cause of mountain gorilla preservation and eventually became the chairman of the Dian Fossey Gorilla Fund, a position she still holds nearly a full Saturn cycle later.

Jupiter in Aquarius

7 January 1926	–	18 January 1927
21 December 1937	–	14 May 1938
31 July 1938	–	29 December 1938
12 April 1949	–	27 June 1949
1 December 1949	–	15 April 1950
16 September 1950	–	2 December 1950
16 March 1961	–	12 August 1961
4 November 1961	–	25 March 1962
23 February 1973	–	8 March 1974
6 February 1985	–	20 February 1986
22 January 1997	–	4 February 1998
5 January 2009	–	18 January 2010
20 December 2020	–	13 May 2021
29 July 2021	–	29 December 2021

Aliens in the classroom

It's finally happened. That thing you never thought would ever happen is happening right now. You don't know where it came from, you don't know what to do with it and words fail you for the first time in your life. Behold, the Jupiter in Aquarius pupils.

To say Jupiter in Aquarius pupils march to the beat of a different drum is a bit of an understatement. These pupils seem to have an internal beat that is completely off whack to fellow pupils or to yourself and indeed seems to have no logical rhythm at all. Teaching them to read will be impossible if you have them sitting in a circle reciting the sounds of every letter the way children usually do. These pupils appreciate inventiveness, experimentation and doing what has never been done before. Stumped for ideas? Ask the pupils. Their creativity will astound, inspire and worry you all at the same time

Through creative play, Jupiter in Aquarius pupils search for ways to ensure that everyone benefits – in their own way – from educational opportunities. Of course, these pupils can't vocalise this premise, but watch them. They excel in teams where they all understand how to take turns being leader. They strive for equality and really do seem unable to differentiate between the genders. In being eccentric, they are calling attention to themselves but give them the attention they seem to want and they run off and hide.

This group of learners requires structure, but only just enough to prevent lessons from becoming a free-for-all. Make sure everyone has the chance to be the teacher and they will appreciate your ability to play the game of fairness. At around the age of six, these pupils will take enormous pride in learning how to read and they will demonstrate their new skills anytime and anywhere – although their choice of reading material can be a little odd (you might want to keep them away from the conspiracy theory sections of the library). These pupils tend to be science-fiction fans so if you have reluctant readers, try anything involving deep space, astronomy or crop circles and you should be able to win them over.

Most pupils enter secondary school determined to follow every rule. Their uniforms are neatly prepared, their books are fresh and their pencils sharpened. Not the Jupiter in Aquarius pupils. They arrive at secondary school determined to break every rule, re-vamp the national curriculum and overturn every tradition. They want revolution.

Once exam time rolls around, all the teachers are tearing out their collective hair because this group is just not interested in changing their ways. They've become beatnik hippies reciting Walt Whitman (who also had Jupiter in Aquarius) and singing Bob Dylan songs. They're organising protest marches and are talking about overthrowing the government. And they're eating everything in sight.

If you're a parent or a teacher and the Jupiter in Aquarius pupils start manifesting these signs during exam season, take a deep breath. The more you push, the more they dig in. Relax. These are smart pupils who do everything a little differently. As exams loom ever closer, you will discover that they have found ingenious ways of looking like they don't care, but they are actually studying like hard core academics. Getting them to surrender their mobile phones might still pose a few problems however.

If you're a teacher with Jupiter in Aquarius, chances are that you have found your way to the House of Commons on more than one occasion. Your teaching methods are questionable, but all your pupils are progressing at the same rate, so everyone is happy. In your free time (which you ensure is plentiful), you scan the night sky for your alien friends, play on the internet all night and join so many groups and have so many affiliations that not even you can keep track of your schedule. As a result of being on the internet so often, your hair has taken on a curiously electric look and your facial expressions seem to have frozen. The kids call you Mr Spock behind your back (even if you're a woman) but they like your eclectic taste in ties and socks – even if you don't wash them very often. By the time you're thirty, you really do live on your own little planet, and by the time you're sixty, you may just want to come home and see what all the earthlings are up to.

Fine-tuning the role of Jupiter

Jupiter in Aquarius is ruled by Saturn, the planet of responsibility and restriction. However, Aquarius is co-ruled by Uranus, the planet of experimentation and innovation (either or both planets can be used). It is often difficult to merge hard-working Saturn with free-wheeling Uranus. It is important to note that Uranus works on a collective basis: Jupiter in Uranus reaches and affects the masses. The interpretations below reflect how a person works towards personal freedom within the confines of society.

Saturn/Uranus in Aries – These pupils naturally work towards independence, perhaps sensing a strong urge to do something to change the status quo. Teachers and other authority figures may be prime targets of mistrust. Those who operate on the edge of society are trusted allies in the fight towards independence.

Saturn/Uranus in Taurus – These pupils naturally work towards stabilising major structures; perhaps sensing huge changes are imminent. Teachers and other authority figures may be relied upon to offer support during times of crisis. Banks and building societies may be viewed as catalysts for change.

Saturn/Uranus in Gemini – These pupils naturally work towards innovating communication systems, perhaps sensing it is imperative to communicate faster and more efficiently. Teachers and other authority figures may be seen as facilitators of this process. Friends and social groups are used to network and distribute information.

Saturn/Uranus in Cancer – These pupils work naturally towards re-forming the way society views family values, perhaps sensing that this basic tradition is on the verge of revolution. Teachers and other authority figures are viewed as an intrinsic part of preventing change. Friends and social groups begin to take the place of family.

Saturn/Uranus in Leo – These pupils work naturally toward avant-garde creativity and self-expression, particularly through vehicles such as mass media. High technology begins to replace traditional authority figures. Youth starts to overtake experience.

Saturn/Uranus in Virgo – These pupils work naturally towards reforming work ethics and innovating health care. This generation, when they came of age led the New Age into alternative medicines. Teachers and other authority figures are seen as dirty or contaminated and as such are rejected.

Saturn/Uranus in Libra – These pupils work naturally towards uniting people by equalising their status. Unusual marriages or new laws regarding marriage are now more acceptable than traditional views. Teachers and other authority figures are seen as allies who try to enforce equality.

Saturn/Uranus in Scorpio – These pupils work naturally towards re-forming attitudes towards sexuality and other forms of subtle power. Teachers and other authority figures are seen as abusing their power on a collective level.

Saturn/Uranus in Sagittarius – These pupils work naturally towards re-forming attitudes concerning religion, education and law. Teachers and other authority figures are seen as those who will not follow conventional law and order as accepted by society.

Saturn/Uranus in Capricorn – These pupils work naturally towards reforming business and government practices. Teachers and authority figures are viewed as those who prevent innovation.

Saturn/Uranus in Aquarius – These pupils work towards changing society. Teachers and other authority figures are viewed as innovators and leaders towards change.

Saturn/Uranus in Pisces – These pupils work towards collectively accepting those who have been marginalised in society. Teachers and other authority figures may be viewed as unexpected martyrs to the harshness and unfairness of society.

Case study – Marilyn Monroe

1 June 1926, 9:30 PST
Los Angeles, California 34°N03'08" 118°W14'34"
Rodden rating: AA; Collector: Rodden
Jupiter in Aquarius, Uranus in Pisces
Saturn in Scorpio, Pluto in Cancer
First Jupiter return: April, August, December 1938
Time between first Jupiter return and last Saturn opposition: 3 years, 2 months
First Saturn opposition: April and June 1941
First Saturn return: October 1955

Jupiter conjunct the Moon in Aquarius usually indicates a chaotic childhood and, more specifically, an erratic mother. Norma Jean Baker lived with foster parents until her mentally unstable mother (who had earlier attempted to smuggle her away from her foster parents in a duffle bag) bought a house and brought her daughter back to live with her in 1933, as transiting Saturn made a series of three oppositions to her descendant. Norma Jean (Marilyn) recalled that her mother had several episodes of screaming and laughing fits which led to her being institutionalised.

Norma Jean was made a ward of the state, with her mother's best friend becoming her guardian. Her guardian told the young Norma Jean

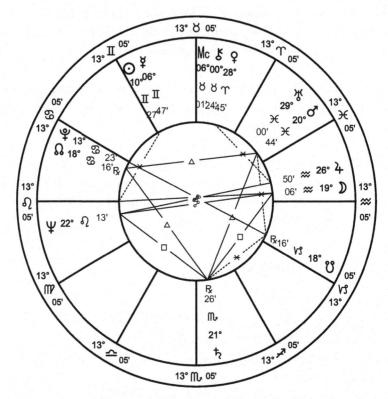

Marilyn Monroe – 1 June 1926

that one day she would become a film star and this stage of her childhood was filled with visits to the cinema and appointments to have her hair curled. When Norma Jean was nine however, the guardian married a man who later made several attempts to sexually assault the young girl; this was in 1937, just after Saturn made a series of conjunctions to her natal Mars in Pisces. Both transiting Saturn and Jupiter made a number of conjunctions to Norma Jean's natal planets in 1942 when she met and married her first husband, James Dougherty. This was probably the only stable time of her life even though, at fifteen, she was under the legal age for marriage.

In 1944, transiting Jupiter in Leo made a series of conjunctions to her natal Neptune and shortly afterwards, she was talent-spotted and the first photographs of her were taken. It was during her time as a model, after some experimentation, that she changed her name to the alliterative Marilyn Monroe. In 1946, as transiting Jupiter was opposite her Venus, her divorce was finalised. In 1947, as she searched for film work, she posed nude for pictures as transiting Jupiter in Scorpio was conjunct her Saturn.

As Saturn in Leo was conjunct her natal Neptune in 1947, she had her slight overbite corrected and later that year, when Jupiter made contact, she was persuaded to have a minor nose job. In March 1952, Jupiter made two squares to her natal Pluto and she was forced to explain her nude photos to the public. Fortunately, the public was sympathetic. Later that year, as Jupiter was conjunct her natal Venus her career really began to take off. She appeared in *Life* magazine and began dating the baseball player Joe DiMaggio.

In September 1954, transiting Saturn opposed her MC at the time when DiMaggio objected to what would become one of her most celebrated scenes, her skirt blowing upwards as a subway train passed. In 1955, just before transiting Jupiter crossed over her ascendant in Leo, the movie *The Seven Year Itch* was released to the public, but by this time she had already divorced DiMaggio.

In 1956, as Jupiter in Leo was conjunct her natal Neptune, she admitted that her marriage to James Dougherty had made her consider suicide[10]. It was also the year she converted to Judaism in order to marry the playwright Arthur Miller. In 1961, as both transiting Saturn and Jupiter made numerous squares to her natal planets, they divorced. Jupiter made its last conjunction to its natal place as Marilyn performed 'Happy Birthday, Mr President' for JFK.

Marilyn died during a series of three transiting Jupiter squares to her Moon in Aquarius.

Jupiter in Pisces

19 January 1927	–	6 June 1927
12 September 1927	–	23 January 1928
15 May 1938	–	30 July 1938
29 December 1938	–	11 May 1939
30 October 1939	–	20 December 1939
16 April 1950	–	15 September 1950
2 December 1950	–	21 April 1951
26 March 1962	–	4 April 1963
8 March 1974	–	18 March 1975
21 February 1986	–	2 March 1987
5 February 1998	–	13 February 1999
19 January 2010	–	6 June 2010
10 September 2010	–	22 January 2011
14 May 2021	–	28 July 2021
30 December 2021	–	10 May 2022
29 October 2022	–	20 December 2022

The deep sea diver

In the underwater world, life is graceful, filled with wondrous beings that live and thrive without the benefit of light. Because of the darkness of the deep sea, much of this realm is unexplored by humans. Except our Jupiter in Pisces friends visit these uninhabitable places in their fertile imaginations and in their often action-packed dreams.

Jupiter in Pisces pupils are very much like fish on dry land in the classroom. The edges of reality are sharp and uncomfortable, the noises deafening and confusing and the limitations of human experience simply too harsh. They seem half asleep most of the time – and they probably are.

If you can resist the urge to shake these pupils awake, you will discover that they are far more aware of their surroundings than you give them credit for. Highly intuitive, Jupiter in Pisces pupils have tapped into your feelings and those of their classmates. They understand you; they want to please you and if you give them a chance, they will find a happy medium that makes everyone comfortable.

At around six years of age, Jupiter in Pisces pupils seem to wake up to the incredible possibilities of words. They choose the words they want in their vocabulary carefully and then use them in ways you never would have imagined. They are dreamers and poets, inspiring and very impressionable. They will accept what you tell them and trust that you know what you're talking about. And they're easily distracted. For these reasons, precision at this age is vital to guide them onto the right path. They may not say much, but they are taking everything in. Content to read or write on their own, they may worry you and their parents with their simple serenity. They completely ignore their more boisterous classmates in favour of games that allow them to play out their fairy-tale fantasies or medieval adventures. These pupils respond well to symbols or archetypes found in stories as opposed to the literal meanings. Reluctant readers may respond well to links to favourite television characters or familiar characters from toys or games from home. Because they tend to thrive on mess and disorder, encourage them to learn to follow a schedule that includes plenty of opportunities to clear up after themselves. No, they won't like it as it interferes with their creative process, but you'll soon tire of the clutter they seem to thrive in.

In secondary school, it is easy for these pupils to become lost in the chaos and confusion. Their timetables might as well be in Sanskrit and the corridors of education resemble a maze. They will be late for every lesson, will forget homework and may not work out what a diary is for until they reach the end of Year 11. Persist in getting them to rely on proven navigational systems rather than on their psychic powers (which are formidable, but usually not in a useful way). Pin their ties to their collars and keep spare buttons, socks, shirts, blazers, PE kits, trousers, skirts, and whatever else they may lose during the course of a single day.

By the time they are ready to sit exams, they have suddenly become even more chaotic with new interests and sudden passions. This stage passes and the next thing they want to do is save the world, or they become fixated on the idea that having children is a great thing to do and they fall madly in love. These pupils have a great deal of compassion and forgiveness and will sacrifice their futures just so they can do something to make the world a better place. Instead of going to college, they will join the Peace Corps or go to Africa or anywhere else there is suffering that needs the gentle touch of a compassionate nature. Of course, we need more people in the world like our Jupiter in Pisces learners. And, as everyone knows, the world is only getting more chaotic. You see? Jupiter in Pisces pupils always win. Eventually.

If you're a teacher with Jupiter in Pisces, you probably haven't seen your planner for a very long time. But that's OK because you know the results of everyone's assessments due to academic osmosis (you pick up the vibes in the classroom). At staff dos, you will be on alcohol rations that seem far too strict and unfair. By the age of thirty, you will have read every single one of Betty Shine's books, had several near death experiences and secretly would rather live in the pandemonium at your school than in a conventional home. Speaking of home, yours is bedlam, mainly because of the sheer number of charity leaflets you keep, the wounded animals (including the two legged ones) you have rescued and the rubbish you keep meaning to recycle. We all know that one day you're going to pull yourself together and save the planet.

Fine-tuning the role of Jupiter

Jupiter in Pisces is ruled by Neptune and co-ruled by Jupiter. In mythology, Jupiter was god of the heavens whilst Neptune was god of the sea. This combination of rulers makes for a grand kingdom in which it is easy to become overwhelmed, sucked in or lost altogether.

Neptune influences are said to be addictive. Like Uranus, Neptune works collectively, affecting many people at once, and its effects may not become apparent until the collective group matures enough to have an effect on society.

Jupiter/Neptune in Aries – These pupils may idealise learning independently and/or the need for teamwork is sacrificed for greater efficiency. Mass media may take the form of teachers and authority figures. There may be an addiction to speed and immediate action.

Jupiter/Neptune in Taurus – These pupils may idealise education for the material gain it brings. Personal power may be sacrificed for greater stability in society. Mother Nature may be the main teacher and authority figure. There may be an addiction to material goods and property.

Jupiter/Neptune in Gemini – These pupils may idealise education for the improvement it brings to communication. Philosophies may be sacrificed for simplified codes. Symbols may be used to teach or to exert authority. There may be an addiction to communicating on a more psychic level.

Jupiter/Neptune in Cancer – These pupils may idealise education because it unites the family. Social status may be sacrificed for emotional freedom. Mother figures may replace traditional authority figures.

Jupiter/Neptune in Leo – These pupils may idealise glamour. Friendship and social groups may be sacrificed for youth and beauty. Young people become authority figures. There may be an addiction to entertainment.

Jupiter/Neptune in Virgo – These pupils may idealise human health. The use of imagination may be sacrificed for a more materialistic approach to learning. There may be an addiction to work and order.

Jupiter/Neptune in Libra – These pupils may idealise human relationships. The need for independent thought is sacrificed for the yearning for teamwork. Couples or pairs are seen as authority figures. There may be an addiction to a search for beauty and harmony.

Jupiter/ Neptune in Scorpio – These pupils may idealise power. The need for stability may be sacrificed for the urge to make profound changes in society. The occult may be seen as having ultimate power. There may be an addiction to the dark side of society.

Jupiter/Neptune in Sagittarius – These pupils may idealise foreign policies, philosophies or religions. Casual conversation may be sacrificed for profound spiritual growth. Authority figures may come from foreign lands or religions. There may be an addiction to holding unusual beliefs.

Jupiter/ Neptune in Capricorn – These pupils may idealise control and order. The rights of women or families may be sacrificed in order to strengthen the work force. There may be an addiction to maintaining traditional or conservative values.

Jupiter/Neptune in Aquarius – These pupils may idealise equality. The rights of the individual may be sacrificed for the rights of the collective. Authority figures may be those that search for alternatives to the accepted view. There may be an addiction to the unusual or unexpected.

Jupiter/Neptune in Pisces – These pupils may idealise sacrifice. Perfection may be sacrificed for chaos. Authority figures may be imaginary. There may be an addiction to what is perceived and accepted as the ideal.

Case study – Jodie Foster

19 November 1962, 8:14 PST
Los Angeles California 34°N03'08"118°W14'34"
Rodden rating: AA; Collector: Wilsons
Jupiter in Pisces, Neptune in Scorpio
Saturn in Aquarius, Uranus in Virgo
First Jupiter return: March 1974
First Saturn opposition: July 1976
Time between first Jupiter return, last Saturn opposition: 2 years, 4 months
First Saturn return: April and June 1991

By the time of her first Saturn opposition, Jodie had already made several television appearances. She is most widely known as the child actress in *Taxi Driver*, *The Little Girl Who Lives Down the Lane*, *Bugsy Malone* and *Freaky Friday*, all released as Jupiter made several oppositions to her natal planets in 1976.

In 1980 and 1981, transiting Jupiter and Saturn in Libra made a total of six conjunctions to Foster's natal MC. Two of these conjunctions took place as John Hinckley Jr. stalked the actress obsessively as she studied for her degree at Yale University. Eventually, on 30 March 1981, he attempted to assassinate then President Ronald Reagan to impress her, leaving four people, including Reagan, wounded by gunfire. The other four conjunctions in Libra took place as details of the full story was exposed to the public.

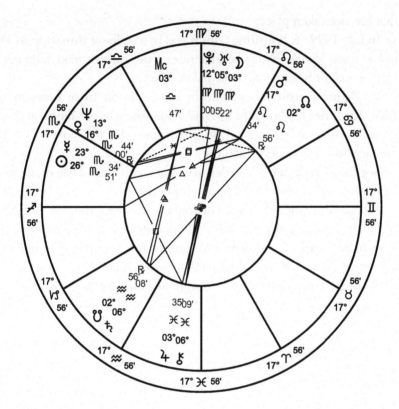

Jodie Foster – 19 November 1962

She is one of the few child actors to successfully manage the transition into adult roles, auditioning for the role of a rape victim in *The Accused* as 'one last try' at acting. The movie was filmed as Jupiter made a series of oppositions to her natal planets and would eventually earn Jodie an Oscar for Best Actress.

During her first Saturn return in 1991, she had starred in *Silence of the Lambs* and had directed *Little Man Tate*, to much acclaim. In 1994, transiting Jupiter made a series of conjunctions with her natal Neptune as she filmed *Maverick* and directed *Nell*. In 1997, during a series of Jupiter oppositions to her natal Mars, she starred in *Contact*, in which she had to act against a backdrop of bluescreen – which she found extremely challenging. In scenes involving a bluescreen the actors have to pretend to be a part of an action scene when in reality the action is added after the scene has been shot. The result is a realistic sequence of something that has not taken place.

In late 1999, as transiting Saturn was in a series of three oppositions to her natal Venus, Foster became one of the highest paid actresses in Hollywood for her role in *Anna and the King*.

As Saturn transited her Pluto by square aspect three times in late 2001-2002, her leading role in *Panic Room* became the most successful movie opening of her career. During this time, she also closed down her production company Egg Pictures.

For the next decade, Foster's career was a very mixed bag of successes and projects that could have been a lot better.

As transiting Jupiter squared her natal Pluto three times in late 2012-2013, she received the Cecil B. DeMille lifetime achievement award; after many years of speculation regarding her sexuality, she used the acceptance speech to come out publicly as a lesbian.

As of 2017 Foster continues to work as a director.

SATURN

Saturn takes about twenty-nine and a half years to complete its journey through the zodiac. However, it reaches a critical stage at its halfway point, known as the opposition, which roughly coincides with the time just before the fifteenth birthday. To be opposite to something means that we are able to step away from that something and look at it from another point of view. We are seeing that something in a new light. We are examining it, measuring it and considering it.

An opposition pulls us in different directions and forces us to make a conscious decision: in Saturn's case, either we fight for what we want or we give up and do something else. This is seldom an easy or uncomplicated process.

In sharp contrast to Jupiter, Saturn is the planet of responsibility. From an early age, the mythological Saturn took life very seriously. Tired of watching his father Uranus devour his brothers and sisters on a daily basis, Saturn castrated his father. Perhaps this is why Saturn grew up into a god who was fearful his own children might overpower him. Consequently, Saturn, like his own father, ate his children. And he had every right to be fearful because his own son Zeus (Jupiter) would eventually disembowel his father in order to free his siblings from his father's stomach.

The fear of failure can drive us to do things we ordinarily would not do. Of course, none of us would eat our own children as Saturn did, but we may push ourselves to our physical, mental or emotional limits in other ways. Or we may just curl up and die.

Saturn's fate teaches us that there are limits to our own power and that sooner or later we will be brought to task for our actions. Saturn represents the reality of our situation and the boundaries to which we are subjected.

For pupils enduring their first Saturn opposition, life can seem a little heavy going. Although they may continue to grow, the majority of the growth process is slowing down by the time of their Saturn opposition. Some pupils experience problems with their teeth and have to wear orthodontic braces (Saturn rules the hard parts of their bodies such as teeth and bones). Although sex continues to interest them, they are starting to understand the consequences of pregnancy and STDs. Sex isn't as funny to them as it was when they were younger.

At the Saturn opposition, the reality of working life is imposed upon them either through responsible jobs like babysitting or Saturday morning chores. In the UK, it is done in a more structured way through work experience, usually in Year 10 when they are fourteen to fifteen years of age. Work experience allows pupils to sample life after the school years by trying out a job they have expressed an interest in. They are interviewed and hired for two weeks and are not paid for the privilege. They usually learn that life at the bottom of the employment food chain is not where they would like to end up. This hopefully gives them an incentive to do well in their exams so they can acquire the qualifications they need to get the job they do want. They start to understand that hard work is well rewarded, either financially or through job satisfaction.

Of course, exams are a metaphor for the Saturn opposition. In the run up to them, pupils will have pared down and chosen their GCSE subjects as opposed to having a variety of taster subjects presented to them as at their Jupiter return a few years previously. As many teachers will attest, there is a world of difference between teaching Year 7 pupils and Year 10 pupils. Year 7s still want to play. Year 10s usually have the idea that they will be tested soon. Very few people can actually sit down and complete an exam without careful preparation. Following the exam, there is a long period of waiting for the results. And finally a proclamation arrives: either they have passed or failed. Throughout our lives we will be examined by someone or some process, such as interviews or other types of examinations. We learn that it takes hard work and practice to master the skills we need to be successful in life.

The following sections describe the learning processes for Saturn in each of the zodiac signs and provide a celebrity example. Typically, celebrities are successful people and it can be useful to see how Jupiter and Saturn manifest at times of success.

Saturn in Aries

26 April 1937	–	18 October 1937
15 January 1938	–	6 July 1939
23 September 1939	–	20 September 1940
4 March 1967	–	29 April 1969
7 April 1994	–	9 June 1998
26 October 1998	–	1 March 1999

The well-armed warrior

Imagine a lone knight.

He rises from the comfort of his bed and begins his daily preparations. After the quickest of washes (using tar soap and cold water), he begins dressing in the suit of armour he has shined to perfection the night before. He then picks up his sword. The sword is heavy and sharp but this is a weapon the knight has used all his life. It fits in his hand as if it had grown in it. Of course, the knight has a horse. It is a massive snorting beast which has killed several previous owners but has been pounded into submission by its current master. The knight and the horse have prepared for battle. Are you ready?

Of course, Saturn in Aries children don't prepare for the battle in the same way as knights, but the sentiment is there. Saturn in Aries is a strongly masculine combination. It's rough and tumble stuff. Non-athletic children will sharpen other skills if they lack physical prowess. Girls in particular are adept at using words – and later sex – as weapons of mastery. Weaker, less competitive children (such as those with Saturn in Pisces) are cannon fodder for these children. Come to think of it, older, stronger and bigger children (Saturn in Taurus) are also in danger. Schools who think they have a strong anti-bullying policy will be put to the test. Saturn in Aries children usually hit hard (be it with fists or words), are devastatingly accurate and, by the time you realise what has happened, irrevocable damage has already been done.

Saturn in Aries children tend not to gang up, or if they do, they will quickly disperse at the first sign of trouble. These children are generals, not foot soldiers. And this is their weakness. Sooner or later, usually around the age of seven, these children realise they are not infallible. They will lose a significant battle. Bones get broken, teeth get knocked out or there's a family tragedy that brings on the tears. Injuries and needing a shoulder to cry on are the badges of shame for these children. They might look and act tough, but they're human just the same.

In the classroom, they are independent learners who will not want teachers or fellow classmates marking their books or assessing their progress. Teach them how to self-assess and give them the tools and knowledge to enable them to improve. Visual aids such as graphs and charts work well, but let the pupils create them using the data they have collected themselves. Be sensitive to their dear little egos – say or do the wrong thing and you will have a never-ending battle on your hands. These pupils are very hard on themselves, so you shouldn't have to be. Give them clear targets to aim for and make a competition of it. Let them know you're going to display the results and that the winners get medals – I mean prizes.

At around the age of fourteen or fifteen, these children suddenly realise that it's not too much fun doing things on their own all the time and they will want to partner up with someone. Anyone will do. Social events become a serious distraction and sexual issues come to the fore. Boys become promiscuous players and girls will catch onto this quickly and stop putting out so readily. But sexual games will play havoc. It's like a scene from *Grease*. The genders polarise. Be open and frank about sex but distract the boys with competitions and encourage the girls to laugh at them – I mean support them. Girls may favour the more aesthetic arts (unless the girls are ultra-sporty, they will be way more concerned about looking pretty and playing hard to get than getting sweaty), so get them competing in ways that don't cause them to get their hair messy or make their mascara run. By the time this phase is over, thes students will be ready to learn that success in itself is very appealing, leads to high-powered relationships and gets them laid by beautiful women or rich men.

If you're a teacher with Saturn in Aries, you've most likely had serious issues around discipline. You expect a lot from yourself and you make it impossible for others to live up to your expectations. For you, losing or under-achieving is unacceptable. Your pupils may be terrified of you or think it a sport to antagonise you. They like to watch the veins in your forehead throb (which will progress to a massive headache later), but they generally do as you say. For a little while anyway. If you play your strengths right, pupils will like your no-nonsense approach and honesty, so long as you don't come across as trying to overpower them with your authority. Your colleagues are in awe of you, your tidy desk and the way you manage the dinner queue. You're an easy target for angry parents. To them, you are the amalgamation of every authority figure who belittled them in the classroom or criticised their athletic prowess. And they will want revenge. Everyone will want to take pot-shots at you but no-one will dare to laugh in your face. At least, this is what you tell yourself. If you're over thirty, you might have realised that walking around with a chip on your shoulder only invites someone to knock it off. Love may hurt at this time – if you're single you might want to get married and if you're married you might want to be single.

Don't beat yourself up over your limitations. If you're over sixty, you might be thinking life would have been better if only you hadn't been so hard on yourself and the people you purported to love. Try to learn this lesson as early as you can. As they say, life is too short to live it in regret.

Fine-tuning the role of Saturn

Saturn in Aries is ruled by Mars, the planet of action, energy and initiative. The influence of Saturn disciplines and hones.

Mars in Aries – These children are driven to be impatient if there is any delay in getting what they want. In their impatience, they often forget what it is they want to achieve. Authority figures are often seen as blockages rather than facilitators. They need continual reminders of clear targets so that they can self-monitor their progress.

Mars in Taurus – These children are driven to display their great reserves of strength and stamina, but they can be plodders if they lack direction. They have a good eye for natural beauty and will search for opportunities to express their sense of beauty and physical order. They need to see their targets regularly and be allowed to be self-driven. Authority figures will often find that they resist encouragement to try harder. Because they are (or have the potential to be) master craftsmen, giving them the materials to create their own progress chart will help to motivate them.

Mars in Gemini – These children are driven to display a great deal of nervous energy. If bored, they can't resist teasing and goading others with their barbed words. Argumentative by nature, they will resist invitations to settle down and work. They love word games and intellectual contests, so authority figures can use this aptitude to keep them entertained and quiet. Predictable routines invite them to show their mischievous side, so try to ensure there is a variety of activities to help keep them on task.

Mars in Cancer – These children are driven to be moody and needy learners if they feel insecure. They whine and whinge if they have to do something they don't feel familiar with. Because they cling to what they know, it can be difficult for them to progress unless there are clear links from one lesson to the next. It can take a long while for them to warm to new authority figures, so stability is best. They are motivated to do well for those they feel close to, so teamwork with other children they know and trust can help to support them.

Mars in Leo – These children are driven to be the centre of attention at all times if they feel they are not noticed. If they are quiet, they're plotting their big entrance. Other children (and sometimes teachers) can resent their melodramatic ways and actively search for ways to knock them down a peg or two. The hardest lesson for these pupils to learn is when to draw attention to themselves and when to wait patiently in the wings.

Mars in Virgo – These children are driven to organise and analyse. They are exacting in their learning natures – and often exasperatingly so. Teachers and authority figures are often treated like they're messing up the place. They will often claim they don't have enough time to finish activities, but then knock themselves out trying to complete everything to perfection. They need clear time limits.

Mars in Libra – These children are driven to form relationships with everyone around them. They actively try to find the good in everyone even if it means their own sense of morality is compromised. They want to see authority figures as their allies and are usually eager to please – unless separated to work on their own. Working independently is a necessary exam skill, so a balance can be found through peer assessment.

Mars in Scorpio – These children are driven to show their personal power. Often they have a do or die attitude that usually gets the desired response, whether positive or negative. They are naturally provocative and authority figures and teachers often find these pupils can hit where it hurts – and in the process damage their chances of learning. These pupils do like winning against the odds, so sometimes it pays to let them work out lessons for themselves.

Mars in Sagittarius – These children are driven to be adventurous and will shake off any attempt at discipline. They tend to be know-it-alls, but often find it difficult to justify their opinions with facts. Teachers and authority figures are often viewed as killjoys, but honest feedback is valued by these learners. They can usually see the need for direction if it can be demonstrated they won't achieve their goals without it.

Mars in Capricorn – These children are driven to be successful. This may sound ideal, but these learners tend to use others to reach their goals and then discard the relationship until needed the next time. They tend to burn their bridges with authority figures. Although generally reliable, these pupils need to be taught basic human kindness and manners.

Mars in Aquarius – These pupils are driven to experiment. They want to re-order current structures and make way for the new age. Revolutions were headed by these types of pupils – and these pupils could do with being reminded that many revolutionaries actually lost their heads. Teachers and authority figures can help by working with them as opposed to driving them towards their goals.

Mars in Pisces – These pupils are driven to be lost in the melee of the classroom. They will put their heads down on the desk the minute the authority figures turn their backs. Given instructions, they immediately forget them. However, if permitted to work with energetic pupils, these learners come to life and become infected with enthusiasm. They need to be kept on their toes – and kept awake through lessons.

Case study – Dustin Hoffman

8 August 1937, 17:07 PST
Los Angeles, California 34°N03'08" 118°W14'34"
Rodden rating: AA; Collector: Rodden
Jupiter in Capricorn, Saturn in Aries
Saturn in Aries, Mars in Sagittarius
First Jupiter return: February 1949
First Saturn opposition: August 1951
Time between first Jupiter return and last Saturn opposition: 2 years, 6 months
Second Jupiter return: January 1961
First Saturn return: April 1967
Third Jupiter return: January 1973
Fourth Jupiter return: December 1984
Second Saturn return: May and September 1996 and February 1997
Fifth Jupiter return: December 1996

Dustin Hoffman began his career as an actor in 1960, just before his second Jupiter return in January 1961. Until his first Saturn return he was cast in off-Broadway shows and made appearances on television. During this time, he was a devoted pupil of the Actor's Studio where he learned method acting. This stage of his life most resembles the lone knight preparing for battle. He carefully honed and practised his craft, emerging from this stage of preparation to achieve his first critical success in the off-Broadway production of *Eh?* which premiered on 16 October 1966. His first significant big break was being cast in the main role of the blockbuster movie *The Graduate* in which he portrayed the angst-filled twenty-one year old Benjamin Braddock. The film was released just after his first Saturn return in December 1966.

In the film, the young Benjamin is famously seduced by the older Mrs Robinson but eventually marries her daughter. Interestingly, in real life, Anne Bancroft, who played Mrs Robinson, is only six years older than

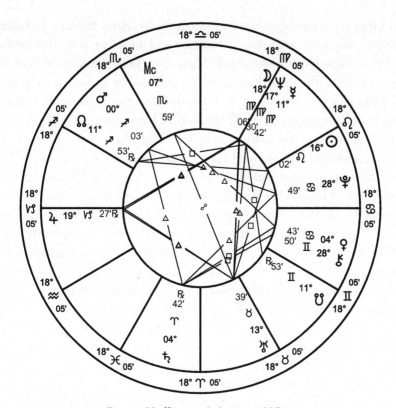

Dustin Hoffman – 8 August 1937

Hoffman. Her Saturn is conjunct Hoffman's Jupiter, her North Node is conjunct his Saturn whilst her Pluto sits snugly on his descendant. Powerful seduction indeed!

Shortly after this, Hoffman starred in his second major movie, *Midnight Cowboy* and afterwards *Little Big Man*, both of which led to BAFTA awards. During the filming, transiting Jupiter made a series of three oppositions to his natal Saturn (November 1968, February 1969 and August 1969). This is Jupiter's reward for doing the work required by Saturn.

By 1978, transiting Jupiter in Cancer was opposite to Saturn in Capricorn as Hoffman filmed multi-BAFTA winning *Kramer versus Kramer*. In this movie the trials and tribulations of a family (Jupiter in Cancer) during a marital breakdown (Saturn in Aries) are portrayed. A few years later in 1981, he went on to star as a cross-dressing, starving actor in *Tootsie*. During the filming, both transiting Saturn and Jupiter in Libra (relationships) were in square to his natal Saturn. Transiting Jupiter magnifies anything it touches and in Libra it is the area of relationships that is highlighted. There is no better exacerbation of the relationship difficulties that can be experienced by Saturn in Aries than a straight actor dressing up as 'Dorothy' and the comedy that ensues from the complications and confusion of having sexual relations with one woman (as a man), falling in love with another woman (dressed as a woman) whilst being pursued (as a woman) by several other men.

Transiting Jupiter was again in conjunction with his natal Saturn as he filmed *Ishtar* with Warren Beatty, a box office flop (and bearer of several Golden Raspberry awards) and *Rain Man*, the story of an autistic savant man who inherits a large sum of money. In sharp contrast to *Ishtar*, *Rain Man* won several major awards for Hoffman, including best picture and best actor. With both movies under the same transit, what made the difference between success and failure for Hoffman?

Ishtar was released just after transiting Jupiter moved into conjunction with Hoffman's natal Saturn. Transiting Jupiter conjunct Saturn in Aries magnifies issues to do with the self – and, from many critics' perspectives, *Ishtar* was a silly, self-indulgent, extremely expensive project that paid over the top fees to two spoiled actors.

However, the theme of self persists in *Rain Man*. Hoffman plays a man who is locked in his own world and is essentially unable to understand the feelings of others. By the time *Rain Man* was released, transiting Saturn was square to its natal position. During the filming, Hoffman employed the lessons he had learned as a method actor a whole Saturn cycle before. Saturn demands precision – and not even 'lucky' Jupiter can worm his way out of that one.

Saturn in Taurus

7 July 1939	–	22 September 1939
20 September 1940	–	8 May 1942
30 April 1969	–	18 June 1971
10 January 1972	–	21 February 1972
10 June 1998	–	25 October 1998
2 March 1999	–	10 August 2000
18 October 2000	–	20 April 2001

The tight-fisted banker

Imagine a fat banker in an opulent room counting his loot while outside, orphans go hungry.

The banker pulls the shades and carefully puts his money away, locks the door and stows the key away safely. He opens his door and, after hearing tales of woe from the orphans, slowly and deliberately peels a few notes from the wad of cash in his wallet. The orphans think he's Santa Claus and this makes the banker smile – not too much of course, because there are greater joys in life than making orphans smile. Like eating for example. A good massage. Counting money. So he closes the door, locks it and takes his money out again.

Most children do not have access to vast sums of money, but this doesn't stop them fantasising about what it would be like. Saturn in Taurus children know that money has to be earned and will readily take on huge responsibilities to secure future fortunes. The entrepreneurial spirit of these children is a wonder to behold, and both genders will be able to outdo their teachers in generating business plans, raising funds and re-investing the money in ways no-one else would have thought about. Unlike Saturn in Aries children, hitting and aggression shouldn't be too much of a problem because these children do not like physical discomfort (and hitting someone often hurts the hitter more than the target). The rare fights will be spectacular and injuries will be likely. Theft and exploitation might be causes for concern, though it might be discovered the victim was in collusion. Treats lifted from lunch boxes will be re-sold at treble the original cost.

However, Saturn in Taurus is generally physically slow and heavy, so offenders usually learn they aren't fast enough to make good thieves. They learn there are better ways of earning cash – and food is best eaten rather than sold. These amazingly creative and resourceful children can turn mundane items into works of art and then sell them. They have a knack for tuning into your likes and capitalising on them. Look in their pencil case and they may have dozens of spare pens or pencils – which they'll loan to another child (or to you) for a price, of course. What drives them and their seemingly instinctive business sense is a fear of losing everything. At about the age of seven, they may have witnessed severe loss of status: Dad went bankrupt, Mum lost her job, or a court case ruined someone's reputation and that person can never raise their head again in public. The threat of having nothing terrifies Saturn in Taurus children, because they think losing money means losing face. Sometimes they're so scared of losing everything that they hide their wealth from everyone else. These are the people everyone thinks to be poor, but when they die, it's discovered they've amassed a fortune.

In the classroom, Saturn in Taurus children can be very unmotivated unless they can see learning will lead to making money somehow. They don't like being assessed unless they can see that the right people will notice – future employers, fellow entrepreneurs or people who have knowledge about investing. And this is where teachers can get them on side: teach them that an education is an investment. Reward them with merits and then reward them again by letting them indulge themselves in their favourite activity: adding up their wealth.

Around the age of fourteen to fifteen, these pupils will suddenly realise they have been led around by the nose by your incentives. Merits become worthless unless they can be used to purchase the things they want – and these kids want top quality stuff. They may resort to dirty tricks to get them – and you will have no idea what is going on because they've learned the art of the under-the-table business deal. Remind them that it's pretty difficult to be productive in detention – or jail. Show them how prospective employers value well-spoken, honest employees. Video record them doing practice interviews and watch how quickly they improve. Gaining material wealth and getting drunk on the power it brings becomes a serious distraction, and this experience transforms them so much that two distinct types of Saturn in Taurus emerge: those who flaunt their wealth and those who become terrified to let anyone know what they have. By the time this phase is over, these pupils will learn the importance of morals and that a lack of them can surely only lead to no-one wanting to do business with them.

If you're a teacher with Saturn in Taurus, you've probably found yourself in the role of fund-raiser or bean-counter because you're trustworthy and dependable. You look the part of the well-heeled business person and have probably made it known you've made some fine investments and can therefore indulge in a little luxury. Conversely, you may be embarrassed by your wealth and go to great lengths to hide it. Your lessons are slow and plodding, making it difficult for more energetic children to get anything out of them. So you just give them more work to do. Colleagues and supervisors try to persuade you to try new techniques, but these just make you suspicious. Your bling – or lack of it – is a frequent topic of conversation, and your pupils will be curious about how you handle your money. Boasting or behaving as if your Be-bop pencil case is the most important thing in the world to you can make you a target for theft, not because you have what anyone wants but because everyone likes to watch you fret over your losses. Nothing beats seeing the normally sedate Saturn in Taurus teacher suddenly click into over-drive. Parents like you because they want to schmooze with you. They think you have connections or the secrets of success. If you're over thirty, you have probably secured all the wealth you will ever need but think it's not enough. By the time you're sixty, you realise there's only so much caviar to consume, fancy holidays to go on, or powerful clothes to wear, before you realise you've been kidding yourself about the true value of life. Remember, you can't take anything to the grave with you.

Fine-tuning the role of Saturn

Saturn in Taurus is ruled by Venus, the planet of love, beauty and harmony. To get a more specific idea of how a person with Saturn in Taurus works towards success, look to the sign Venus occupies.

Note: *Venus rules the signs of both Taurus and Libra. The main difference between Taurus and Libra is that in Taurus there is an emphasis on natural beauty, whereas the emphasis in Libra is on artificially enhancing the natural to make it even more beautiful. Taurus is concerned with maintaining the status quo and resisting change, whereas Libra is concerned with bringing people together.*

Venus in Aries – These pupils love to learn independently. They usually have a child-like simplicity that is appealing but they can be quite impish and delight in getting others to misbehave. They flirt continuously but often flee when the object of their affection returns the favour. Teachers and authority figures should try to keep moving targets forward to ensure these pupils stay interested.

Venus in Taurus – These pupils love to learn kinaesthetically. They like to touch and look over everything. They shake things to see how they sound and will even lick things if they think you're not looking. They are usually greedy to learn and are essentially very resourceful. They like to think teachers and authority figures are dependent on them, so let them do the stationery orders every now and again.

Venus in Gemini – These pupils love to learn through developing their vocabulary. If they are young enough, they will take easily to new languages. Words will become tools later in life. They generally regard authority figures and teachers as being too slow to be much good to them but will appreciate it if there are a variety of things for them to try.

Venus in Cancer – These pupils love to learn history and local knowledge. They like to dwell on what was taught yesterday so there is usually a need to briefly revisit a previous lesson so they feel comfortable. Teachers and authority figures are usually regarded as extended family so changes are not welcomed by these learners.

Venus in Leo – These pupils love to learn dramatically. They like to make big steps towards progress – and they want to know they have been noticed. These pupils will rehearse long sequences of learning steps and will delight in showing off what they can do. Teachers and authority figures should encourage these learners to work with less ostentatious learners because Venus in Leo loves to show off partners as well as their own skills.

Venus in Virgo – These pupils love to learn carefully. They are extremely critical and scornful of others' mistakes, which can mean they are lonely and isolated from other pupils. Teachers and authority figures should encourage them to apply their attention to detail to activities everyone can enjoy: organising parties and outings is one of their specialities.

Venus in Libra – These pupils love to learn with others, but very often there is not a lot of progress to show for it. They usually attend lessons looking their best and follow every social rule to the letter, however they often take advantage of teachers and authority figures. Bargains can be made by promising to let them listen to their favourite music if they meet set objectives.

Venus in Scorpio – These pupils love to learn about how things work. They take a special interest in knowing what things are worth to others. Usually they like to pretend they are above needing or wanting anything. Teachers and authority figures are not usually seen as terribly important – until exam time. Generally these pupils work well if they feel they have a conspiratorial relationship with others.

Venus in Sagittarius – These pupils love to learn about foreign places and philosophies. They save their money and then gamble it or spend it extravagantly. They are restless and eager to learn but require quick and honest feedback to motivate them. Teachers and authority figures are often treated with reverence if they feel time and energy is being invested in them.

Venus in Capricorn – These pupils love to learn how to be successful in life. They have natural and keen business minds but are too money grubbing to be liked by others (and they really don't care if anyone likes them). Usually they have no patience for art, romantic illusions or emotions – unless they think it can get them somewhere. Teachers and authority figures are respected only if they come across as being experienced.

Venus in Aquarius – These pupils love to learn how they can be different from everyone else. They are usually inventive when it comes to devising get-rich-quick schemes. Teachers and authority figures are generally regarded as mugs that deserve to be swindled for conforming to Ofsted.

Venus in Pisces – These pupils love to become absorbed by learning. When they reach the age to go to university, they martyr themselves to education and feel sorry for themselves when the educational system rejects their sloppy study habits. Teachers and authority figures need to help them become organised and more resourceful if they are to survive in the dog-eat-dog world into which they are thrust.

Case study – Bob Dylan

24 May 1941, 21:05 CST
Duluth, Minnesota 46°N47'092°W06'23"
Rodden rating: AA; Collector: Steinbrecher
Jupiter in Taurus, Venus in Gemini
Saturn in Taurus, Venus in Gemini
First Jupiter return: May 1953
First Saturn opposition: January 1953, April and October 1955
Time between first Jupiter return and last Saturn opposition: 2 years, 6 months
Second Jupiter return: April 1965
First Saturn return: June, October 1970 and April 1971
Third Jupiter return: August, October 1976 and March 1977
Fourth Jupiter return: July, December 1988 and March 1989
Second Saturn return: May 2000
Fifth Jupiter return: June 2000

By 1963, transiting Saturn in Aquarius had begun a series of squares to Dylan's Saturn in Taurus. The year before, he had changed his name from Robert Zimmerman to Bob Dylan and had signed a contract with Albert Grossman. Although it is unusual to achieve long-lasting success before the first Saturn return, at twenty-one he was already so successful that he felt he could storm out of the *Ed Sullivan Show* without damaging his career. But then, by this time he had already released two successful albums. By July the same year, he was singing protest songs

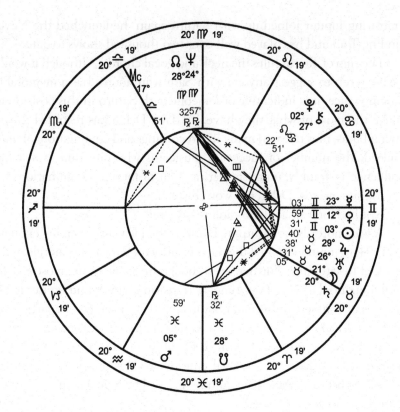

Bob Dylan – 24 May 1941

with Joan Baez at the Washington Monument. Although appearing far less glamorous than the typical successful singer, Dylan displayed the possessiveness typically present in someone with Saturn in Taurus: in his case, this related to his beloved motorbike.

In the summer of 1966, Saturn made two oppositions to Dylan's North Node. Saturn stops us in our tracks and, for Dylan, this manifested in two distinct ways. One, he was booed off stage for using an electric guitar that summer. A few days later, he had a serious motorbike crash that left him unable (or unwilling) to perform for several years.

In 'A Song for Bob Dylan' David Bowie described Dylan's voice as being "like sand and glue". But yet his voice, his songs and his spirit of rebellion have endured across the generations. As the author and poet Joyce Carol Oates described him: "When we first heard this raw, very young, and seemingly untrained voice, frankly nasal, as if sandpaper could sing, the effect was dramatic and electrifying."[11] Nevertheless, as transiting Jupiter joined up with Saturn again, he launched the Never Ending Tour and has played well over two thousand shows to date.

The sign of Taurus rules the neck and vocal chords. Although it would be a stretch to suggest anyone with Saturn in Taurus has a memorable singing voice, it is indicative of someone with Saturn in this position to make the most of what they have. To date, Dylan has recorded thirty-four albums, plus released many live recordings and compilation albums. Indeed, the number of successful musicians who cite him as a major influence is, frankly, quite staggering. Out of fourteen nominations for prestigious awards, Dylan has won thirteen.

Not bad for a singer who can't really sing!

A final note about Saturn in Taurus is the idea of not having enough. In 1994, as Jupiter opposed the natal position of Saturn, Dylan released a book of his etchings. Further, even though he is one of the most prolific and influential artists of our time, as transiting Saturn and Jupiter made a series of contacts to his natal Saturn in 2003, he agreed to participate in several lucrative commercial advertisements. Saturn made a serious square to its natal position in 2007 and shortly after, the Pulitzer Prize jury awarded him a special citation for "his profound impact on popular music and American culture, marked by lyrical compositions of extraordinary poetic power".[12]

Saturn in Gemini

8 May 1942	–	20 June 1944
19 June 1971	–	10 January 1972
21 February 1972	–	1 August 1973
8 January 1974	–	18 April 1974
11 August 2000	–	17 October 2000
21 April 2001	–	4 June 2003

The serious academic

Imagine if Mercury, messenger of the gods, had sandals of lead rather than feathers.

Instead of flying around delivering quick messages and frivolous gossip, his news is usually seriously important and stops everyone in their tracks. This Mercury is the one for whom the phrase "Don't shoot the messenger" was intended. Saturn in Gemini has learned to keep his mouth shut.

Somehow, somewhere Saturn in Gemini children have learned that if they're going to talk, they're going to have to know what they're talking about. They bury themselves in books. Their conversations are full of heavy references to obscure passages and authors. Their homework is always carefully researched; they answer your questions so thoroughly there's no room for argument. They turn every little assignment into a detail-laden thesis. But Saturn in Gemini has its extreme. In mythology, Mercury was the only god who could visit the underworld and return to the land of the living in one piece. Not all pupils with Saturn in Gemini are able to talk about their experiences. The other extreme of Saturn in Gemini is the reluctant pupil who is afraid everyone thinks they are stupid. This pupil is distrusting of teachers and education in general, because to them, learning brings pain. Information flies by too quickly for them to process it to their discerning standards, or they lose interest because everything is moving too slowly. So they find other things to do. Saturn in Gemini pupils pose a particular problem to teachers because their extremes are both difficult to predict and difficult to re-direct. You could be lulled into the notion that these pupils will try anything, could do anything and are therefore ready for anything. And then one day, there you are teaching the finer points of American literature and suddenly you notice your pupils are doodling all over their books, texting on their mobiles or staring out of the window. You've lost them. Some know everything about John Steinbeck and some aren't ready to be dropped into 1930s California. The class polarises with neither side telling you what's wrong. Time for a pop quiz you've prepared ahead of time (because you know what they're like!). Better yet, get them to make up the questions and see if you know the answers. At about the age of seven, these pupils realised that what teachers are looking for is perfection: some other bright spark won the borough's spelling bee or maths competition or got 100% on the science test – and they had failed. They will remember this humiliation and do absolutely anything to avoid such embarrassment ever again. Such a shame, the teachers said, the loser had such potential. Of course, the teachers probably never said this but the Saturn in Gemini pupil understood the experience to mean that they are, and forever more will be, a failure. These pupils fear seeming to be intellectual inferiors. Show them you are an eternal pupil rather than a teacher and you will have taught them that for everyone, some lessons are more difficult than others.

Teachers with Saturn in Gemini pupils will have to watch for the signs of boredom, because by the time they are fourteen or fifteen these children will have seen knowledge and higher education worshipped like a god and it will give them an inferiority complex. How will they ever measure up? Some will have their confidence knocked so badly they will be rendered speechless. Others will plunge headfirst into heavily academic work for which they are not ready. This phase will pass and these pupils will learn to steady their pace, focus their interests and choose a subject they can specialise in.

If you're a teacher with Saturn in Gemini, you probably have a bad back from all the heavy books you carry around with you. You're the pub quiz champion but you still fear someone else is smarter than you – and that fear extends to being frightened your pupils will out-do you. So you pile on the homework and mark it with such scarily scathing remarks that even your best pupils come up with creative excuses for not doing it. Parents know you have a way with the critical word and so they avoid you. Take some time and listen to yourself: we know that you have a PhD in particle physics, fellowships with several top universities worldwide and can recite *pi* to two hundred digits forwards and backwards. You're smart enough. Get some fresh air, will you? At around the age of thirty, you will probably want to stop teaching kids and start teaching adults. You'll get your book published and everyone will fawn over it. By the time you're sixty, you will have amassed a library of books you have written based on a lifetime of research. But you will realise that words are just words and that maybe the word "stupid" doesn't even exist at all.

Fine-tuning the role of Saturn

Saturn in Gemini is ruled Mercury, the planet of communication and travel. To get a more specific idea of how a person with Saturn in Gemini works towards success, look at the sign Mercury occupies.

Mercury in Aries – Generally these pupils have active minds that need to be exercised regularly. Their interests are usually short but intensely lived. They are generally straight talkers who thrive on intellectual competition and provoke immediate reactions from others. These pupils need to be taught to listen so that they can develop their promising eloquence.

Mercury in Taurus – Generally, these pupils rely on their common sense rather than on new information. They can appear to be slow-minded, but their stubbornness and reluctance to take on new facts hides a sound and patient mind. They are practical and tend to know much about business. Their fear of losing money can often mean they become stuck in patterns that are no longer working for them. They need to be encouraged to move onto different interests.

Mercury in Gemini – Generally these pupils have enormous amounts of nervous energy but they lack the confidence to express themselves. Some keep their nervous hands busy with numerous, productive projects; others waste their ample mental energies by flitting from job to meaningless job. They fear boredom. They need to be grounded with worthwhile activities and be shown practical ways of working off nervous energy (such as physical exercise).

Mercury in Cancer – Generally these pupils suppress their emotions to the extent they are like a shaken up bottle of cola: eventually the lid will not be able to hold the inevitable explosion. They pick up on everything around them including irrelevant facts and they rely on their memories (which can be distorted). They fear emotions because they are often drowning in them. They need authority figures to help them focus on the big picture rather than the trivial.

Mercury in Leo – Generally these pupils are proud of their intellectual achievements. They tend to be passionate writers and speakers but although they come across as confident and tend to be bossy, very often they have a paralysing fear of failure. They tend to focus only on what they are good at and it can be difficult to persuade them to diversify. They need to be encouraged to develop their creativity.

Mercury in Virgo – Generally these pupils are very analytical and often focus on one particular talent. They are able to ingest huge amounts of information but can spit out what is immediately relevant (much to everyone's relief). They fear mess. They are so serious, they often need to be encouraged to set time aside to play and be a little silly.

Mercury in Libra – Generally these pupils are very sociable and bend over backwards to accommodate everyone. They are very adept spin doctors and diplomats but ultimately lose their own sense of self. They fear upsetting others and making enemies. They need to be encouraged to dig a little deeper into self-knowledge so they understand what is important to them.

Mercury in Scorpio – Generally these pupils work towards controlling their environment. They do this by ensuring they understand how everything works – and that includes understanding how other people think. They fear being found out and need authority figures to help them focus their targets of intrigue into worthwhile projects.

Mercury in Sagittarius – Generally these pupils work towards finding answers. They can be irreverent and garrulous in their attempts, and consequently upset other people. They fear being tied down intellectually and tend to be eternal pupils. They need authority figures to help them focus on what they feel most strongly about.

Mercury in Capricorn – Generally these pupils work towards stabilising themselves mentally. They can be extremely resistant to learning new topics. They take scepticism to new heights because they fear that change means shoddy workmanship and extravagant spending. They need authority figures to help them loosen up and try new things.

Mercury in Aquarius – Generally these pupils work towards grasping innovative ideas. They are way-out thinkers that other people regard as mere cranks. They fear things staying the same because they know that if things remain the same, they will never fit in. They need authority figures to help them choose experiments that are worthwhile.

Mercury in Pisces – Generally these pupils work towards using their intuition to learn. They are natural mediums to the spirit world but are like fish out of water in the material one. They fear throwing anything away lest their rubbish turns out to be valuable. They need authority figures to help them develop organisational skills.

Case study – Julia Child

15 August 1912, 23:30 PST
Pasadena California 34°N08'52"118°W08'37"
Rodden rating: AA; Collector: CAH
Jupiter in Sagittarius, Jupiter in rulership
Saturn in Gemini, Mercury in Virgo
First Jupiter return: December 1923
First Saturn opposition: June and September 1927
Time between first Jupiter return and last Saturn opposition: 3 years, 7 months
Second Jupiter return: December 1935
First Saturn return: May 1942
Third Jupiter return: November 1947
Fourth Jupiter return: November 1959

Fifth Jupiter return: October 1971
Second Saturn return: July and November 1971 and April 1972

With Saturn in Gemini on her ascendant and Jupiter on her descendant in Sagittarius, Julia Child's adventures with the two planets are more obvious.

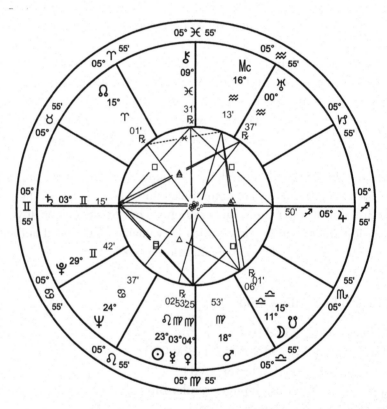

Julia Child – 15 August 1912

For example, Saturn, normally noted for restriction, had the opposite effect on Julia, who grew to an imposing six foot two. She regarded being too tall as a handicap and by the time of her first Saturn return in 1942 had accepted that she would remain unmarried. She had not yet discovered her love for France or French cooking, the two interests which paved her road to success. It wasn't until she met Paul Child, who she later married, that her life opened up to the promises of Saturn.

The descendant typically represents the signals we unconsciously send out to people that attract them to us. Jupiter in Sagittarius is ever buoyant, exuberant and fortunate. In the mid-1940s, Julia was awarded for her work with the OSS in China, and amongst her many virtues was her inherent drive and cheerfulness. Her delightful nature attracted a man who would introduce her to fine cuisine.

In 1946, Jupiter the ruler of her descendant was square to Uranus the month she finally married her gastronome husband. We can hear the astrology echoing through Julia's words when she said: "I was lucky to marry Paul. He was a great inspiration, his enthusiasm about wine and food helped to shape my tastes...I would have never had my career without Paul Child." [13]

Towards the end on 1948, as transiting Saturn made a series of aspects to its natal position as well as to Mercury and Venus, the Childs moved to France. Paul carried on with his work with the US government, whilst Julia wondered what to do with herself. Eventually Paul was posted to Paris in 1948. They shared their first French meal together near Rouen: sole meunière. The moment was a defining one for Julia:

> "It arrived whole: a large, flat Dover sole that was perfectly browned in a sputtering butter sauce with a sprinkling of chopped parsley on top. The waiter carefully placed the platter in front of us, stepped back, and said: "Bon appètit!" I closed my eyes and inhaled the rising perfume. Then I lifted a forkful of fish to my mouth, took a bite, and chewed slowly. The flesh of the sole was delicate, with a light but distinct taste of the ocean that blended marvellously with the browned butter. I chewed slowly and swallowed. It was a morsel of perfection." [14]

Occurring 3 November 1948, at about 2:30 pm in Rouen France,[15] Julia came to refer to this meal as "the moment of sensual delight." From this moment, Julia knew she wanted to replicate the recipes she had tasted. To do this, she would have to master not only the art of French cooking (transiting Saturn conjunct Venus), but also the French language and the metric system (transiting Saturn conjunct natal Mercury).

The sign of Gemini mimics rather than invents and translates to be understood by as many people as possible. *Mastering the Art of French*

Cooking, Volumes 1 and 2 published by Knopf in 1961 and 1970 respectively (written with Simone Beck and Louisette Bertholle), was a seminal work containing detailed drawings and precise attention to detail. Its publication allowed everyday people to create master class standards of culinary art. And all this in America at a time when the height of haute cuisine was TV dinners! Just after publication, transiting Jupiter made a number of conjunctions to her natal Uranus, signifying the sudden and profound changes occurring in Child's life. Jupiter also made a series of three squares to her natal Saturn. The opportunities presented to her following the publication of the book would force Julia to change in ways she never could have imagined: appearing on television nearly fourteen years after the moment of sensuous delight (half a Saturn cycle).

It was during this time that her unforgettable, tremulous, Saturn in Gemini voice was unleashed to audiences. Gemini is a playful sign and Saturn's presence does little to quench the repressive sense of humour. On her live shows, she fluttered about her television kitchen, knocking things over and encouraging the cooks at home to be as messy as they wished. She dried lettuce leaves by waving them around, splashing herself, the cameras and her crew with water. She beheaded huge fish with giant meat cleavers, brandished knives like something from a medieval nightmare and introduced the poultry she was about to use by title and purpose for cooking. She mixed eggs with a comically oversized whisk and sloshed them everywhere. Once, when she tried to flip over a potato pancake, half of it missed the pan and hit the stove. She excused her error by explaining to the live studio audience that she didn't have the courage of her convictions. In time, several of her passions would be revealed to viewers: the perfection of French cooking, a love of good wine, a staunch defence of the liberal use of butter, a clean kitchen towel and the importance of using fresh ingredients. And of course the "bon appetit!" that ended every show.

Astrology charts continue to tell their story even after the native has died. Child passed on to the big kitchen in the sky in 2004 but *Julie/Julia*, a movie about her life in France and the blogger Julie Powell's attempt to replicate all of the recipes in *Mastering the Art of French Cooking* in one year, was released on 7 August 2009, just as transiting Jupiter made its second of three oppositions to her natal Sun.

Saturn in Cancer

21 June 1944	–	2 August 1946
2 August 1973	–	7 January 1974
18 April 1974	–	17 September 1975
15 January 1976	–	5 June 1976
5 June 2003	–	16 July 2005

Super mum

Imagine coming into a home that is not only the most comfortable place to be, but where you can eat whatever and whenever you like.

Fun, right? Just shift your feet so mum can sweep under your feet. Ketchup? She gets it for you. Can't hear the TV for the hoover? She moves to another room, giving you a chance to check out your surroundings. Around you are lots of animals with things wrong with them. There's a cat with three legs, a blind dog and a guinea pig with the mange. The doorbell rings and more children come in. Mum's a childminder. Like the animals, there's something wrong with the children: they're brats and all cry too much. Mum comes in and feeds them and they're quiet – for the moment.

"Toilet, dear?" she asks you.

As a matter of fact, nature is calling you. To your alarm, mum follows you. If that weren't bad enough, she hovers around the door and offers to wipe your bum for you. Not so much fun anymore, is it?

Saturn in Cancer pupils have difficulty in knowing the difference between mandatory care and outrageous over-indulgence because they have issues with emotional boundaries. They know what should be done but often don't feel like doing it because they are worried that some whale off the coast of Ethiopia is in danger of extinction and that is far more important than maths, English and science. They do seem to like history though, especially if it involves allowing them to recite every wrong ever committed by a tyrant. They're good at getting to grips with family trees and are particularly adept at analysing housing structures. They don't mind detention, because it gives them a chance to think about how they will be better parents than their own parents.

Issues with home and family cut very deeply with Saturn in Cancer pupils. Divorce or deep relationship problems leading to a change in family structure, particularly around the age of seven, may have been a problem. The Saturn in Cancer pupil may be a young carer or think he or she has to take on a family responsibility that shouldn't be their concern. They are very secretive and loyal to their families (no matter what kind of family it is) and it is likely that teachers will be completely oblivious to the responsibilities these pupils have taken on their shoulders. Needless to say, very often homework is not high on their list of priorities because they are too busy feeling sorry for themselves and the state of the world. What kind of place is this to bring up children, they might ask. And so they go about looking for causes or something else to worry about. They will look up to you if you show them you share their worries but be aware that these pupils will know if you're a sucker for sob stories.

Motivating Saturn in Cancer pupils usually involves getting them to care about issues. It might help them to know the root causes of the problems they are trying to solve. Guide them in their research but don't be sucked into doing it for them. They should respond well to being put into support groups, both in the role of a supporter and the supported. You as a teacher may have to play the role of a parent or need to feign reliance on the pupil to get them thinking. Give them tasks they can take care of and take pride in, but be aware that anything involving emotional commitment may require your support.

At fourteen to fifteen, these pupils begin to fear the future, and depression (in its many forms) may raise its ugly head. These pupils need to know there is a light at the end of the tunnel: there will be a job for them, their family will respect them for their endeavours and yes, there is a point to taking exams. Once they bite the bullet, suddenly, these pupils will stop being overwhelmingly needy and will come up with innovative ways of seeing themselves out of an academic rut.

If you are a teacher with Saturn in Cancer and you don't yet have children, you will be unfailingly worried about your pupils. Do they eat enough? Can they use the washer/drier? Do they have enough money? All teachers find teaching emotionally draining at some point, but you take it to the extreme. You want them to have a better childhood than you did because you couldn't live with the guilt if they didn't. Therefore, you overindulge them and do things for them that they should do for themselves. Parents will equally see your soft touch, and unless you are firm with your expectations, they will overwhelm you with their concerns, thus making them yours. If you do have your own children, you may be so wrapped up in your own world that you keep your pupils at arm's length and neglect them. For either extreme, keeping your emotions in check is a priority. Depression is a serious illness, one that should not be ignored or allowed to gestate. Thirty is usually the age when family responsibilities lead to feelings of being overwhelmed and you may feel others have treaded into your territory. By sixty your territory (however you define it) has security to rival that of Fort Knox.

Knowing when to open the door to your life, and when to shove unwelcome guests through it (shutting it behind them of course), is your greatest challenge.

Fine-tuning the role of Saturn

Saturn in Cancer is ruled by the Moon which moves through the zodiac at about 14 degrees per day. Thus a chart set for noon may not accurately signify which sign the Moon is in. If the Moon is in the early degrees of a sign, there is a possibility that the Moon may have been in the previous sign at the actual time of birth. Likewise, if it is in the latter degrees, it may be in the next sign. Therefore, you might need to look at both signs. To get an idea of how a person works towards success, look at their Moon sign.

Moon in Aries – These pupils may have formed the idea that they somehow don't belong in their families and they have to constantly battle to prove who they really are. Consequently they dislike the soppiness of family life and prefer to strike out on their own. As learners, they welcome and then conquer new experiences easily. Although they try to pretend they don't need anyone, they really need teachers and other authority figures to be around when they can no longer pretend they are above all emotions.

Moon in Taurus – These pupils may have formed the idea that family is everything and therefore any proposed change to the status quo is a threat. They dislike extravagance because it is a waste of carefully cultivated resources, and they dislike throwing anything away because it might be needed in the future. They need teachers and authority figures to help them understand the true cost of everything.

Moon in Gemini – These pupils may have formed the idea that family is just some rumour they heard. They talk about family loyalty yet they don't really understand what it means. To them, communication is the putty that holds everyone together, not blood. Consequently they feel comfortable wherever they are – as long as the conversation is stimulating and they don't feel bogged down. Teachers and other authority figures need to help them prioritise what is important to them.

Moon in Cancer – These pupils may have formed the idea that family is everything. They will do anything to protect their loved ones – and these pupils are fatally sensitive to perceived threats. They don't like to learn new things just in case they uncover something about their past that will go against what the family thinks or believes. Teachers and authority figures need to help them develop independence and self-reliance.

Moon in Leo – These pupils may have formed the idea that being the centre of attention is the only way to avoid being overlooked completely. They over-react to everything – and they even take the understatement too far to go unnoticed. These learners need their teachers and authority figures to help them address, and then act upon, their shortcomings.

Moon in Virgo – These pupils may have formed the idea that the only emotions worth expressing are the perfect ones, which of course don't exist. Instead they express their worries by making long to-do lists, and get enormous satisfaction through ticking things off, because it really is one less thing to worry about in their search for perfection. These learners need teachers and authority figures to help them to stop behaving as if everything smells bad.

Moon in Libra – These pupils may have formed the idea that they need other people in order to understand themselves. They compare themselves, as well as their emotions, to everyone. These learners need teachers and authority figures to help them develop a good sense of who they are as individuals.

Moon in Scorpio – These pupils may have formed the idea that the only way to show someone you love them is to kill for them or die for them. Their intensity can be more than a little disconcerting. These learners need teachers and authority figures to help them see the bright side of life.

Moon in Sagittarius – These pupils may have formed the idea that the emotional highs and lows they get from the thrills they seek are fun for everyone. They like to gamble on whether people might react to their over-the-top-provocations, but whether they win or lose isn't really what is fun. These learners need teachers and authority figures to help them to accept responsibility for their actions.

Moon in Capricorn – These pupils may have formed the idea that the only acceptable form of progress is made through traditional hard graft. They take comfort in the material world of work, and cling to social status as if it were only thing keeping them afloat. These learners need teachers and authority figures to help them reserve their spartan emotions for the things that really matter.

Moon in Aquarius – These pupils may have formed the idea that family and emotions are passé. They fear that if they become like everyone else with emotions they will discover they really don't fit in this world. These learners need teachers and authority figures to help them see that the search for uniqueness does not have to be lonely.

Moon in Pisces – These pupils may have formed the idea that everyone is family and therefore everyone needs protection. They fear that if they shun someone, they will (eventually) discover that same person will be their mother in the next life. These learners need teachers and authority figures to help them to face up to reality.

Case study – Cher

20 May 1946, 7:25 PST
El Centro, California 32°N47'31" 115°W33'44"
Rodden rating: AA; Collector: CAH
Jupiter in Libra, Venus in Gemini
Saturn in Cancer; Moon in Capricorn
First Jupiter return: November 1957
First Saturn opposition: January 1961
Time between first Jupiter return and last Saturn opposition: 3 years, 2 months
Second Jupiter return: October 1969
First Saturn return: July 1975
Third Jupiter return: October 1981
Fourth Jupiter return: September 1993
Fifth Jupiter return: January, February and August 2005
Second Saturn return: August 2004, February and March 2005

The family identity, and understanding where one comes from is terribly important to someone with Saturn in Cancer. Cher was born Cherilyn Sarkisian. Her parents divorced when she was fourteen months old and, when her mother re-married, little Cherilyn was adopted by her new step-father and her last name became LaPiere.

Cherilyn stumbled her way through school and was labelled as a pupil who did not live up to her potential. At sixteen, when her first Saturn opposition coincided with a Jupiter opposition to her natal Saturn, it was discovered that she had been dyslexic all along. This problem did not stop her winning an Academy Award, a Grammy Award, an Emmy Award, three Golden Globes and a Cannes Film Festival Award amongst others for her work in film, music and television. She is the only person in history to have achieved this.

Natally, the pupil we know and love as Cher has natal Jupiter square Saturn. In itself, this suggests a blockage to the learning process. Natural growth and exploration is inhibited by the circumstances represented by Saturn. In Cher's case, Jupiter is in Libra, the sign of relationships whilst her Saturn is in Cancer. What does a child with these significators do? They throw themselves into a relationship. And so, rather than

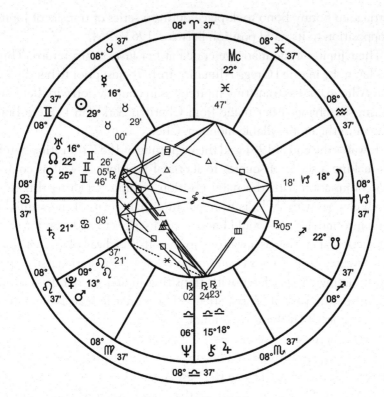

Cher – 20 May 1946

leaving school with any qualifications, the young Cher entered into a relationship (Jupiter in Libra) with Warren Beatty. Because Cher's needs as a pupil were ignored by her parents and neglected by her teachers, her dyslexia was not only undiagnosed, but was left completely untreated. As Cher's other successes demonstrate, dyslexia does not need to be a detriment to success but it does need to be dealt with. Today, there are many, many ways of getting help for dyslexia. Cher's experiences highlight the importance of early diagnosis of it and developing a mindset to overcome, rather than submit to, this learning difficulty.

Relationships are a theme in Cher's life: she was married twice but has had several significant relationships. "My relationships usually last a few years," she has said. "When I'm involved with a man, other men are fascinated with me, but the minute I'm single again, half of those men disappear because they don't have the balls to really want me."[16] Her first marriage to Sonny Bono took place during a series of transits of Jupiter in opposition to its natal position between 1963-1964.

Their Jupiter-cycle marriage ended at her first Saturn return. Three days later, she married Gregg Allman.[17] In 1978, just prior to her divorce from Allman, and as transiting Jupiter was in conjunction with her natal Saturn, she changed her name from Cherilyn Sarkisian LaPiere Bono Allman to the monosyllabic moniker, Cher.

Towards the end of 1981 and the beginning of 1982, transiting Saturn was making a series of squares to its natal position, as well as coming into conjunction with the natal position of Jupiter. During this time, her challenges with dyslexia were put into sharp focus: if she wanted to break into movies, she would have to read scripts to audition for parts. Her successful casting as a waitress in the off-Broadway play *Come Back to the Five and Dime, Jimmy Dean, Jimmy Dean* was the start of a successful turn to acting. A year later, with transiting Jupiter on her descendant, she earned the part of Meryl Streep's blue collar lesbian roommate in *Silkwood*, for which she was nominated for an Academy Award for best supporting actress. These successes led to others. In 1985, she played the mother of a severely disfigured boy in *Mask* as transiting Saturn opposed her Sun. For this role, she won the Best Actress Prize at the Cannes Film Festival. In 1987, she appeared on the David Letterman show singing 'I Got You Babe' with her ex-husband, as transiting Jupiter squared her natal Saturn. The same year she also starred in a further three films: *Suspect*, *The Witches of Eastwick* and *Moonstruck*.

Like Dolly Parton (who also has Saturn in Cancer), Cher has been a gay icon for much of her career. Thomas Rogers of *Salon* magazine commented that "Drag queens imitate women like Judy Garland, Dolly Parton and Cher because they overcame insult and hardship on their path to success, and because their narratives mirror the pain that many gay men suffer on their way out of the closet."[18] Saturn in Cancer toughens up the feminine edges, adds resilience and brings uncompromising tenacity to a sensitive nature. Although Cher struggled to accept her only daughter's lesbian sexuality and eventual transition to being a man, in due course she became one of LGBT's (lesbian, gay, bisexual and transsexual) most ardent supporters. "I did have a problem saying him or her but the important thing is that my child is happy. I have two sons. I never thought that would be but you go through life and you get what you get. You get what belongs to you."[19] In 1998, after another series of Saturn oppositions to natal Jupiter, she was named one of the 'top twenty-five coolest women' by USA LGBT-interest magazine *The Advocate*.

As one would expect of someone with Saturn in Cancer, Cher is a dedicated humanitarian. In addition to her work with LGBT, she is National Chairperson and Honorary Spokesperson of the Children's Craniofacial Association, and has a charitable foundation in her name.

Saturn in Leo

2 August 1946	–	19 September 1948
4 April 1949	–	29 May 1949
17 September 1975	–	15 January 1976
5 June 1976	–	17 November 1977
5 January 1978	–	26 July 1978
17 July 2005	–	2 September 2007

The reluctant pop star

Imagine the lead singer of the most famous boy band in history. He is sitting in his dressing room with his head in his hands listening to the roar of the waiting crowds. His manager comes in to see how he's getting on.

"I can't do it," the star wails.

"Baby, you'll be fine," the manager coos. "Everybody loves you, man!"

"I can't do it," the star says again. "Not with this hair!"

Pupils with Saturn in Leo may be the smartest kids in the school but they need to hear you say that. Often. It can be very difficult to get these pupils to try something different, because they are paralysed by the shame of looking ridiculous in front of you, their peers, their parents, other teachers, the prime minister, Bob Dylan, or His Divine Holiness Lord Krishna Himself. For these pupils, life is lived out on the world stage and is therefore up for scrutiny by anyone who happens to be passing by even if no-one is paying any particular attention.

At around the age of seven, these pupils had someone else's will imposed on them and consequently they have become terrified of losing control again. It's irrelevant if Mummy was right in forcing them into stage school or Daddy made them go to swimming lessons. The point is that the Saturn in Leo child learned that he wasn't good enough, that he needed fixing and therefore he cannot be trusted to make his own decisions. These children need you to tell them that it's okay to be different and to hold an unpopular opinion (as long as it can be backed up!) or to put ketchup on their chocolate puddings, because they wouldn't do such things otherwise. To Saturn in Leo children, popularity is everything and they would be completely and irrevocably mortified if they didn't fit in. Unfortunately, everyone in the class is probably thinking the same thing, so the jostling to be king/queen of the classroom begins.

Saturn in Leo children quickly learn where their strengths are – be it verbosity, sporting prowess, knowing who their allies are or understanding the weaknesses of their enemies. Once the battle has begun, there's no stopping it until the metaphorical dead bodies are carried away. This is why it's so important for teachers to be comically blunt and fawning with their compliments. Did a pupil not do his homework? Tell him: "What a shame! I was so looking forward to you showing me what you've learnt." Shining the spotlight on good behaviour works well too; compliment the children who are behaving.

Parents' evenings are usually the opportunity for teachers to get their own back on naughty pupils. Be careful of doing this with Saturn in Leo children as they so badly want to impress their parents. A few petty negative comments can not only make the child hate you forever and thus rebel against any of your future efforts, it could also cause massive rows between the parent and child that won't be easily healed.

At fourteen to fifteen, the Saturn in Leo child will face immense changes that essentially rip up their internal rule book. Technology is brought in, the exam board changes; a new pupil arrives who is instantly the most popular person in the school. They realise they don't know or even like themselves any more. Terror has struck the hearts of Leo in Saturn pupils, but of course, their pride prevents them from seeking support and, quite suddenly, it's like the lights have been turned off. It may take some deliberate withdrawal from the limelight for these pupils to realise it is what is within them that makes them such remarkable people. Once this stage is over, these pupils learn to be more sensitive to others because they know what it is like to be hurt. They really are so generous of heart that they could never deliberately hurt someone who is vulnerable.

If you're a teacher with Saturn in Leo, you probably tend to favour pupils most like you so that you can coach them towards the perfection you will never achieve. Fortunately for you (or so you think), all your pupils want to be like you. It is nice to have your shining classroom stars, but lay off a bit because the kids think you are rather overbearing;

some might even think you're kind of creepy. Especially when you wear a Batman suit on Mufti Day. Parents find you a little over the top too: what are you implying about their methods of parenting? By the time you're thirty and you have children of your own, you'll realise what a tremendous responsibility parenting is. It hurts you to see them make the same mistakes you did and so you go to great lengths to fix your child. If you don't have children, you turn the critical mirrors onto yourself and loathe your reflection. Put the botox down and come to the playground with the rest of the teachers. We like you, crow's feet and all. By the time you're sixty, you will probably have finally learned that the world doesn't revolve around you. And then you can really have some fun.

Fine-tuning the role of Saturn

Like everything else with Leo, finding the ruler of Saturn is not difficult: it is their sun sign and is obvious from just the date of their birth. To get an idea of how Saturn in Leo works towards success, look at their star sign.

Sun in Aries – These children fear that everyone will see that they don't know what they're doing. So they try to do things faster than everyone else in the hope of concealing their self-doubt. Although they don't like to seem like they need help, they need teachers and other authority figures to remind them to slow down, to take a breather, or just to conserve energy for what really matters.

Sun in Taurus – These children fear that everyone will think they are poor. So they try to put on ostentatious shows of wealth or, conversely, they take great pains to hide their valuables. They need teachers and authority figures to help them understand the true value of the things that really do matter.

Sun in Gemini – These children fear that no-one will understand how really clever they are (or that everyone will see how not clever they are). They jump at every opportunity to show off their considerable vocabulary and conversational skills. They need teachers and authority figures to help them apply their knowledge in a resourceful way.

Sun in Cancer – These children fear that others will see how much their family means to them and try to take them away. They become clingy to their nearest and dearest (this extends to home and country too). They need teachers and other figures of authority to protect and comfort them so they can be brave enough to step outside their homes and familiar experiences.

Sun in Leo – These children fear that they will be overlooked because they are not good looking or intelligent enough. They want to be noticed for all the good things they do. They need teachers and authority figures to stroke their fragile egos by praising their good points but also to help them improve their bad points.

Sun in Virgo – These children fear that they will be contaminated by everyone else's imperfections. They like side-stepping life's messy ways and truly enjoy cleaning up after everyone, as long as they can wash themselves afterwards. They need teachers and authority figures to encourage them to leave well enough alone and focus on what really needs to be fixed.

Sun in Libra – These children fear that everyone will see or think that no- one likes them. They want to make friends with everyone and try to see the value in even the most unpleasant characters, often compromising their own sense of values. Although they will always shun poor manners and brutish behaviour, they need teachers and authority figures to help them develop their own sense of value and style.

Sun in Scorpio – These children fear that everyone will see what really motivates them: they are afraid that if they don't succeed, they won't survive the experience. For them, everything is a matter of life or death but they know this is a secret they must not tell others because it would bring almost certain defeat. They need teachers and authority figures to help them lighten up and to stop taking everything so seriously.

Sun in Sagittarius – These children fear that everyone will think they're boring and laden with responsibilities. They're scared they are going to miss out on an invitation to the next big adventure. They need teachers and authority figures to help them stay focused on their long term goals.

Sun in Capricorn – These children fear that everyone will see them as irresponsible and unworthy of a good job or position in society. They want to impress everyone with how hard they work and how seriously they take life. They need teachers and authority figures to help them to learn the noble art of schmoozing and networking at parties.

Sun in Aquarius – These pupils fear that everyone will think they're just like everyone else. They want to be noticed for their innovative thinking and manners. They need teachers and authority figures to help them conduct their experiments safely.

Sun in Pisces – These pupils fear that everyone will see them as harsh and rejecting critics. They want everyone to be accepted and will do everything they can to ensure no-one is left out. They truly hate to see suffering – but don't mind if others think they are suffering. They need teachers and authority figures to remind them that martyrs tend not to live long enough to see that they make a difference.

Case study – Elton John

25 March 1947, 2:00 GDT
Pinner, England, 51°N36' 000°W33'
Rodden rating: DD; Collector: Rodden
Jupiter in Scorpio, Pluto in Leo
Saturn in Leo, Sun in Aries
First Jupiter return: January, May and September 1959
First Saturn opposition: January 1962
Time between first Jupiter return, last Saturn opposition: 3 years
Second Jupiter return: July and August 1971
First Saturn return: October and December 1975 and June 1976
Third Jupiter return: December 1982
Fourth Jupiter return: November 1994
Second Saturn return: July 2005
Fifth Jupiter return: November 2006

By dissociate aspect, Elton John has Saturn in Leo trine Jupiter in Scorpio. He began playing the piano at his first Jupiter square at the age of three and began formal piano lessons by his first Saturn square at seven. By his first Jupiter return, he had impressed his Royal Academy of Music instructors by playing a four page Handel composition after hearing it played only once. By his first Saturn opposition, his parents had divorced, his mother re-married and the young Reginald Dwight was hired as a pianist in a local pub. Elton's chart is a good example of how Saturn and Jupiter, when well-aspected, can work together to bring out success in the chart.

In 1967 a series of transiting Jupiter squares to the natal position saw the beginning of Elton's musical partnership with Bernie Taupin, with Elton writing the music for Bernie's lyrics. By 1973, at the release

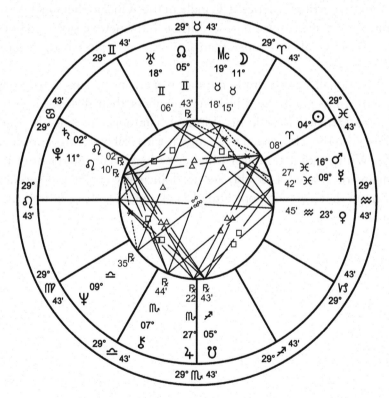

Elton John – 25 March 1947

of *Goodbye Yellow Brick Road*, Elton had released an incredible seven albums as transiting Jupiter was opposite to its natal position. During this prolific time, Elton's fashion style became increasingly flamboyant. He has often said his wild stage costumes and performance were his way of letting go as a result of a restrictive childhood.[20]

In 1977, as Jupiter opposed itself and Saturn opposed his Venus, Elton announced he was retiring from performing, but after a brief hiatus, continued to write music. He re-emerged with *Less than Zero* in 1983, on cue with a series of transiting Saturn squares to the natal position. His Jupiter return of 1994 brought him a Grammy Award for Disney's *The Lion King* ('Can You Feel the Love Tonight?').

Jupiter's next opposition to natal Saturn brought the emotional difficulties ensuing from the deaths of two close friends, Princess Diana and Gianni Versace. On hearing of Diana's death, he contacted Bernie Taupin to re-write the lyrics of 'Candle in the Wind' for her funeral, two Jupiter cycles after its first release. Although the new version won him a Grammy and sold more copies than any other song, Elton has performed it live only once.

Traditionally, Saturn rules the hair so perhaps it's not so surprising Saturn in Leo pupils are a little touchy about their manes. Elton has gone to extremes to hide his thinning hair, apparent since his early career even though he tried to disguise it with elaborate wigs and clever hats. Whilst speculation over whether he had a hair transplant or not remains rife, those of us who are not follicularly challenged can only shrug our shoulders and hope Elton John keeps on writing his wonderful music.

Saturn in Virgo

20 September 1948	–	3 April 1949
29 May 1949	–	20 November 1950
8 March 1951	–	13 August 1951
17 November 1977	–	5 January 1978
27 July 1978	–	21 September 1980
3 September 2007	–	29 October 2009
8 April 2010	–	21 July 2010

The pregnant virgin

Imagine a heavily pregnant woman who is incredibly self-sufficient. She has built her own immaculate house, grows her own vegetables and is impeccably healthy. She is, in every possible way, walking perfection.

Saturn in Virgo children are very discerning learners who will refuse a steady diet of junky fiction, artistic pursuits that get them messy, or music practice that offends their virginal ears. They won't use pencils that aren't sharpened to a perfect point, ink pens with ink that blots their meticulous work, or papers that have dents. Their uniforms must be immaculate and, if you look in their bags, they will have spare socks and underwear, plasters, baby wipes and an economy size bottle of anti-bacterial disinfectant. Their notes are perfectly taken verbatim (which can be quite alarming to the teacher) and they will insist that everyone sticks to the homework schedule. For lunch, they eat their hygienically-wrapped wholemeal bread sandwiches and the fruits they have carefully peeled. Just in case they aren't getting the right vitamins, they wash their vitamin supplements down their perfect throats with vegetable juice, freshly squeezed and decanted into a thermos bottle that has been previously sterilised.

Now I ask you, how long will it be before this child is pushed into the nearest mud puddle?

The challenge for Virgo in Saturn pupils is tolerating us imperfect, lesser mortals. If you get within five feet of them to offer your assistance, their little button noses twitch in anticipation of your human odour. But they are always willing to help you improve. They will tidy your bookshelves, organise your desk, research the best place to have dinner that night (and even make the reservation for you) and help you get that nasty bubble gum stain off the back of your favourite pair of trousers. Hell, you could even give them a green pen and get them onto that pile of marking. For Saturn in Virgo pupils, the issues are about shunning mediocrity and demanding perfection, but ultimately it's about controlling their environments. When they were about seven, something came into their lives that was completely impossible to control: they may have developed a rare, exotic bug or a parent's religious conversion threw the family into turmoil or perhaps the family packed up and moved to a different country or they may have experienced an injury due to someone else's recklessness. The possibilities are pretty endless, because there are so many different ways of disturbing a Saturn in Virgo's immaculate pursuit of order.

For these reasons, Saturn in Virgo pupils appreciate established routine – and they'll think better of you for providing it. Teachers won't need to provide pencil sharpeners, tissues, spare pens, markers, glue, hair ties, plasters, paper clips or spare shoelaces because these incredibly self-sufficient pupils are better organised than you. All you really need to do is make sure you wash your hands before you mark their work and they are generally good to go.

At about fourteen or fifteen, these pupils encounter the chaos of exam revision. Which revision session should they go to? What are their targets? What are the examiners looking for? Suddenly these perfect pupils are in a major freak out. They are so busy trying to re-organise themselves that they forget to wash and put on clean clothes. They start to stink, turn crusty at their edges and a film of moss starts to develop on their teeth. And then they start to get sharp again. They learn to prioritise and do what's important first – and that's usually looking after their bodies.

If you're a teacher with Saturn in Virgo, chances are that your relentless pursuit of delivering perfect lessons, encouraging your pupils to concentrate on important information rather than trivia, as well as your reputation for impeccable time-keeping means you are the head teacher. Parents are scared of you but they respect the high standards you set. In other words, everyone resents you and goes out of their way to avoid you. This is okay by you because being a head teacher is a difficult job, but someone has to do it and it might as well be you because you're so much better than the rest of us. By the time you turned thirty, you probably thought it was time to tighten the screws a little more, or you realised that allowing a little mess in your life provides you with the opportunity to get the cleaning products out. By the time you're sixty, you will realise that you've worked hard enough, so it's now time to let someone else take over so you can retreat into your own perfect world and let us mucky pups get on with it.

Fine-tuning the role of Saturn

Mercury rules Virgo as well as Gemini. However, in Gemini, Mercury's ability to change and adapt is more apparent. In Virgo, Mercury's preference for precision and its interest in health matters is clearer.

Mercury in Aries – These pupils think that they need to work harder and more quickly. They are usually incredibly efficient, but are often very hard on themselves. Equally, they can be quite harsh towards other people as well and can attract quite a lot of antagonism. These pupils need teachers and authority figures to remind them that a little humility is sometimes needed to get others to listen to their advice.

Mercury in Taurus – These pupils think that they need to take their time and do a thorough job on everything. They normally have a very good work ethic, but can get hung up on details and not finish anything. These pupils need teachers and authority figures to help them decide when enough is enough.

Mercury in Gemini – These pupils think that they need more to do and frantically add items to their already substantial to-do lists. They usually display a lot of nervous energy that makes everyone else jumpy. These pupils need teachers and authority figures to encourage them to do one thing at a time and do it well.

Mercury in Cancer – These pupils think that they haven't expressed their true feelings clearly enough, so go completely over the top with talking about their emotional crises, as well as those of everyone else in the family. And there's always some sort of crisis that requires their tender loving care or protection. These pupils need teachers and authority figures to help them overcome their fear of the unknown.

Mercury in Leo – These pupils think that they are not perfect enough to be seen by anyone. They spend hours in front of the mirror fixing their hair or dreaming about new plastic surgery techniques. If they can't achieve perfection, they complain bitterly until someone compliments them on how wonderful they look. These pupils need teachers and authority figures to remind them that all that glitters is not gold.

Mercury in Virgo – These pupils think there is always room for improvement and are not afraid to give criticism even when it's not welcome. Consequently, they often feel unappreciated and undervalued. These pupils need teachers and authority figures to show them where their critiques are appreciated and when to let things lie.

Mercury in Libra – These pupils think that everyone enjoys a party. In fact, they came up with the idea of a 'working party'. Does work always have to be so dull, they wonder. These pupils need teachers and authority figures to help them plan achievable targets and make sure they reach them.

Mercury in Scorpio – These pupils think that only they know everything about life and death. They see themselves as sole survivors of an intellectual train crash, so their arguments can be a little intense at times. These pupils need teachers and authority figures to help them pick and choose their intellectual battles.

Mercury in Sagittarius – These pupils think that they have the intellectual freedom to say and do whatever they like. They provoke everyone they meet, cause massive upset and then shrug it off as if it doesn't matter to them and shouldn't matter to anyone else. These pupils need teachers and authority figures to get them to take responsibility for what they say by backing up their opinions with solid facts.

Mercury in Capricorn – These pupils think only they have the skills and resources to handle important projects. They ooze intolerance of lesser mortals and consequently lesser mortals do whatever they can to ensure their 'superior' looks like a failure. These pupils need teachers and authority figures to help them to share their vision with others.

Mercury in Aquarius – These pupils think that they have the right to do what they like. Although they tend to be original thinkers, they frequently alienate others with their drive to rebel against the commonly excepted mores of society. These pupils need teachers and authority figures to help support their journey towards independent thinking.

Mercury in Pisces – These pupils think there's so much perfection in the world that they're entitled to be the ones allowed to make a mess. Consequently, they attract even more mess, until they disappear under it completely. These pupils need teachers and authority figures to help them to reflect on the little details of life that will allow them to have the peace and quiet they like so much.

Case study – Olivia Newton John

26 September 1948, 6:00 GDT
Cambridge, England 52°N13' 000°E08'
Rodden rating: A; Collector: Rodden
Jupiter in Sagittarius, Jupiter in rulership
Saturn in Virgo, Mercury in Libra
First Jupiter return: January 1960
First Saturn opposition: April 1964
Time between first Jupiter return, last Saturn opposition: 4 years, 1 month
Second Jupiter return: December 1971
First Saturn return: August 1978
Third Jupiter return: December 1983
Fourth Jupiter return: November 1995
Second Saturn return: September 2007
Fifth Jupiter return: November 2007

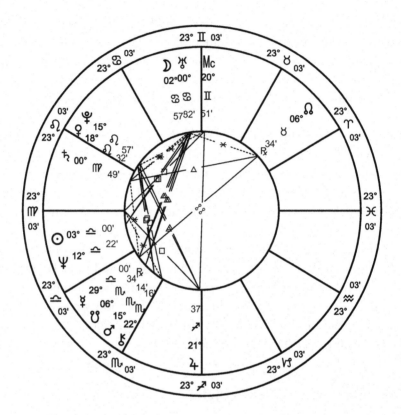

Olivia Newton-John – 26 September 1948

By the time of her first Saturn opposition, Olivia Newton John had discovered her passion for music and was part of an Australian girl band called Sol Four. After winning a television contest, she received the prize of a trip to England and began a successful recording career. Throughout 1966, transiting Jupiter was opposite her natal Jupiter and Saturn hovered over her descendant. She released her first major hit 'Till You say You'll Be Mine' and then formed a singing partnership with Pat Carroll.

By the time Jupiter opposed her natal Saturn in 1974, she had won three Grammies (one in 1973 for 'Let Me Be There' and two in 1974: Best Record for and Best Performance for 'I Honestly Love You') and had taken part in the Eurovision Song Contest, placing fourth after ABBA's 'Waterloo'. Meanwhile, she caused all sorts of outrage to the American country music stage when she, as a foreigner, out-performed some of the genre's more established stars. In this scenario, Jupiter represents the young, foreign upstart whilst Saturn represents the old guard. She eventually won their support, but not without a whole lot of griping.

Of course, Olivia is best known for her performance in the musical *Grease*, shot just prior to her first Saturn return. Initially, at the age of twenty-nine, she felt she was too old for the part of the virginal Sandy, however the lyrics of 'Look at me I'm Sandra Dee' seem totally appropriate for someone with Saturn in Virgo.

Sandy's transformation from virgin to spandex clad vamp by the end of the movie echoed the road Olivia would take in her own career as she ditched her buttoned-up, frilly blouses in favour of leather gear for the cover of her next album, *Totally Hot*. In 1982, with Jupiter in Libra sitting provocatively on natal Mars in her second house, she had just released her album *Physical*, the single of which was a saucy little number about the joys of sex (I mean exercise) that wiped the billboards of squeaky clean Debby Boone's 'You Light up My Life'.

Sadly, Jupiter's conjunction to her ascendant in Virgo coincided with her battle with breast cancer and her father's death. She cancelled all tours to focus on her health, but upon recovery, as Saturn opposed itself in Pisces, she embarked upon several humanitarian causes, including breast cancer research. For her second Saturn return and fifth Jupiter return in 2007, she focused on raising funds to help build her own cancer and wellness centre in Australia, re-married, and in 2009 bought a $4.1 million home... in Jupiter Inlet, Palm Beach County, Florida.

Saturn in Libra

7 October 1921	–	20 December 1923
7 April 1924	–	13 September 1925
20 November 1950	–	8 March 1951
21 September 1980	–	29 November 1982
7 May 1983	–	24 August 1983
30 October 2009	–	7 April 2010
22 July 2010	–	5 October 2012

Industrial-sized scales

Imagine scales that can weigh anything, elephants or mites, liquids or gasses, planets or pebbles to the nearest micro gram.

Saturn in Libra pupils are so busy comparing themselves to their peers that they completely forget the essay you assigned last week is due today. Before they raise their hand to give their feeble excuses, they take a final opportunity to check their hair. After all, the (potential) significant other might be watching.

"Yes?" you ask.

"I would have done the essay but you didn't explain it properly," they say sweetly. It doesn't matter that you had produced an entire lesson that practically wrote the essay, their lack of work is your fault.

"Oh, that's okay then," you counter, "I'll explain it again in e-lab-or-ate de-tail af-ter school."

"Can't, miss," they say, consulting their diaries, "I'm otherwise engaged."

Saturn in Libra pupils are not terribly easy to teach because they are so preoccupied with finding someone to offset their fear of loneliness. They don't feel whole unless they are with someone who fills in the gaps of what they think they don't have. To them, there is no such thing as a casual relationship. Putting them in pairs to complete class work is as good as forcing them to recite marriage vows. These pupils are pretty impossible to convince that independent study is the way of the future. They (politely) groan at the prospect of controlled assessments (but really can't be bothered to protest too strenuously), or immediately make plans to turn a study session into a social occasion before you have even finished explaining what to do. When they were about seven, they may have heard about an elderly aunt who was dead for two years before someone found her, or it might have been that their mother was so pre-occupied with her job that they felt neglected; or perhaps there was a cataclysmic crack in the family structure like the parents splitting up.

Saturn in Libra, with its focus on relationships with others, tends to be more complicated for girls simply because boys are conditioned from an early age to be independent. As society continues to change, this imbalance will eventually redress itself.

Saturn in Libra pupils are a lot smarter than they let on, but they like to pretend they are the opposite of what you would expect. Treat them as if they were insane and you might get some decent work out of them. They often don't realise that their instinctual need for balance often means they take up subjects they are not very interested in or they partner up with people who aren't good influences on them. So, by the time the pupils are fourteen or fifteen, we get the pretty but not-too-bright cheerleader from a good home taking organic chemistry and dating the forty year old drug addict who is on the sex offenders list. What's wrong with her? For starters, she's doing it to gauge your reaction and to see what you will do about it. She can't see her own value, so you will have to do it for her: getting other people to do their dirty work is a Saturn in Libra speciality. You will have to tell her that her boyfriend is breaking the law and you are putting her on the child protection list immediately. That done, the next thing to do is to explain to her that in order to master organic chemistry, she needs to get to grips with the table of elements tout de suite (don't lose your temper if she says she doesn't know what it is). She will, of course, blame you for screwing up her life and for wrecking the most important romance she will ever have. She'll tell her friends you are her worst enemy and that everyone should hate on you by not attending your revision classes. She'll get other teachers involved by complaining about how you had no right to interfere with her education by implying that she's stupid. She'll pretend you are her worst enemy and you will just have to hold your ground until she realises she isn't so attractive when she's scowling. Thankfully, by the time real exam pressure hits, she will see the value of hard, steady work and if you really were patient with her mistakes, she will trust you when you say that good exam scores can help her get a good job and she will be able to buy all the pretty things she wants.

If you are a teacher with Saturn in Libra, you will be extremely uncomfortable watching pupils make mistakes in relationships. You will see yourself as the referee between fights, the matchmaker of doomed romances, the objective middle ground between disputes and inevitably the only teacher in the school who tries to play marriage counsellor between warring parents. Don't kid yourself. You most likely haven't learned that you can never get other people to magically morph into what you want them to be. By thirty, you are probably still working out that he-(or she)-that-will-never-change is a perfect reflection of the qualities you dislike in yourself. By sixty, you have probably become everything you always said you never would, but have learned to like yourself anyway.

Fine-tuning the role of Saturn

For the Saturn in Libra pupils, the best discipline comes from others. Understanding the strengths and weaknesses of this class of pupils can help teachers to focus on developing specific strengths, whilst improving particular weaknesses.

Venus in Aries – These pupils typically attract those who are able to act independently. They show affection spontaneously and like to tease other pupils to get them to chase them. They need to feel that they can commit to a long-term project. Teachers and other authority figures can facilitate this process by ensuring they understand what they are committing to, how long it should take and what they can do with the knowledge once they get it.

Venus in Taurus – These pupils attract those who offer stability. They are typically self-indulgent and need to know the people around them can meet their needs. They also need to know that what they commit themselves to do can benefit them and enable them to buy the nice things they want. Teachers and other authority figures can facilitate this process by ensuring they can see the long-term benefits of study.

Venus in Gemini – These pupils attract those who stimulate their minds. They need to know trivial details and will gossip forever if they are allowed to. They need to know that they will learn lots about different types of subjects. Teachers and other authority figures can facilitate this process by showing them an overview of a course and helping them to see what they will learn.

Venus in Cancer – These pupils attract those who express their feelings easily. They need to feel comfortable with the people around them or they will not interact. They need to know that what they are learning will help them improve their home life, or future home life, so they feel secure. Teachers and other authority figures can facilitate this process by showing them how what they are learning is just building on knowledge they already have.

Venus in Leo – These pupils attract those who are creative. They need to know that even their faults are worthy of admiration. They won't do anything that will make them look stupid in front of others, and they need to feel confident they will be successful. Teachers and other authority figures can facilitate this process by showing them what skills they already possess and encouraging them to believe in themselves.

Venus in Virgo – These pupils attract those who demand perfection. They need to know that their analytical and critical skills are useful to others. They tend to be slave drivers and can be exceptionally harsh on their friends and family. Teachers and other authority figures can capitalise on this process by ensuring they are engaged with their own emotions as well as those around them. Ask them frequently how they feel about what they are working on.

Venus in Libra – These pupils attract those who want to socialise. They are a challenge to get to work, but they don't want confrontation. Challenge them if they start to slack off, but do it in a polite way. Once they are turned off a project, it can be nearly impossible to engage them again. Teachers and other authority figures can facilitate the process of keeping them committed by allowing them to use all the pretty folders they like and occasionally letting them preen at their desks.

Venus in Scorpio – These pupils need to attract people who can cope with their intense work habits. They want to feel something for what they're doing. They need key words or phrases that will stick in their minds. Teachers and other authority figures can facilitate this process by encouraging these pupils to bring their work to life. Let them see how what they are studying works in the real world.

Venus in Sagittarius – These pupils attract those who like to take chances. They are risk-takers and like to play chicken with the exam board. These pupils need to understand the consequences of failure or of putting things off until the last possible second. Teachers and other authority figures can facilitate this process by not worrying on their behalf and by making them accept full blame or credit for their marks.

Venus in Capricorn – These pupils attract those who work hard. They pupils admire excellent workmanship and the kudos that goes with it. Typically, they take a mature approach to studying and usually set a good example to pupils who are faltering. Teachers and other authority figures can facilitate this process by pairing them with pupils who need to apply rigour to their studies.

Venus in Aquarius – These pupils attract those who like to experiment. They do not like to do things the same way all the time. They appreciate innovation and scorn tradition. They will work if they are allowed to try out new techniques. Teachers and other authority figures can facilitate this process by allowing them some freedom and then letting them share how they have benefited from doing things differently.

Venus in Pisces – These pupils attract those that cause chaos and so will benefit from classroom learning partners who encourage them to be more organised and structured, but are strong enough to avoid getting sucked into the mayhem. Teachers and other authority figures can facilitate this process by ensuring there are clear instructions for good outcomes and solid structures for organisational purposes.

Case study – Christopher Reeve

25 September 1952, 3:12 EDT New York
40°N42'51" 074°W00'23"
Rodden rating: A; Collector: Rodden
Jupiter in Taurus, Venus in Libra
Saturn in Libra, Venus in Libra
First Jupiter return: July and November 1964 and March 1965
First Saturn opposition: April 1968
Time between first Jupiter return, last Saturn opposition: 3 years, 8 months
Second Jupiter return: June 1976
First Saturn return: October 1981
Third Jupiter return: June 1988
Fourth Jupiter return: May 2000

In 1956, as transiting Jupiter was in conjunction with Christopher's Chiron, the marriage of his parents broke down and his father re-married shortly after. In 1959, as Saturn was conjunct his Chiron, his mother re-married and Christopher and his brother were placed in a highly selective, elite private school. He excelled in sports but by his Jupiter square at nine, he had found his passion for acting. At fifteen, just after his first Saturn opposition, he was accepted as an apprentice in a theatre festival where his maturity helped him fit into a group of older pupils.

Christopher won a place at the prestigious Julliard School and became firm friends with the actor Robin Williams as Jupiter formed a series of three squares to his natal MC. He continued to perform in a variety of plays, but by the time of his second Jupiter return in 1976 he was ready for something more. In 1977, transiting Saturn in Leo crossed over his ascendant, Pluto and South Node and squared his natal Jupiter as he was preparing for the role of his life as *Superman*. Reeves had intuitively tapped into his natal Saturn in Libra when he acknowledged that the masculine image was changing and that he would interpret the role with greater gentleness and vulnerability. All he needed was a pair of tights! Even though he was in touch with his feminine side, he still threw himself into a two month body-building regime that packed thirty pounds of muscle to his slender frame. Touchingly, as Jupiter made the

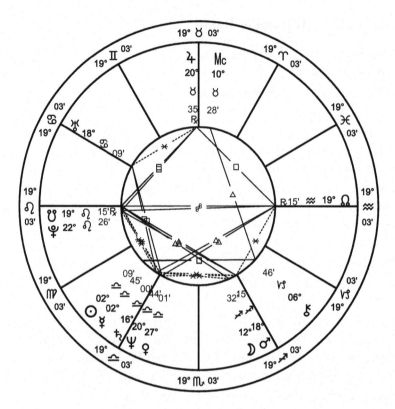

Christopher Reeve – 25 September 1952

same transits to the planets in 1979, he became a track and field coach for the Special Olympics. As Jupiter was conjunct Jupiter in 1988, he announced that after several sequels, he was finished playing the man of steel after a complete Jupiter cycle.

Following *Superman*, Christopher found it difficult to find his niche. His relationship with the mother of his two children had fallen apart and he turned down the lead role in *Pretty Woman*. In 1992, as Jupiter was in conjunction with his Sun and Mercury in Libra, Christopher's career re-surfaced with *Remains of the Day*, and his son with Dana Morosini was born. By the time of the movie's release in November 1993, his Jupiter was in conjunction with his natal Saturn in Libra.

Jupiter in Sagittarius was conjunct his natal Moon a few weeks before his tragic horse riding accident, which left him a quadriplegic and unable to even breathe on his own. He had taken up horse riding as he filmed *Anna Karinina* during Saturn's opposition to natal Jupiter towards the end of 1984. As with all the other sports he had taken up, he wanted to compete, and this time it was as an equestrian. Following his injury, Christopher considered suicide but by the end of the year, with the support of his wife and with transiting Jupiter conjunct his Chiron, Christopher was breathing without the aid of a ventilator.

In 1996, Saturn made a series of oppositions to his Sun and Mercury, and Christopher appeared at the Academy Awards show to a long standing ovation, as well as appearing on the front cover of *Time* magazine. He was still everyone's man of steel. In 1998, transiting Jupiter made a series of squares to natal Jupiter as his book *Still Me* (Arrow Books, 1999) was published and he made his directorial debut with *Rear Window*.

In 2000, he had started to gain motor control as well as being able to sense hot and cold temperatures on his body. Astrologically, there was a Saturn/Jupiter conjunction in Taurus on his natal Jupiter. After making such remarkable progress, his doctor asked if he had any more surprises for him. And on command, Christopher moved his index finger. "I don't think Dr. McDonald would have been more surprised if I had just walked on water," said Christopher in an interview.[21]

In October 2004, he was treated for sepsis with a course of antibiotics which are thought to have caused a cardiac arrest. Jupiter again passed over his Sun and Mercury in Libra, and Christopher Reeve, who brought such sensitivity and vulnerability to the role of the Man of Steel, died shortly after.

Saturn in Scorpio

20 December 1923	–	7 April 1924
14 September 1925	–	2 December 1926
22 October 1953	–	12 January 1956
14 May 1956	–	9 October 1956
29 November 1982	–	6 May 1983
24 August 1983	–	17 November 1985
6 October 2012	–	22 December 2014
16 June 2015	–	18 September 2015

Badass scorpion

Imagine being in a room with the biggest scorpion you have ever seen. You're not going to get too close to it are you? You'd keep your eye on it every second. No matter how you want to dress up (or dress down) the nature of a scorpion, sooner or later you're going to have to admit this thing has you under its control.

Pupils with Saturn in Scorpio are pretty frighteningly ambitious and they're fairly certain you're going to do things their way. Let them out of your sight for a second and you're done for. You know and they know. Such is their control over you.

Or so they'd like to think.

Astrology represents the entire human life cycle and that includes bodily functions most of us would be happy not to discuss. Ever. However, sex, death and going to the toilet have to be assigned to a sign, and that sign would be Scorpio. Girls with Saturn in Scorpio will have no problem with shouting out across a mixed classroom, in front of a male teacher (the older the better), that her period is due or what she got up to with which boy the night before. It's more fun for her if the male teacher quickly heads for the toilet, apologising profusely for his insensitivity out of sheer embarrassment. Boys will ask female teachers (the younger the better) seemingly genuine questions on sex education and then laugh like crazy afterwards at her blushes (bottom humour seems to be particularly hysterical). If you teach this group, you're going to have to batten down the hatches and prepare to be tossed about on the ocean of teenage sexuality. Prepare to learn something you missed out on when you took sex education at their age. For girls, Saturn in Scorpio is about torturing the male gender with what they can never have, because they're in control of their own bodies, thank you very much. For boys, Saturn in Scorpio is about threatening the female gender with what they could do if they really wanted to. For teachers, this really does mean you should never leave yourself in a position where your intentions could be twisted and manipulated into something far more sinister than you ever realised.

There is a positive side to this challenging group and that is they are good researchers. They like mysteries and puzzles and can grasp an author's intended purpose with ease. They'll most likely enjoy the gothic fiction genre. They dislike trivia or poking about the surface of a subject.

They probably won't openly flirt in the classroom (group work is tricky too) but will drink each other's blood in private. Joking aside, these pupils will master material you present to them if you can show them that you can manage the lesson without being side-tracked by their attempts to distract you. No doubt you will often have to explain the importance of what they're learning and lead them in analysing and working out how things are done. Your job is to show them how to use their copious reserves of control to discipline themselves in order to improve their status quo. They have a notion that they are not well liked and they try to work out how they can use this to their advantage. Some will let it all hang out and some will bottle it all up. You need to help them work out which method is appropriate for the situation.

These pupils fear the unexpected and hate wishy-washy teachers who are content to let computers do all the hard work. At about the age of seven they learned that everyone really is out to get them. Perhaps they were caught out doing something that shamed them and everybody laughed at them. They learned that your friends can truly be your worst enemies, so it's best to keep them at arm's length. The only true threat to their power is being ganged up on, so they will strenuously avoid any chance of that happening.

By the age of fourteen to fifteen, these pupils still haven't quite learnt to lighten up but they do appreciate the bright side a bit more. Long walks in the countryside might appeal to them and it could be difficult to persuade them to sit inside the classroom and do their work. Loitering around the corridors could be a problem too. Suddenly, after years of trying to pretend they are above human needs, they start to get hunger pangs and eat their parents out of house and home. They stop skittering around the place avoiding sunlight and start to appreciate the value of making contacts and opening up their horizons. They start to learn they have valuable, important knowledge and an eye for analysis that could be useful in the world. Most importantly, if you taught them well, they will have learned how to use their power constructively.

If you are a teacher with Saturn in Scorpio, you are probably very quick at finding someone's weakness without revealing any of your own. You're like Ofsted inspectors with an agenda to shut down a malfunctioning school. Everyone's afraid of you (parents included) because of what they think you might know (even if you know absolutely nothing). If you could just use your ability to capitalise on helping your colleagues to acknowledge their weaknesses without destroying their spirits, you would be an invaluable asset to the staff team. Like Saturn in Scorpio pupils, you have a dark side that is best hidden from the head mistress but you also have so much more to give if you could just trust your colleagues enough to let them bring out the best in you. Around the age of thirty, you probably had a secret revealed to disbelieving ears. By the time you've reached sixty, you probably will agree with what George Bernard Shaw said about making the skeletons in your closet dance.

Fine tuning the role of Saturn

The primary role of Saturn in Scorpio is to learn how to express power effectively. This energy needs to be focused by the person in authority or it can be misused. Scorpio is ruled by both Mars and Pluto; either or both can be used for fine-tuning.

Mars/Pluto in Aries – These pupils usually have an abundance of self-control and think that they can have control over you as well. Don't look into their eyes for too long, but let them have a stretch or get a drink of water. They can sometimes become so obsessed with their work that they forget they're human. They need teachers and authority figures to appreciate their superhuman ability to concentrate on a task and can be good examples to other pupils.

Mars/Pluto in Taurus – These pupils need to control their environment so they are comfortable and can kid themselves that they are at a five star hotel instead of a classroom. They want to prevent changes from happening. They like to know that what they are learning will help them get the job they want. Teachers and authority figures can help them by getting them to investigate underhand business deals in the current news. And by allowing them to occasionally get away with eating in the classroom.

Mars/Pluto in Gemini – These pupils need to control the conversations around them. They like to drop verbal bombshells to get a reaction from others. They need to know that what they say has an effect on other people, even though it might be something quite bland. Teachers and authority figures can help them by getting them to investigate effective communication processes in world news topics. And by blowing their shallow minds with a good story or joke every now and again.

Mars/Pluto in Cancer – These pupils need to feel in control of the emotional ambiance of wherever they are. They are extremely sensitive to everyone's weak points and will exploit this knowledge when everyone is least expecting it. They also like to think they control the security of any given situation. Teachers and authority figures can help by getting them to investigate the power struggles between different countries or races of people. And by reminding them that their family will be very disappointed if they don't start paying attention.

Mars/Pluto in Leo – These pupils like to feel they can control who does and does not receive attention in the classroom. They like to have all the positive attention and of course, the people they don't like are held up for ridicule. Teachers and authority figures can help by getting them to investigate power struggles between leaders of different nations. And by holding up a mirror (either an actual one or a figurative one) and telling them they don't look so attractive when they're being nasty.

Mars/Pluto in Virgo – These pupils manipulate situations by carefully analysing what is going on before they take action. Their carefully aimed verbal bombshells can break hearts and obliterate a lesson plan. Teachers and authority figures can help by getting them to investigate health care reforms in different countries or governments. And by convincing them that such viciousness is sure to take a toll on their health.

Mars/Pluto in Libra – These pupils manipulate situations by controlling the social nuances of the classroom. They can turn long-term friends against each other and persuade enemies that they really love each other, just to create a diversion to avoid algebra. Teachers and authority figures can help them to better use their power by getting them to investigate the power struggles between people on a personal level. And by reminding them that they never know who they might end up with if they carry on behaving the way they do.

Mars/Pluto in Scorpio – These pupils manipulate the personal power between people. They are masters of subtlety and can get a whole class worked up with just a few seemingly innocent statements. Teachers and authority figures can help by getting them to research sex scandals in the news.

Mars/Pluto in Sagittarius – These pupils try to control the environment by being as offensive and insensitive as possible. For them, it doesn't take a whole lot of work as they are naturally born with their foot in their mouths. They are also very naturally energetic and frequently engage in horseplay that gets quickly out of hand. Teachers and authority figures can help by getting them to research religious scandals.

Mars/Pluto in Capricorn – These pupils try to control their environment by manipulating their social status (outright lying about it). They'll say their father is the MP for such and such and that he pays your salary, but you later find out that their dad works for a fast food chain. Teachers and authority figures can help by getting them to investigate the successes of prominent businessmen and women.

Mars/Pluto in Aquarius – These pupils try to control their environment by constantly changing rules and expectations. They are natural rebels and can cause total chaos with just a short speech on how pupils should be equal to their teachers. Teachers and authority figures can help by getting them to investigate historical fights for freedom.

Mars/Pluto in Pisces – These pupils try to control their environment by weirding everyone out with general confusion and their thoughts on the afterlife. They conduct séances at break and lunchtime and keep a pack of tarot cards in their lockers. Teachers and authority figures can help by getting them to investigate psychic phenomenon and asking them to justify their beliefs.

Case study – Annie Lennox

25 December 1954, 23:10 GMT
Aberdeen, Scotland 57°N10' 002°W04'
Rodden rating: AA; Collector Rodden
Jupiter in Cancer, Moon in Capricorn
Saturn in Scorpio, Mars in Pisces
First Jupiter return: September 1966, January and May 1967
First Saturn opposition: June, November 1970, March 1971
Second Jupiter return: August 1978
First Saturn return: November 1984
Third Jupiter return: August 1990
Fourth Jupiter return: July 2002
Fifth Jupiter return: July 2014
Second Saturn return: December 2013, June and August 2014

Annie Lennox's chart is notable for its Saturn/Venus conjunction in Scorpio. She was a lonely, unhappy child particularly as she struggled for independence from her over-protective father as she became a teenager. For Saturn in Scorpio, issues over control are very likely and Annie's Venus conjunct Saturn emphasises this tendency.

Annie had piano lessons from the age of seven, around the time of her first Saturn square. As Jupiter opposed Saturn in 1964, she won second prize in a singing contest at a Butlins holiday camp. She won a place at the Royal Academy of Art and Music several years later where she studied flute and classical music. Jupiter again opposed Saturn in 1977 when she began performing with Dave Stewart in The Tourists.

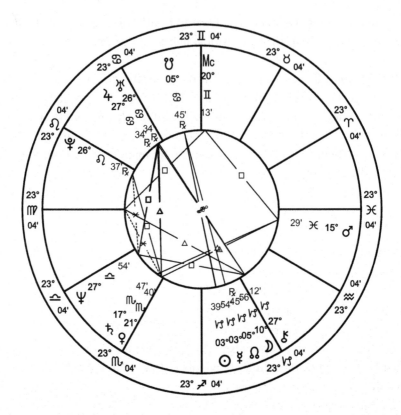

Annie Lennox – 25 December 1954

The duo changed their name to The Eurythmics and released their first album, *In the Garden* in October 1981 as Jupiter was square to its natal position. The following year, as Saturn was square to Jupiter, Annie suffered a nervous breakdown probably brought on by the stress of managing so many of their music responsibilities on their own. By the end of 1982, they were preparing for the release of *Sweet Dreams* during transiting Jupiter's movement over her natal Saturn. Jupiter would transit her IC several months later when they released *Touch* in December 1983.

Throughout 1984, as Annie's androgynous image became known worldwide, Jupiter was very busy indeed with conjunctions to Annie's Sun, Mercury, North Node and Moon — and just to show how much fun it was, went retrograde and then forward again over the same planets. During this time, their album *Touch Dance*, featuring re-mixes from *Touch*, was released, withdrawn, re-named, re-released and then rejected by their audiences. Annie's first Saturn return the next year was a happier time with *Be Yourself Tonight* securing four number ones, and the delivery of their jaw-dropping performance of 'Would I Lie to You?' at the 1985 MTV Video Music Awards.

Although The Eurythmics have never officially broken up, they decided to give themselves a rest after Jupiter had repeated his crazy forward, retrograde, forward-motion again antics by opposition (over the same planets) six years later in 1990. It was also her third Jupiter return and she had given birth to a healthy baby girl (a stillborn son was born during a transit of Jupiter in opposition to natal Saturn in Scorpio in 1988).

In 1992, Annie released *Diva* as transiting Saturn was square to its natal position. The album entered the charts at number one and won Best Album at the BRITS in 1993 and was nominated for an Academy Award. Saturn's opposition to Pluto had seen Annie seize power in the fickle world of pop music and repeat her success with the following year's *Medusa*. The Eurythmics reunited briefly as first Saturn and then Jupiter opposed her natal Saturn in 1999.

At the end of 2005, as Jupiter was conjunct her natal Saturn, *The Ultimate Collection* of Eurythmics hits was released. In 2007, as Saturn was conjunct her natal Pluto, she released her fourth solo album *Songs of Mass Destruction*.

Saturn in Sagittarius

3 December 1926	–	30 November 1929
13 January 1956	–	14 May 1956
10 October 1956	–	5 January 1959
18 November 1985	–	13 February 1988
11 June 1988	–	12 November 1988
23 December 2014	–	15 June 2015
19 September 2015	–	20 December 2017

The defence lawyer

Imagine a lawyer who has been assigned a case for a murder suspect. On the morning of the trial, the lawyer finds irrefutable evidence of his client's guilt. When the court is called to order, the lawyer stands and faces the judge saying: "This man deserves everything he has coming to him."

The blunt righteousness of children with Saturn in Sagittarius can be quite breath-taking, and is far more obvious in religious conviction and moral debate. Religion and politics are breeding grounds for extremely intense arguments and disagreements. There will be black eyes and bloody noses during the election seasons. These children risk exclusion to ensure their right to speak their minds.

At around the age of seven, these children probably witnessed extreme injustice that led to suffering or some form of incarceration. At their very hearts, these children fear being denied freedom because they (or someone else) lacked the courage of their convictions. Their faith in the justice system has been seriously shaken. They will hate your wishy-washy, sit-on-the-fence opinions meant to placate the entire classroom. You will be goaded into offering your views on capital punishment and they will laugh in your face. Put evidence under their noses and they suddenly act as if you meant to hurt their tender little compassionate feelings. Don't fall for it. More than any other pupils you teach, Saturn in Sagittarius pupils need to take responsibility for their opinions. They need to be encouraged to base their theories on reliable resources rather than ecclesiastical rantings, extreme examples of injustice or operative laws in Timbuktu. In other words, get their heads out of the clouds and make them have a good look at the reality around them.

Because Saturn in Sagittarius children fear loss of freedom, it can be hard to get them to take the educational bit and saddle. Detention will scare them, but they will wear you out with their arguments of their innocence. Trying to punish them is like punishing yourself ten times worse. Instead, show them the real injustice of the breadline. The Salvation Army (and other religious organisations) always needs volunteers and pupils with Saturn in Sagittarius can see what religious compassion, hard work and a frugal lifestyle can achieve. These pupils will learn that the line between being solvent and being destitute is a very fine one indeed. Do prepare yourself beforehand for their outrageous and even offensive commentary on unemployment, homelessness and poverty. Remember they are pupils who are learning about these things (they can be so priggishly self-righteous it's easy to forget) and they are probably badly regurgitating something their parents have said or something they picked up in church or from the TV crime series *Cracker*. Let them discover alternative views and then get them to badger their MPs to make changes to the law.

Around the age of fourteen or fifteen, these pupils will hear of new ideas and they may suddenly want to change the GCSE courses they so carefully chose the year before. They are completely confident that they're smart enough to catch up with all the coursework and exam practice required to complete their new interests. You and your colleagues will spend a lot of time and energy trying to persuade them to stick with their commitments, but these risk-takers will want to gamble their success away. Fortunately, this phase ends and these pupils slowly realise there is value to sticking to familiar territory once the exam pressure really starts to bite. These guys are visionaries and academic failure does not appeal to them because it jeopardises their chances of achieving further education.

If you're a teacher with Saturn in Sagittarius, you are probably not known for your grace or elegance or for your ability to keep a secret. Colleagues carrying mugs of coffee give you ample room to pass by and the head teacher has learned that private conversations with you will be broadcast the next day. You may notice no-one asks you for your opinion (though it doesn't stop you from giving it!). At around the age of thirty, some crisis in your faith may have caused you to really wonder what life is all about. You may do some travelling, heavy academic research or start attending church again. By sixty, after you have been just about everywhere, you realise the God you have been searching for all your life actually resides quite peacefully in the soul of every being.

Fine-tuning the role of Saturn

Saturn in Sagittarius is ruled by Jupiter. To get a better idea of how a person works towards success, examine their Jupiter placements.

Jupiter in Aries – These pupils work for opportunities to explore their bravery. They are the ultimate risk-takers, and inevitably they take quite a few knocks, but miraculously never seem to do serious damage to themselves. Because of their often breath-taking and careless activities, others seem to avoid them. These pupils need teachers and authority figures to help them prepare their safety nets – or even do it for them.

Jupiter in Taurus – These pupils work for opportunities to explore their resources. They are usually very good at making money and equally adept at spending it. But they don't waste money, they re-invest it to get even more money. These pupils need teachers and authority figures to help them have faith in the abundance of life.

Jupiter in Gemini – These pupils work for opportunities to learn. They devour books at break-neck speed and are probably your best pupils. However, their knowledge can be superficial but because they speak and write with such confidence, it can be easy to overlook that beneath the huge volumes of work they produce, they haven't actually made solid points. These pupils need teachers and authority figures to help them dig deeper and have more faith in what they are trying to say.

Jupiter in Cancer – These pupils work for opportunities to care for others. They are cautious learners, and it can be tricky to get them to explore new territories if lessons aren't linked together well. Natural philanthropists, they know that everyone likes to feel at home and they will try to accommodate the needs of all. They spoil others with their kindness and can feel taken advantage of. These pupils need teachers and authority figures to help them feel comfortable with and have faith in saying "no".

Jupiter in Leo – These pupils work for opportunities to show off. They need to be the centre of attention and they make themselves huge targets for sabotage by others. They often make the mistake of assuming everyone is as generous as they are and discover too late that others don't share their great faith. These pupils need teachers and authority figures to help them share the limelight and believe that others are just as important as they are.

Jupiter in Virgo – These pupils work for opportunities to analyse details. They can get completely tangled in the minutiae and finer points of lessons, therefore missing the objective completely. Consequently, they are often over-worked (or complain that they are). These pupils need teachers and authority figures to help them to have faith in the bigger picture.

Jupiter in Libra – These pupils work for opportunities to socialise with others. Born diplomats, they can get themselves in tangles by being too loyal to too many people. They enjoy art and culture but can be put off by facts and figures. These pupils need teachers and authority figures to help them to have more faith in themselves.

Jupiter in Scorpio – These pupils work for opportunities to control life. They are master manipulators and can be very heavy going and driven to see how far they can push themselves and others. They live life on the edge – often with one foot in the grave. These pupils need teachers and authority figures to help them uncover their hidden resources and let everyone else discover their own.

Jupiter in Sagittarius – These pupils work for opportunities to learn and philosophise. Unfortunately, they can come across as opinionated and irreverent and other people can't resist the urge to knock them off their high horses. But fortunately (for them), they get right back up again.

They are boisterous learners. These pupils need teachers and authority figures to help them have faith in quiet and stillness.

Jupiter in Capricorn – These pupils work for opportunities to further their careers. They are not afraid of hard work but do not like diversions from tradition. They are practical and are often worried about what they don't have. These pupils need teachers and authority figures to help them have faith in change.

Jupiter in Aquarius – These pupils work for opportunities to liberate and experiment. They eschew rules and regulations. They rant against fascism and dogma and worship democracy. However, they overlook that they themselves sound dogmatic at times. These pupils need teachers and authority figures to help them have faith in discovering their own beliefs.

Jupiter in Pisces – These pupils work for opportunities to explore the mystical. They are dreamy and kind but can be too dependent on others. They see the good in others and seem to truly believe there is no such thing as bad people. Deeply spiritual, they like peace and quiet. These pupils need teachers and authority figures to help them get their heads out of the clouds and face a few home truths about the world.

Case study – Shirley Temple-Black

23 April 1928, 21:00 PST
Santa Monica. California 34°N01'10"118°W29'25"
Rodden rating: AA; Collector: Wilsons
Jupiter in Aries
Saturn in Sagittarius
First Jupiter return: January 1940
First Saturn Opposition: July 1943
Time between first Jupiter return and last Saturn opposition: 3 years, 6 months
First Saturn return: December 1957
Second Saturn return: February, May, November 1987
Fourth Jupiter return June, November 1987, January 1988

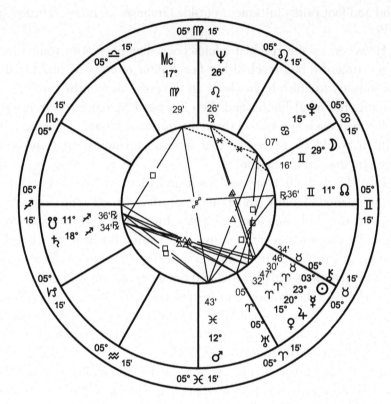

Shirley Temple-Black – 23 April 1928

Shirley Temple is best remembered for her role in the film *Bright Eyes*. Released at the end of 1934, as Jupiter opposed its natal position, she played the role of a little orphaned girl who becomes embroiled in a custody battle between her godfather and cranky uncle (but resolved the problem by suggesting everyone live together).

The following year, she featured in *Curly Top* as transiting Jupiter was conjunct her natal Saturn. Again, she played an orphan who is a key player in the romance between her older sister and an anonymous beau. In 1937, during transiting Jupiter's squares to its natal position and Saturn's conjunction with Uranus in Aries, she again played the part of an orphan in *Heidi*. Shirley was a beautiful, charming child whose image was used for dolls, dishes and clothing. From 1935-1938, she was the top box-office draw in the relatively new world of cinema. She even left her hand and foot prints in cement outside Grauman's Chinese Theatre in 1935.

However, as she reached adolescence, her popularity waned and by the time she had reached her first Jupiter return, she had left the film industry to finish high school. In the previous months, Saturn was conjunct her natal Jupiter and then her natal Mercury and transiting Jupiter had made a series of three hits to natal Uranus. Imagine how awful it would be to realise that growing up meant that suddenly everyone stopped loving you!

In 1945, as Jupiter opposed itself and Mercury (three times) and Saturn squared Mercury (three times), Shirley married at just seventeen years of age. Although she had a daughter during the marriage, the union did not last to its fifth anniversary. During the final throes of the marriage, Saturn made three squares to its natal position in Sagittarius, three conjunctions with her MC and three oppositions to natal Mars in Pisces. Perhaps she did not want to marry in haste and repent at leisure. A short time later she remarried, this time to Charles Alden Black (reputedly one of the richest young men in California), but this time the marriage lasted until his death in 2004.

In 1957-58, during a time of three Jupiter oppositions to the natal position, she returned to television in *Shirley Temple's Storybook*.

What does a former child star with Saturn in Sagittarius do when the acting parts dry up? Shirley turned her attention to politics and ran (unsuccessfully) for the Republican House of Representatives in 1967 as transiting Jupiter was conjunct her natal Neptune. The start of her fourth Jupiter return brought success, as she was appointed a US ambassador to Ghana in 1976 and then as an ambassador for Czechoslovakia in 1989, as transiting Jupiter opposed natal Saturn.

Saturn in Capricorn

1 December 1929	–	24 February 1932
14 August 1932	–	20 November 1932
5 January 1959	–	10 January 1962
14 February 1988	–	10 June 1988
13 November 1988	–	6 February 1991
20 December 2017	–	22 March 2020
1 July 2020	–	17 December 2020

The ultimate businessman

Imagine a man in an office. Everything is built for purpose, not for comfort. The clock on the wall says it's eleven o'clock at night.

To understand a Saturn in Capricorn pupil, it is best to understand what 'work' means. Work means you are doing something that may not be completely unpleasant, but you would still not choose to do it on a Saturday morning. Work means you are doing something you know will pay off in the long run otherwise you wouldn't bother to do it: there is an intrinsic or extrinsic reward. Work often means you are denying yourself some sort of comfort. You got up early or you have to sit in an uncomfortable chair or get your hands dirty or hurt your back moving something. Work implies some sort of purposeful action. If you are doing work, you are applying some sort of force to get something to change.

Pupils with Saturn in Capricorn seem to wholeheartedly disbelieve in Newton's First Law of Motion as they constantly need to test it out to see if it really works. They use a sledgehammer to crack a walnut, throw stones in glass houses and bark orders rather than make polite requests. Manners and other social niceties are not seen as requirements, parents and other authority figures are seen as being generally redundant and if something isn't hurting, you're not working hard enough. They tend to over-do everything and have a curiously mature attitude to responsibility. In fact, you may get the dizzying idea you are teaching your re-incarnated grandparents. Most disturbingly, Saturn in Capricorn pupils are far more professional than you are.

At the age of seven, these pupils may have got the distinct idea that the only person they can trust to do a job well is themselves. Other people just let them down or did a shabby job because they weren't in a position to supervise them. Consequently, they will hate working with other mere children and may need to be constantly reminded that their peers are also capable of great feats of research, can present ideas to a high standard and work just as hard as they do. These pupils love structure. They worship structure. They will love you if you provide structure. They adore your carefully scaffolded essay plans and crystal clear learning objectives. For this very reason, it's important to stand back and let them come up with their own game plans. Let them come up with a strategy for getting from A to Z. Direct them to play and invent (try not to cringe when they insist that you mark them for how well they do it). Use music and art to inspire them and tell the business studies teacher to stop acting so smug. More than any other pupils you will teach, Saturn in Capricorn children really need to loosen up. They need you to prove to them that the world is not the hostile place they have been led to believe it is. Show them opportunities that don't lead to making money and that people won't think less of them if they take a day off.

About the age of fourteen to fifteen, these pupils suddenly discover emotions, the primary emotion being fear. Suddenly, they start needing their mothers more and can't wait to go home. They spend long lunchtimes with you seeking reassurances, but nothing you say can dry their tears of terror of the examinations officer. They fret over children they don't yet have (well, hopefully) and carry elaborate architectural plans for the house they want to build. They put on weight through comfort eating or lose weight because their stomach is in constant knots. Fortunately, they start to believe in themselves again. They get a new hairstyle or buy some jewellery with the money they've been hoarding since their birth. When the exam results come, they will not be disappointed in themselves because this group has always known hard work pays off.

If you are a teacher with Saturn in Capricorn, you are a slave-driver and would be a good head teacher, an examinations officer or an Ofsted inspector. If you've learned how to balance your home and work life by the time you're thirty, you're a very wise person indeed. But you probably haven't, so everyone avoids you because you're so irritable and grumpy all the time. By the time you're sixty, you're probably worn out but eligible for early retirement and can then enjoy your second childhood as you missed out on the first one because you were working so hard.

Fine-tuning the role of Saturn

Saturn in Capricorn is ruled by Saturn. Saturn is at its most potent in the sign of Capricorn.

Case study – Sean Connery

25 August 1930, 18:05
Edinburgh, Scotland 55°N57' 003°W13'
Rodden rating: AA; Collector: Rodden
Jupiter in Cancer, Moon in Virgo
Saturn in Capricorn, Saturn in rulership
One Jupiter return: August 1942 age 12
Three Saturn oppositions: August 1944, Jan, April 1995
Time between first Jupiter return and last Saturn opposition: 2 years, 8 months
First Saturn return: November 1960
Second Saturn return: January 1988
Fourth Jupiter return: June 1990

Sean Connery was small in stature, but, like many boys, shot up around the time of his Jupiter return in Cancer at twelve. His Jupiter and Saturn transits were slightly unusual during adolescence: his one and only Jupiter return was slightly later than average and his final Saturn opposition was earlier than average. Though more research needs to be done in charts with similar traits, the short space of time between Connery's Jupiter return and final Saturn opposition may have accounted for his sudden growth spurt. He has boasted that he lost his virginity around the time of his first Saturn opposition to "an older woman in an ATS uniform" when he was fourteen.[22]

Although his size and talent for football attracted the attention of scouts, just before his second Jupiter return, and as Saturn made a series of oppositions to his North Node, Sean decided to become an actor

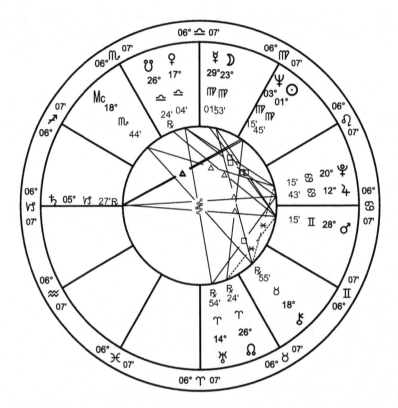

Sean Connery – 25 August 1930

because "I realised that a top-class footballer could be over the hill by the age of thirty and I was already twenty-three. I decided to become an actor and it turned out to be one of my more intelligent moves."[23] Even before his first Saturn return, Sean was showing the wisdom and maturity of Saturn in Capricorn: he had the self-discipline to refuse the temptation of playing out most young men's dream as a footballer, and instead choose a career that had more longevity.

After playing numerous small roles, Sean played in the Disney fantasy *Darby O'Gill and the Little People* as Saturn made its three returns to its natal place in Capricorn. Already an imposing six feet two inches, Sean's height was emphasised by comparisons to his co-stars who were portraying leprechauns.

His big break came as Jupiter made a series of oppositions to Neptune in Virgo when he was cast as James Bond in *Dr No* in 1961. As James

Bond fans know, the character has an impeccable, discerning nature in his attire, his choice of weaponry and, of course, he always gets the most beautiful women. Ian Fleming, the creator of the James Bond books, had serious doubts over Sean's suitability for the role. He felt Sean was too unrefined and too much like an overgrown stuntman.[24]

However, after intense tutelage from the director Terence Young, who taught Sean how to eat, walk and talk, everyone agreed Sean was a perfect James Bond. Sean played Bond off and on until his Jupiter made a series of three oppositions to his Saturn. *Never Say Never Again* (released in 1983) was his last turn as the spy. He was not always happy playing Bond and frequently turned his eye to other, more removed parts. "I'm fed up to here with this whole Bond bit," he said in a 1965 interview, just after the start of his fourth Jupiter cycle.[25]

A Saturn opposition to natal Jupiter in 1989, as well as Saturn's second return in early 1989, provided him with an opportunity to hang up his associations with cufflinks and shaken martinis forever: he played the father of Indiana Jones in *The Last Crusade* and shortly thereafter a commanding officer in *The Hunt for Red October*.

Saturn in Aquarius

25 February 1932	–	13 August 1932
20 November 1932	–	14 February 1935
11 January 1962	–	24 March 1964
17 September 1964	–	16 December 1964
7 February 1991	–	21 May 1993
1 July 1993	–	28 January 1994
23 March 2020	–	30 June 2020
18 December 2020	–	7 March 2023

The mad scientist

Imagine Victor Frankenstein in the moments before he animates his new creation. Your whole life has led up to this moment. But will your creation be the stuff of dreams or nightmares?

With Saturn in Aquarius pupils, you can never really predict how they'll turn out because they are adept at doing exactly the opposite of what you say. You assign them a straightforward essay and they turn in an indecipherable piece that turns out to be secretly coded. But it's not a bad piece of work. It's just not what you asked for. To understand these pupils, you need to understand Victor Frankenstein. Victor was a bright pupil who got it into his head he could do things better than his teachers. Eventually, he got it into his head he could do better than God, and decided to replicate human life. And it was a disaster, not because it didn't work but because by breaking a few little old rules (like grave-robbing for body parts, driving himself insane with exhaustion and enraging the church for starters), his experiment turned out a lot better than he thought it would. The creature could learn to speak and read, for example. He was also incredibly ugly and no-one liked him but hey-ho. The creature was harshly judgemental of Victor, who had created him then abandoned him, thus leaving him to learn the cruel ways of society without any sort of parental support. Saturn in Aquarius pupils have to learn to be accountable for their actions and be ready to accept that if they bend a few rules, they will have to bite the bullet and accept the consequences. This is a hard lesson for all pupils, but especially so for

Saturn in Aquarius pupils who get it into their heads that they are not really human and therefore don't have to follow the same rules humans do.

Saturn in Aquarius pupils generally hate the bodies they have to live in. At around seven, there may have been some sort of physical limitation imposed upon them that has led them to believe it isn't too much fun doing normal things like eating on a schedule, using the toilet when required, sleeping or staying in bed when you're sick. Perhaps the family was deeply entrenched in traditional values and forced these on the child, thus denying him/her of their own individual rights to develop unique identities.

Consequently, by the time Saturn in Aquarius pupils meet you, they think they have grown propellers on their heads. They become fascinated with high-tech gadgets, scientific experiments and conspiracy theories. They watch for aliens and hang around in crop circles hoping to make contact. They're so odd, and so above the pain of rejection (so they like to pretend), that they isolate themselves from their peers and spend hours on the internet searching for other weirdoes who share their opinions. Other weirdoes validate their hypotheses and, as they say, a monster is created. In the classroom of Saturn in Aquarius pupils, it won't pay to make them honour home and country and force them to sing 'God Save the Queen'. But if you refuse to do it, suddenly they're clearing their throats and singing patriotic songs like nightingales. Saturn in Aquarius pupils can fix your mobile phone, show you how to upload digital voice recordings and change the settings on your iPod, but they will think Ernest Hemingway was just another fat old Yank who drank too much. So you have to show them how his writing influenced and revolutionised twentieth century writing. You have to teach them that you have feelings – something you have probably spent your whole career trying to conceal. It's difficult contradicting your own values and beliefs to antagonise Saturn in Aquarius pupils into trusting you're not just another teacher cramming the same old regurgitated rubbish down their throats. But by seeing things in a different light, and doing things in a different way, you are learning new things just like they are. Teaching Saturn in Aquarius pupils is always exciting, challenging and refreshing, because very often they are the ones who are teaching you.

At fourteen or fifteen, self-consciousness cripples these brainiacs, and the pain of being just another nerd with glasses starts to hurt them. They start grooming. They discover mirrors and ugly ducklings suddenly become the swans of fairy tales. But they neglect their studies because it flattens their hair, or they can't get to classes on time because they didn't get their beauty sleep, or they discovered someone who admires them and they just can't get enough of them. Soon this phase passes, and by the time examinations come, they discover the joy that precision can bring to their experiments. They start learning a newer, more innovative vocabulary that has their teachers scrambling for their dictionaries. They produce ground-breaking research that challenges presiding dogma and through by-passing the limitations society imposes on us, they can make new discoveries so our collective neighbourhoods can break for freedom.

If you're a teacher with Saturn in Aquarius, you probably wear a lab coat and secretly collect data about the colours other teachers wear on a Monday. But you ardently believe that everyone is equal and will be the first to fire off if you think management have indicated otherwise. Everyone loves you at Ofsted inspection time because you're not afraid to tell the inspectors where to get off – and you have creative ideas for how they could do it. You're not afraid of the head teacher because you know the union will back you. By thirty, you will probably have the strong urge to take a sabbatical and invent something. By sixty, you've learned that the simplest, most natural things are often the most delightful: a baby's smile, the laughter of children, love and wholemeal bread. You've discovered it isn't so bad being human after all.

Fine-tuning the role of Saturn

Aquarius is ruled by both Saturn and Uranus (either or both can be used for fine tuning). Uranus rules anarchy, and every teacher or parent knows that dealing with more than one rebellious teenager can be tricky. Knowing how pupils (or children) might try to gang up on you to try to get out of homework or chores is being one step ahead.

Saturn/Uranus in Aries – These pupils work to rebel by uniting individuals to fight a common cause. Although formidable opponents, they are not natural team players and their impatience makes them reckless.

Teachers and other authority figures can capitalise on their lack of staying power. They will lose the energy to persist.

Saturn/Uranus in Taurus – These pupils work to rebel by pooling businesses and resources. Although they become temptingly big targets to shoot at, they find it difficult to change direction, and can be persistent in their desire to take over everything. Teachers and other authority figures can capitalise on their slowness. Failing that, give them lunchtime detentions or take their allowance away.

Saturn/Uranus in Gemini – These pupils work to rebel by networking, often with digital technology. They are argumentative but lose their focus easily. Teachers and other authority figures can capitalise on their short attentions spans. Punish them by making them sit in silence.

Saturn/Uranus in Cancer – These pupils work to rebel by drawing on people's commonalities. They're very perceptive of what everyone needs and have very good memories. Teachers and other authority figures can capitalise on their sensitivity to the emotional needs of others. Punish them by eating biscuits in front of them without offering to share.

Saturn/Uranus in Leo – These pupils work to rebel by spotlighting issues they think no-one else is aware of. They like to embarrass others. They also think they are always right. Teachers and other authority figures can capitalise on their difficulties working with other people by offering random bits of praise. Eventually they start turning on each other. Punish them by not letting them use their mirrors.

Saturn/Uranus in Virgo – These pupils work to rebel by upsetting the normal routines. They like to try new ways of doing things so they seem one step ahead and therefore smarter than anyone else. Teachers and other authority figures can capitalise on their fear of germs by blowing their noses in front of them.

Saturn/Uranus in Libra – These pupils work to rebel by splitting or re-assigning partnerships. They have a good sense of social norms but like to see what will happen if they upset them. Teachers and other authority figures can capitalise on their fear of being on their own, by making them sit in detention all by themselves.

Saturn/Uranus in Scorpio – These pupils work to rebel by uniting powers. They form unlikely alliances and are adept at finding common purposes. Teachers and other authority figures will find them slippery and exceptionally wilful. Be nervous when they're quiet, cautious when they're noisy (they're using diversion tactics) and never let them think you're on to them.

Saturn/Uranus in Sagittarius – These pupils work to rebel by uniting philosophical views and they will keep working until they think everyone agrees with them and then promptly change their stance. Give them an inch and they'll take a mile, so always ensure there are clear boundaries in everything. Teachers and other authority figures can capitalise on their fear of making commitments and taking on responsibilities.

Saturn/Uranus in Capricorn – These pupils work to rebel by uniting work forces. They are adept at getting everyone else to do their work whilst they chat about the latest developments in high-speed travel. Teachers and other authority figures can capitalise on their fear of waste by pointing out environmental hazards and waste by-products.

Saturn/Uranus in Aquarius – If left without supervision and guidance, these pupils will find it difficult to follow instructions. Directions and criterion for success must be explicit and praise should be given following procedures. However, this group will appreciate time to conduct group projects and experiments which can then be extended into allowing them time and space to conduct further independent research.

Saturn/Uranus in Pisces – These pupils work to rebel by dissolving boundaries. Never be tempted to give this group any sort of directions and then trust them to follow through. They will get lost or abducted, or will find where the booze is secretly hidden. Teachers and other authority figures can capitalise on their fear of order by making them do the same small task over and over until they get it perfect (although they may actually enjoy this!).

Case study – Joan Collins

23 May 1933, 3:00 GDT
London United Kingdom 51°30' 00°W10'
DD rating; collector: Rodden
Jupiter in Virgo, Mercury in Taurus
Saturn in Aquarius, Uranus in Aries
First Jupiter return: September 1944
Three Saturn oppositions: August 1947, March and May 1948
Time between first Jupiter return and final Saturn opposition in adolescence: 3 years, 8 months
First Saturn return: February 1963
Fourth Jupiter return: December 1991, January and July 1992
Second Saturn return: April, July, September 1992

Because of the rebellious nature of Aquarius, it can be a little difficult to pin down Saturn in Aquarius – unless you pretend you really aren't all that interested.

Joan Collins grew up in an affluent household in Maida Vale, London, attended an independent day school for girls and later did a degree at RADA – a high pedigree education. However, Joan's father was hard to please and despite the mountains of money he invested in educating his daughters, he was often critical of them.

And so we may start to get the idea that Joan's rise to fame was not a result of an excess of money and social connections (though there were plenty of both) but perhaps more of a by-product of trying to please daddy or trying to prove him really wrong.

Joan's acting debut was in Ibsen's *A Doll's House* in 1946, a first post-Jupiter return, pre-first Saturn opposition achievement. It is a remarkable debut and a fitting one for someone with Saturn in Aquarius, because the play is largely seen as a sharp criticism of nineteenth century marriage norms. Thus, *A Doll's House* is a good choice of role for someone who eventually married five times.

Although very beautiful, a popular pin-up and signed to Rank, a very good British studio, for the next several years Joan's early promise as an actress was unfulfilled. She complained bitterly about the studio's concentration on building up the career of its male clients.[26] In 1955,

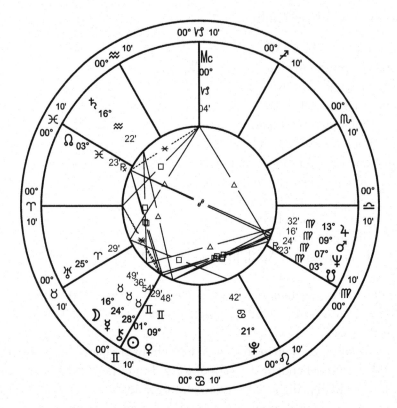

Joan Collins – 23 May 1933

as Saturn squared its natal position and Jupiter opposed Saturn's natal position, she had finally broken Hollywood with *Land of the Pharaohs*. From there, she made appearances in many American TV shows but it was for her role as Alexis Carrington in *Dynasty* that she is remembered by everyone. Happily for astrologers, her 1968 Jupiter return saw her singing a zodiac themed song in the British film, *Can Hieronymus Merkin Ever Forget Mercy Humppe and Find True Happiness?*

Saturn's conjunction to natal Jupiter in 1978 could have meant the end of her acting career as many actresses have complained that they struggle to find roles once they reach their forties, and Joan turned to writing to supplement her floundering career and appeared in many commercials, most notably for Cinzano. However, just after her third Jupiter return, Joan won a role in *Dynasty* and brought us a new brand of female archetype previously unseen in film and television: the rich, powerful and very beautiful Super Bitch. At around the time of her next Saturn square, she posed for *Playboy* at the grand old age of fifty, thus proving it isn't only the twenty somethings that have it going on. Saturn in Aquarius refuses to bow down to the expected social mores and instead creates its own rules.

Saturn in Pisces

15 February 1935	–	25 April 1937
19 October 1937	–	14 January 1938
24 March 1964	–	16 September 1964
17 December 1964	–	3 March 1967
22 May 1993	–	30 June 1993
29 January 1994	–	7 April 1994

The frogman on dry land

Imagine a deep-sea diver, still in his diving suit and flippers, in a library. You ask him what he's doing. He answers: "I'm looking for a book to help me conquer my fear of water."

Like the frogman in the library, Saturn in Pisces pupils often feel dreadfully out of place in a classroom. They have the vague feeling they should be learning something but feel out of their depth. Used to the comfort their imaginations bring to them, they are often very disappointed that the pictures they draw or the stories they write are painfully inadequate when compared to the ones in their heads. Highly intuitive, they find it shocking that they can't communicate telepathically. Loud noises make them jump out of their skins and being in a classroom with twenty-nine boisterous and deafening children makes them hug themselves and make rocking motions to escape the commotion. Give them a ruler and scissors and they talk quietly to them, and later pretend the ruler and scissors are talking to each other, whispering sweet nothings and promising each other eternal devotion. Saturn in Pisces pupils will always find a way to escape the harsh reality of the classroom.

Pupils with Saturn in Pisces fear being overwhelmed and swept out to sea. They are content to paddle on the shores of education but often won't take the full plunge. Teaching them to overcome their fears is often as easy as reminding them to stop panicking and let their feet touch the floor. They forget the water isn't as deep as they had feared. At the age of seven, they may have been reluctant (but not incapable) of being able to read and write. To them, letters and numbers are pathetic, meaningless squiggles. They could come up with much better symbols. Thus these reluctant pupils become wonderful artists, if left to their own devices. But, of course, leaving pupils to their own devices is not part of the educational repertoire, where every moment is supervised and pointless meandering is not permitted. And so the teacher feels forced to instil some serious discipline and the pupil is left with the idea that learning is painful. They are often tested in sink or swim conditions where the consequences of not passing the test are so frightening that they have no choice but to make feeble attempts to keep their heads above water until someone feels sorry for them and rescues them. Or not. Because of their experiences in the educational system, Saturn in Pisces pupils very often become teachers, as they think they can save their own pupils from similar experiences.

Teachers with Saturn in Pisces pupils need to pay particular attention to the ebb and flow of their pupils' interests. They don't have to pander to their every whim, but they need to be aware that there are frequent opportunities to squeeze in advice on how to take notes (they tend to write down everything verbatim, but because they can't keep up, they give up), how to organise themselves ('organise' to them means keeping everything) and how to self-monitor their progress (they'll hate it, but if you don't help them they won't do it for themselves). Teaching a classroom of Saturn in Pisces pupils can feel like persuading fish to use their legs and walk on dry land. It's against their nature to appreciate structure and order and it means getting them to plunge into those big thoughts of theirs and persuading them there has to be something rattling about in there that can help them. Once you convince them to trust and use their own resources, these pupils will have the confidence to share their ideas with others. They will laugh good naturedly at their careless mistakes if you give them the tools to make it better next time. They want to make you happy, so make it clear to them how to do that. Give them the time and space to reflect on what they should do next. Very often, these pupils will inspire you with their hidden strengths or stimulate your sense of compassion for the suffering in the world. Through their tears, these pupils will let you know that they appreciate you and that they think you are the greatest thing in the world. But they'll never come out and say it, so make sure you tell them when they get it right.

At fourteen or fifteen, these pupils become afraid that their disorganised notes are wholly inadequate and they employ the most inefficient study method known to man: cramming. Two years of study become condensed into one month of intense swotting up. For the first time in their lives, they pass with flying colours and use their library cards with such gusto that they wear them out. And then they fall in love. Romantic fools that they are, they start fantasising about getting married before the object of their affection has even kissed them. Exam season comes and goes and soon the Saturn in Pisces pupil forgets all about them – unless you or their parents (or other authority figures) have taught them the value of step by step processes.

If you're a Saturn in Pisces teacher, chances are everyone knows they can find you in the pub because you've just worked out what your planner is for – and there's nothing to ease the suffering of having to plan more than anesthetising yourself a little first. And there you'll be, furiously back-dating your lesson plans for the inspection the next day. Morning briefings? *Was I supposed to be there?* you ask. Your colleagues know that you very often won't have a clue about what's going on, but they like you because you're such a nice person. Parents completely take advantage of you because they know you're secretly still frightened of authority figures. By thirty, you've probably finally found a cult to join or a place to retreat to. Or you've found something interesting to study and have embarked on a half-baked quest to become an outstanding scholar in that subject. But you still haven't broken your bad habit of 'cramming' for exams. By sixty, you will have returned to the sea to swim with the dolphins but you will have learned that it's more fun to take the rest of us with you and show us how it's done. In our imaginations, of course.

Fine-tuning the role of Saturn

Saturn in Pisces is ruled by Neptune and co-ruled by Jupiter; either or both planets can be used. In mythology, Jupiter was god of the heavens whilst Neptune was god of the sea. This combination of rulers makes for a grand kingdom in which it is easy to become overwhelmed, sucked in or lost altogether. Neptunian influences are said to be addictive. Like Uranus, Neptune works collectively, affecting many people at once and may not become apparent until the collective group matures enough to have an effect on society.

Jupiter/Neptune in Aries – These pupils may think they can save the world through learning independently and/or the need for teamwork is sacrificed for greater efficiency. Mass media may be the teachers and authority figures. There may be an addiction to speed and immediate action.

Jupiter/Neptune in Taurus – These pupils may think they can save the world by stabilising financial institutions. Personal power may be sacrificed for greater stability in society. Mother Nature may be the teacher and authority figure. There may be an addiction to material goods and property.

Jupiter/Neptune in Gemini – These pupils may think they can save the world by making improvements in education. Philosophies may be sacrificed for simplified codes. Symbols may be used to teach or to exert authority. There may be an addiction to communicating on a more psychic level.

Jupiter/Neptune in Cancer – These pupils tend to idolise the family structure (in whatever guise this may take) and they should be encouraged to work out not only where their loyalties lie but why. The perpetual search for the perfect mother (or father) figure can lead these pupils into very surreal territory and an occasional reality check is often necessary to pull them back from the brink and prevent them from falling over the edge.

Jupiter/Neptune in Leo – These pupils may think they can save the world by idealising glamour. Friendship and social groups may be sacrificed for youth and beauty. Young people become authority figures. There may be an addiction to entertainment.

Jupiter/Neptune in Virgo – These pupils may think they can save the world by idealising or seeking to perfect human health. The use of imagination may be sacrificed for natural products. The search for perfection becomes the authority figures There may be an addiction to work and order.

Jupiter/Neptune in Libra – These pupils may think they can save the world by idealising or searching for perfect human relationships. The need for independent thought is sacrificed for the yearning for teamwork. Couples or pairs are seen as authority figures. There may be an addiction to a search for beauty and harmony.

Jupiter/Neptune in Scorpio – These pupils may think they can save the world by idealising or searching for perfect power. The need for stability may be sacrificed for the urge to make profound changes in society. The occult may be seen as having ultimate power. There may be an addiction to the dark side of society.

Jupiter/Neptune in Sagittarius – These pupils may think they can save the world by idealising or searching for perfect foreign policies, philosophies or religions. Casual conversation may be sacrificed for profound spiritual growth. Authority figures may come from foreign lands or religions. There may be an addiction to holding unusual beliefs.

Jupiter/Neptune in Capricorn – These pupils resist change and find it exceedingly hard to 'go with the flow' if they feel their need for order and structure is threatened. They need to learn that not all small changes necessarily lead to big changes and that very often small adjustments can improve on a system rather than completely destroy it.

Jupiter/Neptune in Aquarius – These pupils may idealise equality. The rights of the individual may be sacrificed for the rights of the collective. Authority figures may search for alternative versions of the truth. There may be an addiction to the unusual or unexpected.

Jupiter/Neptune in Pisces – These pupils may idealise sacrifice. Perfection may be sacrificed for chaos. Authority figures may be imaginary. There may be an addiction to what is perceived and accepted as the ideal.

Case study – Keanu Reeves

2 September 1964, 5:41 EET
Beirut, Lebanon 33°N53'035°E30'
Rodden rating: C; Collector: Rodden
Jupiter in Taurus, Venus in Scorpio
Saturn in Pisces, Neptune in Scorpio
First Jupiter return: June 1976
First Saturn opposition: November 1977, January and July 1978
Time between first Jupiter return and last Saturn opposition: 2 years
Second Jupiter return: May 1988
First Saturn return: April and July 1993
Third Jupiter return: May 2000
Fourth Jupiter return: April 2012

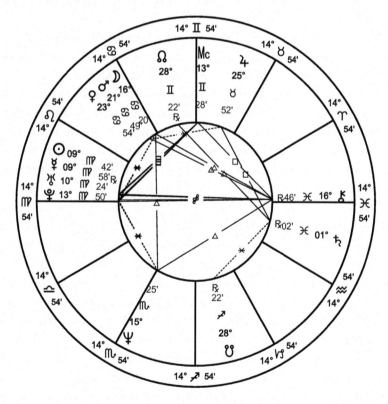

Keanu Reeves – 2 September 1964

Keanu's mother's frequent marriages and divorces meant the young boy changed schools several times at crucial stages of development. Although not everyone benefits from a traditional style of education, to a pupil with Saturn in Pisces, already difficult to keep on track, a lack of routine can mean they have a ready-made excuse not to excel at school. Keanu was diagnosed as dyslexic, a condition not helped by an unstable education, and he left school without a diploma. Although he had minor successes early in life (such as playing Mercutio in *Romeo and Juliet* just after his first Saturn opposition), he was relegated to playing dumb or spaced out teens such as Ted in *Bill and Ted's Excellent Adventure* and its franchise films (1989-1991), Tod in *Parenthood* (1989) and, in a small role, as Chevalier Raphael Danceny in *Dangerous Liaisons* (1988). However, at his first Saturn return in 1994, he began starring in far more serious, meatier roles such as in *Speed* and other high budget Hollywood films – with many of the roles casting Reeves as the character who saves the world.

Speed was filmed during Reeves' single Saturn return and released to eager audiences as transiting Saturn made a series of oppositions to his natal stellium in Pisces. Although he had the world at his feet (appropriate for Saturn in Pisces!) with his success in *Speed*, he continued to make very odd choices in roles that were viewed as highly experimental rather than as roles to cement his position as top male lead. He even refused $11 million to make *Speed II* in order to play the title role in small production of *Hamlet* in Manitoba (although it was a highly acclaimed performance) and to tour with his band Dogstar.

The Matrix, released 31 March 1999 was another turning point in Reeves' career. In early 1998, transiting Jupiter began a series of oppositions with his natal planets in Virgo as pre-production preparations began for the film. Reeves' had been suffering spinal injuries and was still recovering from surgery when filming began. Despite this, he continued to train intensely and by the summer of 1999 as Saturn made a series of oppositions to his natal Neptune, the altered reality movie made Reeves one of the most bankable actors in Hollywood.

Keanu's third Jupiter return brought him much success with *The Matrix*. However, sadly, the Jupiter/Saturn conjunction of 2000 occurred near his natal Jupiter and coincided with the awful death of a stillborn daughter and, a year later, the death of the child's mother.

Despite the tragedies, Reeves continued to act and received a star on the Hollywood Walk of Fame as transiting Saturn made a series of conjunctions with his natal Mars and Venus in Cancer. The re-make of *The Day the Earth Stood Still*, released in December 2008 (released two Saturn returns following the original of 1951), saw Reeves cast as the inverted Klaatu, an alien in human form.

Although he still remains a highly recognizable actor, his profile hasn't as yet matched the success of his work just after his first Saturn return. However fans should bear in mind that his second Saturn return, a series of three, begins in early 2023.

THE VARIATION OF
JUPITER AND SATURN CYCLES
IN ONE ACADEMIC YEAR

To demonstrate the variation in the Jupiter and Saturn cycles between the first Jupiter return and the first Saturn opposition, let us examine the charts of three well known celebrities who more or less grew up in front of us.

Theoretically, Angelina Jolie, Drew Barrymore and Leonardo DiCaprio could have (if they had lived in the same cities at the time) been in the same Year 7 class, as they all would have turned the age of eleven before 1 September 1986. DiCaprio, born 11 November 1974, was the oldest in the group. Barrymore, born 22 February 1975 was the next oldest and, born 4 June 1975, Jolie was the youngest. As an added bonus, their birthdays are evenly distributed throughout this school year.

The secondary school is perceived as one big adventure as pupils have spent their entire educational experience in one classroom with one teacher with people they have known for most of their lives. As an aside, most school years have (roughly) half the year group with Jupiter in one sign and the other half with Jupiter in the next.

The bricks

To understand how this year group learns, a perusal of the ephemeris shows that on 1 September 1974 Jupiter was in Pisces, moving retrograde until early November. Jupiter moved into Aries on 19 March 1975, indicating this year group would have about half of its members with Jupiter in Pisces and the younger half with Jupiter in Aries. Or, we might expect the older half to have more mystical or spiritual leanings, and that their personal philosophies towards expanding their personal boundaries at Jupiter's return would be an accepting one. If a year group's Jupiter sign is known, then it gives a clue as to what kind of discipline is required to guide them. As any astrologer will tell you, there is a world of difference between the signs of Pisces and Aries. Jupiter in Pisces pupils may have needed a steadier hand to guide and direct them. The younger half of the year group, with Jupiter in Aries, may have been more precocious and more boisterous than the half with Jupiter in Pisces. The younger pupils would need to be encouraged to work together (patiently!) with other pupils, to slow down and commit to finishing projects and to be careful of rushing into things without considering the consequences. Simply by considering Jupiter, an idea of how to handle this year can be established.

The mortar

As Saturn is further away from the Sun, its orbit is longer than that of Jupiter and it therefore moves more slowly through the zodiac. Saturn spends about two and a half years in each sign, meaning that most years have Saturn in the same sign. For our celebrity examples, on 1 September 1974 Saturn was in Cancer, moving direct until the end of November, moving retrograde (see the next section on forward and retrograde motion for an explanation) until mid-March and remaining in Cancer until the end of the academic year. With the entire year having Saturn in Cancer, it may be expected that family conditions may have left this year group emotionally inhibited or even repressed in some way. There may be a family crisis around the time of the opposition. It may also be a feature of this year group to have issues around safety and security. Those with Saturn in Cancer may fret about the past, but they may feel a lot better if they know they don't bring the mistakes of the past into the future.

Forward and retrograde motion

Although the motions of all the planets and celestial bodies are predictable from our point of view on earth, they do not move in a simple straight line. Sometimes, they appear to speed up, slow down or even move backwards at various times of year. For this reason, it is important to have an awareness of how the planets are moving.

Something else that must be kept in mind when examining Jupiter and Saturn is that owing to the forward, stationing and retrograde motions of the planet, the number of return and opposition hits, as well as the time between them, can vary. There is a chart for the celebrity examples at the end of this section that shows how many returns or oppositions were present in adolescence.

Specific examples

Leonardo di Caprio
11 November 1974, 2:47 PST
Los Angeles, California 34°N03' 118°W15'
Rodden rating: AA: Collector: Clifford

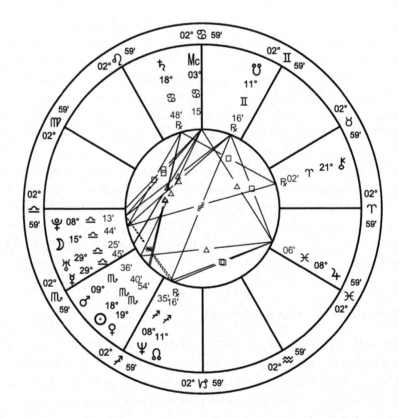

Leonardo di Caprio – 11 November 1974

Jupiter in Pisces
Saturn in Cancer ruled by Moon in Libra
First Jupiter return: March 1986, age 11 years, 4 months
Final Saturn opposition: (series of 3) Oct 1990, 15 years, 11 months
Time between: 4 years, 7 months

Leonardo DiCaprio was the first of the celebrities to have his Jupiter return (26 March 1986), some five months before he would have entered secondary school. His parents had divorced when he was still a baby and post Jupiter return, but pre-Saturn opposition, he appeared in commercials and educational films. It wasn't until after the first Saturn opposition (27 January 1990) that he made his break into television and later the big screen. He spent nearly four years in the growing phase between the first Jupiter return and first Saturn opposition, and was nearly sixteen when the last of three Saturn oppositions took place. It was as if he needed time to prepare himself for the responsibilities that fame and fortune would eventually bestow upon him. DiCaprio is a very good example of a Hollywood megastar who has not imploded on his own success. Owing to the retrograde motion of transiting Saturn, he had three oppositions, the final one being when he was nearly sixteen. Not much is written about DiCaprio before his first Jupiter return – it's almost as if he arrived on silver screens already matured, his childhood obscured by some kind of Jupiter in Pisces mystery. After the success of *Titanic* (a wonderful Jupiter in Pisces film!), DiCaprio had to carefully choose his projects and not allow himself to be swept away in the enthusiasm of directors who wanted to cast him in the wake of his successes.

Drew Barrymore
22 February 1975, 11:51 PST
Culver City, California 34°N01' 118°W24'
Rodden rating: AA; Collector: Wilsons
Jupiter in Pisces
Saturn in Cancer ruled by Moon in Cancer
First Jupiter return: February 1987, age 12 years
Final Saturn opposition: Dec 1989, age 13 years, 10 months
Time between: 2 years, 10 months

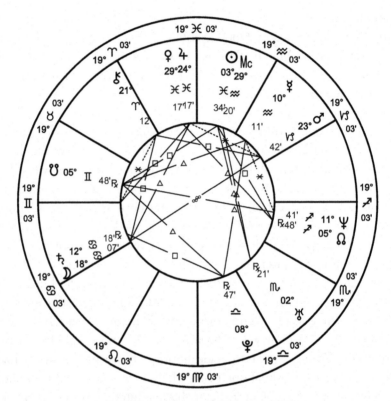

Drew Barrymore – 22 February 1975

Drew Barrymore, also the child of a single parent, most obviously lived out the Jupiter in Pisces excesses: she was already smoking, drinking and taking drugs by the time of her first Jupiter return (5 February 1987) because her mother, apparently, didn't mind that she did these things because she had addiction problems herself. Note that although three months separate Drew and Leonardo in age, Drew's first Jupiter return took place only a couple of weeks after Leonardo's. As she was a household name from the age of five (thanks to ET), her awkward era between her first Jupiter return and first Saturn opposition was played out in a dramatically public way – something interviewers like to remind us of. Barrymore did not choose to be an actress; it was imposed on her or overcame her in true Jupiter in Pisces style. Barrymore also had to find a reality in the chaos of her mother's addiction in the time between her Jupiter return and Saturn oppositions.

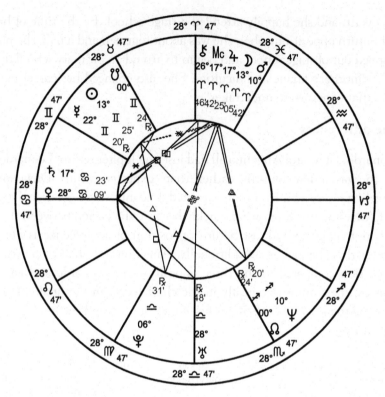

Angelina Jolie – 4 June 1975

Angelina Jolie
4 June 1975, 9:09 PDT
Los Angeles, California 34°N03' 118°W15'
Rodden rating: AA; Collector: Rodden
Jupiter in Aries
Saturn in Cancer ruled by Moon in Aries
First Jupiter return: May 1987, age 11 years, 11 months
Final Saturn opposition: Jan 1990, age 14 years, 7 months
Time between: 2 years, 8 months

Angelina Jolie's parents had also split up by the time she entered
adolescence. However, Jolie had Jupiter in Aries, immediately setting
her apart from DiCaprio and Barrymore. From a young age, she seemed
to know what she wanted: to be an actor like her parents. Her first
Jupiter return was just before her twelfth birthday, an average age for

the event, and she happily attended a stage school. By the time of her first Saturn opposition, when she was about fourteen and a half, she had dropped out of stage school and begun to attend an ordinary school due to her mother's financial difficulties. She also changed her career path from that of actress to undertaker!

The differences

Leonardo, Drew and Angelina all had just one Jupiter return. Leonardo's return was a few months earlier than expected whilst Drew and Angelina's were a bit later than expected. In contrast to Leonardo, Drew and Angelina had to grow up quickly because the period between their first Jupiter return and last Saturn opposition of adolescence is much shorter than Leonardo's. Additionally, Angelina only had one Saturn opposition compared to the three oppositions of Leonardo and Drew. This can be seen astrologically in the chart below in the final column showing the period between the first Jupiter return and the final Saturn opposition.

Jupiter return Saturn opp	Age at Jupiter return	Hits	Age at Saturn opp	Hits	Time between 1st Jupiter return and last Saturn opp in adolescence
Leonardo 11 Nov 1974	Pisces Mar 1986 11y 4m	1	Cancer Feb 1990 15y 3m; Sept 1990 15y 10m; Oct 1990 15y 11m	3	4y 7m
Drew 22 Feb 1975	Pisces Feb 1987 12y 0m	1	Cancer Mar 1989 14y 1m; Jun 1989 14y 4m; Dec 1989 14y 10m	3	2y 10m
Angelina 4 Jun 1975	Aries May 1987 11y 11m	1	Cancer Jan 1990 14y 7m	1	2y 8m

Problems with the brickwork

Except in very unusual cases, most parents only have to deal with one or two adolescents at any one time. They will often know when there is a problem with their adolescent because there is a change in behaviour. By understanding when their child is going through the changes brought on by hormones and other factors, they can help to ease the growing process.

By contrast, teachers of adolescents may have hundreds of pupils to deal with. Although many of these pupils will grow up with only a few hitches, there are always a few who need extra support. For these pupils who are struggling, it is useful to examine their birth charts more closely. Children who drink or use drugs excessively are usually easy to spot. Their behaviour is erratic, their attendance is appalling and their physical appearance is alarming. Drew's problems during adolescence were picked up not only by the people who cared for her but also by the national press who bellowed out her problems for the whole world to hear. On closer inspection of her chart, it can be seen that her natal Mars and Moon are implicated in the first Saturn opposition (8 March 1989): transiting Saturn was conjunct her natal Mars and in opposition to her natal Moon. Saturn/Moon contacts can add a depressive element to the personality, and sadly Drew attempted suicide during this time. Because Saturn's opposition took place in the sign of Capricorn (conjunct Mars in Capricorn and also opposite the Moon in Cancer), Drew needed stable, family support which her mother was unable to provide at that time. Thankfully for her, the singer, and advocate of sobriety David Crosby allowed Drew to stay with him and his family. After a period of time with him, Drew began proceedings to become legally emancipated from her mother. Drew has written extensively of this stage of her life in her aptly named autobiography *Little Girl Lost* which was published just after her final Saturn opposition in 1990.

Like Drew, Angelina came from a family of actors. During adolescence she has indicated she was continually bullied (the only one of the sample celebrity group to make this complaint) for her unusual features and underweight frame. Although she only experienced one Jupiter return and one Saturn opposition (at the times we would expect), Jolie was a strange child who didn't really fit in amongst her peers. Had she been in a mainstream school, she would have stood out as a troubled pupil. On closer investigation of her chart, it can be seen that her natal Jupiter is square to her natal Saturn, a difficult aspect that takes practice to handle effectively, which a young adolescent would not know how to do. Her natal Moon and Mars are in conjunction with Jupiter (and thus also square to Saturn) and both planets oppose Pluto. At the first Jupiter return, transiting Jupiter would have set off a number of intense issues for Angelina. She began cutting herself to release the tension she felt and she decided to completely change her career path. During the time between her first Jupiter return and final Saturn opposition, Angelina decided to give up her acting aspirations as she wanted to be a funeral director and even took embalming classes. She did eventually work through these issues and return to acting. As Angelina's recent shocking disclosure of her decision to have an elective double mastectomy was announced, the planet Uranus was transiting this sensitive point of her chart. Jolie's difficulties with family relationships (particularly with her father and brother) are well documented. She had to learn the Saturn in Aries lesson of balancing between the needs of the self and those of others.

Thankfully, the right type of support was available for Drew and Angelina. Although they may look back on their adolescence as a time of great troubles, they survived the experience.

Let us examine cases where other adolescents weren't so fortunate. The English word 'adolescence' has its root meaning in the Latin word *adolescere* which simply means to grow up. Although we typically associate adolescence with the teenage years, the changes towards maturity can begin earlier and later. In Western culture, the stereotypical focus tends to be on sexual development with the more significant cognitive and psychological development overlooked. Western culture's pre-occupation with breast size and its sole focus on their sexual role, as well as worry and obsession over penis size, means that the transitional stage into adulthood is fraught with furtive comparisons to more mature peers and worry over slow development.

The average onset of puberty is ten or eleven years of age for girls and twelve or thirteen years for boys.[27] Environmental and hereditary factors play a large part in when adolescence occurs and for how long it lasts. The major hallmarks of adolescence appear to be focused on menarche for the girls and ejaculation for the boys. Here there is the emergence of a huge gender divide: whilst girls are taught to be private or even ashamed about their monthly cycles, boys are encouraged to be boastful about their sexual prowess. Girls are conditioned to be careful of unwanted pregnancy, whereas boys are seemingly permitted to simply be boys in the ever static adolescent games of sexual inequality.

Interestingly, studies show that girls who mature earlier than their peers are more likely to have unwanted pregnancies and are more likely to be exposed to alcohol and drugs.[28] Thus girls who begin adolescence earlier are also more likely to perform less well in school.[29] Boys who mature more quickly than their peers are more likely to be sexually active earlier and to take sexual risks before they have developed the necessary cognitive skills to cope.[30]

Perhaps it is because girls develop first, and for a couple of years are bigger than their male counterparts, that they are more prone to eating disorders, and perhaps because boys are so competitive over their development, their perception of being smaller or more inadequate can lead to an obsession with violence or domination. It is rare for boys to be anorexic and rare for girls to become interested in guns. Further, during the growth spurts girls put on body fat, whereas boys put on muscle. For some of these reasons, anorexia and other forms of self-harm tend to be issues for young females, and a fascination with violence, or outward forms of expressing violence, tend to be issues for boys. In astrology, we might attribute these tendencies to Venus in the charts of girls and Mars in the charts of boys. Much more comment could be made of these astrological factors, but for the purposes of *Growing Pains* the emphasis will be on Jupiter and Saturn.

Anorexia

Anorexia is not a new disease but is a dangerous condition that has received much attention since Karen Carpenter succumbed to its effects at the age of thirty-two in 1983. The usual victims of anorexia are young women who typically exhibit signs of the disease during adolescence. Although the root causes of anorexia are complicated, the general issues of it tend to centre on self-control and body image.

Karen Carpenter
2 March 1950, 11:45 EST
New Haven Connecticut 41°N18'29" 072°W55'43"
Rodden rating: AA; Collector: Steinbrecher
Jupiter in Aquarius ruled by Uranus in Cancer
Saturn in Virgo ruled by Mercury in Aquarius
First Jupiter return: February 1962, age 11 years, 11 months
Last Saturn opposition: February 1966, age 15 years, 11 months
Time between: 4 years

In Karen's timed chart, it can be seen that her natal Pluto and Moon are in conjunction in the sign of Leo. Not only are there issues of extreme control, her self-image is particularly sensitive. As Mercury and Jupiter in Aquarius are opposite the Moon and Pluto, these issues are triggered by her Jupiter returns.

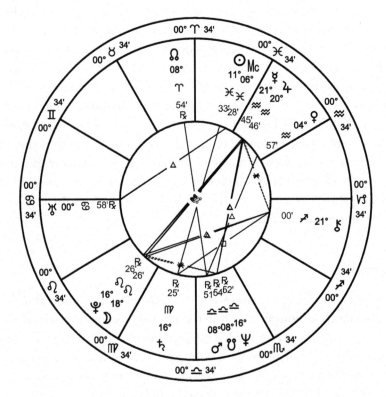

Karen Carpenter – 2 March 1950

Natally, Karen's Jupiter was in the sign of Aquarius, which is ruled by Uranus in Cancer. Because Uranus is conjunct her ascendant, Karen may have held unusual views about family. For example, she lived at home with her parents until the age of twenty-six and had an unusually close relationship with her brother.

Karen's first Jupiter return was followed by a Saturn conjunction with natal Jupiter, indicating her growth cycle was immediately followed by a blockage. It is as if her body was given the signal to grow and then immediately given the signal to stop. Additionally, her cycles of growth appear to be tied into Jupiter's conjunctions to Saturn by transit. In her lifetime, transiting Jupiter made three conjunctions with Saturn. The first was just after the age of six, the second was just after her first Saturn oppositions when she began her extreme diets and the third was when she wed her husband in August 1980, just months after her first Saturn return.

During her first Saturn oppositions, Karen had begun making her first recordings as part of the Richard Carpenter Trio alongside her pianist brother and bassist Wes Jacobs. In her chart, Saturn is opposite her Sun, and thus issues of self will be triggered by transiting Saturn. Sometime after this Karen began dieting and, if we are to believe *The Karen Carpenter Story*, the reason she began dieting was because she had been referred to as Richard Carpenter's chubby sister. This triggered a life-long obsession with extreme weight management that ultimately led to her untimely demise at the age of thirty-two.

In her natal chart, Saturn in Virgo was in opposition to her Sun in Pisces, indicating that it may have been difficult for Karen to appreciate her soft and sensitive nature. Saturn in Virgo requires precision and accuracy, traits that a Sun in Pisces just doesn't understand. As Saturn continued his journey through Karen's chart, this theme of incongruence contributed to her lack of self love and acceptance. During every single Saturn transit, she evaluated her position in life and made a critical decision about her self-worth. In 1978-79, The Carpenters were at the height of their career. In addition to transiting Jupiter conjunct to natal Saturn, during this time Saturn made three oppositions to Karen's natal Sun and then completed its own return.

In September 1982, as transiting Saturn was conjunct Neptune and in a trine aspect to her natal Jupiter, Karen controversially gained thirty pounds on medically-supervised intervention. She died of heart irregularities a few months later.

Lena Zavaroni
4 November 1963, 0:45 GMT
Greenock, Scotland 55°N57' 0004°W45'
Rodden rating: AA; Collector: Wright
Jupiter in Aries, ruled by Mars in Sagittarius
Saturn in Aquarius, ruled by Uranus in Virgo
First Jupiter return: May 1975, age 11years, 6 months
Final Saturn opposition (series of 3): July 1977, age 13 years, 8 months
Time between: 2 years, 2 months

By the time Lena experienced her first Jupiter return a few months after her eleventh birthday, she was already a star, having won the talent

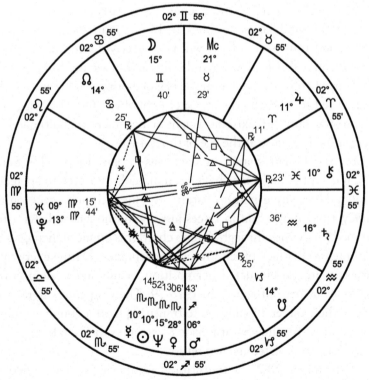

Lena Zavaroni – 4 November 1963

show *Opportunity Knocks* and then travelling to America to perform on the *Johnny Carson Show*. She was a beautiful, if precocious child, the owner of a phenomenal voice. She knew exactly what she wanted to do with her life.

With Jupiter in Aries, Lena would have been naturally exuberant and ambitious. Her energy and enthusiasm would have been contagious, and probably irritating to less energetic personalities. During the period of time between her Jupiter return and Saturn opposition, she began to grow rapidly, a trait that did not go unnoticed by her costume fitters who complained that they had to continually let the seams out of her clothes.

As noted in the Saturn in Aquarius section, as her Saturn opposition took hold, Lena began to hate her body. Natally, Lena had Saturn in Aquarius and all the problems of self-consciousness became apparent in an extremely short period of time in the two years and two months between her first Jupiter return and first Saturn opposition. Anorexia took hold and with the final Saturn opposition at the age of just thirteen years and nine months, her growing phase was significantly short. She later said the costumes prevented her from developing as a woman.

A more detailed look at her birth chart reveals she has a concentration of planets in Scorpio, indicating issues of control would be prominent in her life. Her natal Jupiter is on the receiving end of some very intense attention from Uranus, Pluto, her Sun, Mercury and Neptune. Of course, with the first Jupiter return, this intensity would have been stimulated by Jupiter. At Saturn's first opposition, the same type of energies would lead to self-doubt and a need to test her sense of self-control. With Saturn's ruler in Virgo, much of the testing could have been carried out in terms of health issues and day to day routine.

Sadly, opportunity knocked but the reality of seeing one's self with any sense of balance was lost on this wonderful talent.

Jupiter return Saturn opp	Age at Jupiter return	Hits	Age at Saturn opp	Hits	Time between 1st Jupiter return and last Saturn opp in adolescence
Karen 2 Mar 1950	Aquarius Feb 1962 11y 11m	1	Virgo May 1965, 15y 3m; July 1965 15y 5m; Feb 1966 15y 11m	3	4y 0m
Lena 4 Nov 1963	Aries May 1975 11y 7m	1	Aquarius Nov 1976 13y 0m; Dec 1976 13y 1m; July 1977 13y 9m	3	2y 2m

Boys who kill

During the 1990s, school shootings were prominently reported in the newspapers. Nearly all school shootings are carried out by adolescent boys. Research into why teenage boys kill their classmates and teachers indicates that whilst profiling yields little useful information, there are similarities amongst the shooters. For example, shooters don't snap one day and start shooting – they make plans, acquire weapons and they talk to their friends about their plans. In the months leading up to their crimes, they also try, unsuccessfully, to fit in with their peers. It is also common for behavioural medication to have been prescribed, indicating that the problems were evident before the crime took place. This really does mean there are no surprises about which boys might be prone to commit violent crimes.

Barry Loukaitis
26 February 1981
Seattle, Washington USA 47°N36'23" 122°W19'51"
Noon chart (time unknown)
Jupiter in Libra ℞, Venus in Aquarius
Saturn in Libra ℞, Venus in Aquarius
First Jupiter return (series of 3): Nov 1992, age 11 years, 9 months
Saturn opposition: Mar 1997, age 16 years, 1 month
Time between: 4 years, 3 months

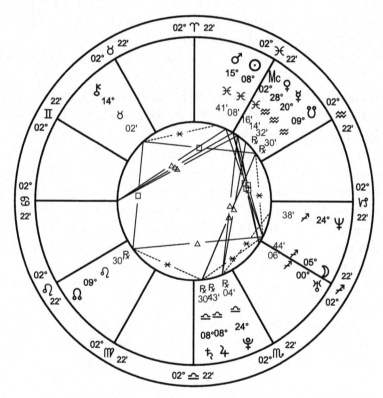

Barry Loukaitis – 26 February 1981

Barry's Jupiter and Saturn are conjunct to within only about 13 minutes
of arc degree, and both were in retrograde motion at the time of his
birth. This means that every Jupiter and Saturn transit triggers this
configuration. Usually a favourable aspect between Jupiter and Saturn is
viewed in a positive light: it usually denotes steady growth, a respect for

law and order and great potential for success because of the understanding of hard work bringing good fortune. As Barry was an honour student, there indeed was a promising future.

With both Jupiter and Saturn in Libra, issues around relationships would be the most prominent themes of his growth cycle. With the ruler of both planets being Venus in Aquarius, Barry would have come across as an eccentric to his peers. He may have felt he was different to everyone else but someone with Venus in Aquarius likes to belong to a group. He would have needed to be assured that it is okay to be different. From his birth chart set for noon, it can be seen that his natal Moon is conjunct Uranus in Sagittarius. He may have suffered from erratic mood swings and perhaps viewed his mother as unreliable.

His first Jupiter return was in November 1992, the second of the series of three was in April 1993 and the final one was in July 1993. His single Saturn opposition was in March 1997, making the period between the first Jupiter return and Saturn opposition about four years, three months. During this time frame, Barry's parents separated and then divorced following his mother's discovery of his father's infidelity. She often spoke to Barry about killing herself, and even told him he would also have to kill himself on the allotted day, 14 February 1996. Instead, on 2 February 1996, Barry dressed himself up as a gunslinger, walking into his school and murdered two of his classmates and his algebra teacher. During the time of the murders, Barry's Jupiter was in a square aspect to his natal Jupiter/Saturn conjunction.

He was given two life sentences and an additional 205 years without the possibility of parole in September 1997, about six months after his Saturn opposition. During his trial, it emerged that Barry was severely bullied by his classmates, was a fan of violent films and books, was on behavioural medication and had a family history of depression.

Kipland Kinkel
30 August 1982
Springfield Oregon 44°N02'47" 123°W01'15"
Noon chart, time unknown
Jupiter in Scorpio, ruled by Pluto in Libra
Saturn in Libra, ruled by Venus in Leo

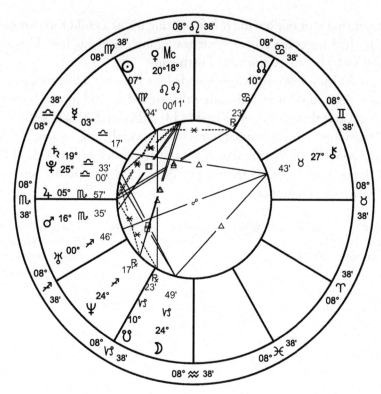

Kipland Kinkle – 30 August 1982

First Jupiter return (series of 3): December 1993, age 11 years, 5 months
Final Saturn opposition (series of 3): March 1998, age 15 years, 7 months
Time between: 4 years, 3 months

Kipland "Kip" Kinkel, an extreme example of the problems that can be
experienced in adolescence, murdered his parents when he was fifteen
years old. Kinkel was born on 30 August 1982 with Jupiter in Scorpio
and Saturn in Libra. He experienced his first Jupiter return in December
1993 at 11 years four months, but owing to the forward and retrograde
motions of transiting Jupiter, experienced three returns, the final one in
July 1994. He also experienced three Saturn oppositions, the first in July
1997 at age fourteen years eleven months and the final one at fifteen
years seven months in mid-March 1998.

Kip's Saturn is conjunct Pluto. Both are likely to be square to his
Moon in Capricorn and his natal Mars and Jupiter are in Scorpio, all
echoing issues of power. Because of power issues (either having it and

not wanting it or not having it but wanting it), as a child Kip may have felt he had no control over what was going on in his life. This may explain why he was so fascinated with guns.

On 20 May 1998, he was suspended for bringing a loaded gun into school. As a punishment, his father threatened to send him to boarding school. Later that afternoon, Kip shot his father in the back of the head and when his mother returned home from work, she was also fatally shot by her son. The following day, Kip went to school and shot dead two fellow pupils and injured twenty-two others. He is currently serving a 111 year prison sentence.

Jupiter return Saturn opp	Age at Jupiter return	Hits	Age at Saturn opp	Hits	Time between 1st Jupiter return and last Saturn opp in adolescence
Barry Loukaitis 26 Feb 1981	Libra Nov 1992, 11y 9m; Apr 1993 12y 2m; Jul 1993 12y 5m	3	Libra Mar 1997 16 y 1m	1	4y 3m
Kip Kinkel 30 Aug 1982	Scorpio Dec 1993 11y 4m; Jun 1994 11y 10m; Aug 1994 12 y 0m	3	Libra Jul 1997 14y 11m; Sep 1997 15y 1m; Mar 1998 15y 7m	3	4y 3m

Dyslexia

Dyslexia is a learning difficulty that affects the fluency of a person's ability to read and write. Certain languages such as English, French and Arabic are more difficult to read because of complex orthographies. Spanish, Finnish and Italian have more shallow orthographies and so are easier to master. Interestingly, Japanese has a shallow orthography but because it uses the logogram symbols rather than letters, different types of dyslexia present themselves to readers of that language.

Pupils learn to read around the age of six. This is the time of their first Jupiter opposition. The process of learning to read typically involves rote learning of the letters and corresponding sounds. The mastery of this early stage of reading is usually dependent on the planet Mercury's placement in the chart. However, the later stage of learning to read, putting sounds and letters together to form words, requires the leap of faith of Jupiter.

About a year after the first Jupiter opposition is the first Saturn square. Saturn rules the teeth, so it can be very easy to spot a seven-year-old as the front milk teeth are usually missing. The learning process at this stage requires the practice of the newly acquired reading skills. Although some educational theories do not begin teaching children how to read and write until after the first Saturn square, children in mainstream schools who don't display signs of a mastery of their language by the first Saturn square should be referred for further learning help and support. It only stands to reason that children who have not mastered the written language will fall further and further behind. And usually things come to a head by the Saturn opposition at fifteen when preparations for exams begin in earnest.

Most importantly, children who have dyslexia should be encouraged to practise their reading and writing skills rather than use it as an excuse to give up.

Kip at the age of six

Kip's problems started well before the final Saturn opposition and it is worth looking at his early education to gain an insight into the astrological significations. His late August birthday would have meant that he was the youngest member of his class when he started in September 1987. He was born into a family of academics, his parents both being Spanish teachers. His Mercury is in Libra so working with a partner in the rote learning stage of reading may have helped him (although Mercury in Libra is so sociable he would need constant encouragement to keep him on task!). Just after Kip's first Jupiter opposition at the age of five, in April 1988, the family moved to Spain where he attended a non-English speaking school. The teachers in Spain regarded him as immature and lacking in physical and emotional development. When he returned after this sabbatical year to start school in September 1990, just before his final Saturn square (of three), his parents agreed to make him repeat the first grade. This would have meant that he would have gone from being the youngest child in the classroom to being the oldest child. A few years later, he was diagnosed with dyslexia and received extensive educational support. Thus Kip's learning disabilities, as well as his age, set him apart from his peers.

Keanu Reeves

Keanu's Mercury in Capricorn usually indicates a methodical approach to the rote learning phase of reading. However, his Mercury makes an awkward contact to his natal Jupiter. Additionally, Keanu's Jupiter in Taurus opposes his Neptune and Moon in Scorpio. Just before his first Jupiter opposition shortly before his sixth birthday, Keanu's Saturn was conjunct his Jupiter, indicating there may have been a lack of faith in the reading process. He may have looked at the letters and shrugged his little shoulders. Saturn was conjunct his Jupiter at his first Jupiter opposition and then for the third time a few months later. The Saturn/Jupiter opposition in June 1971 was square his natal Saturn. This is an incredible blockage to his education and his teachers should have been a bit more attentive to his learning needs! Unfortunately, although he was diagnosed with dyslexia, he did not receive a high school diploma.

Cher

Cher's Mercury in Taurus usually indicates a hands-on approach to the rote learning stage of reading. One of the methods recommended by Maria Montessori involves cutting out letters from sandpaper to aid kinesthetic learning and Cher may have benefited from doing this.

Mercury is in an uncomfortable aspect to Jupiter and Chiron so she may have found the learning-to-read process painful. With both Mars and Pluto in a square aspect to Mercury, she has a strong sense of survival which perhaps explains how she succeeded – despite her dyslexia – and perhaps also helps to explain how she was able to conceal the fact that she was having problems with reading. Saturn in Cancer opposes her natal Moon and is square to Chiron/Jupiter. When she had her first Saturn square a few months before she turned seven, there may have been family difficulties that distracted her. Cher's dyslexia remained untreated.

Jupiter return Saturn opp	Jupiter return	Hits	Saturn opp	Hits	Time between 1st Jupiter return and last Saturn opp in adolescence
Fergie 27 Apr 1975	Aries Mar 1987	1	Cancer Mar, June, Dec 1989	3	2y 9m
Robert Downey Jr 4 Apr 1965	Taurus Jul, Nov 1976, Mar 1977	3	Pisces Nov 1978, Feb, Jul 1979	3	3y 0m
Oprah Winfrey 29 Jan 1954	Gemini Jul 1965	1	Scorpio April 1970	1	4y 10m
Steve Jobs 24 Feb 1955	Cancer Aug 1966	1	Scorpio Jul, Oct 1970, April 1971	3	3y 11m
Pamela Anderson 1 Jul 1967	Leo Oct 1978, Jan, Jun 1979	3	Aries Oct 1981	1	3y 0m
Tom Hanks 9 Jul 1956	Virgo Oct 1967, Feb, Jun 1968	3	Scorpio May 1971	1	3y 7m
Madonna 16 Aug 1958	Libra Nov 1969, Jun, Jul 1970	3	Sagittarius Aug, Nov 1972, May 1973	3	3y 6m
Hillary Clinton 26 Oct 1947	Sagittarius Feb, Apr, Oct 1959	3	Leo Apr, Jul, 1963 Jan 1964	3	4y 2m

Jupiter return Saturn opp	Jupiter return	Hits	Saturn opp	Hits	Time between 1st Jupiter return and last Saturn opp in adolescence
Sigourney Weaver 8 Oct 1949	Capricorn Jan, Feb 1961	2	Natal Virgo Apr, Sept 1965, Jan 1966	3	5y 0m
Marilyn Monroe 1 Jun 1926	Pisces Apr 1938 11y 11m; Aug 1938 12y 2m; Dec 1938 12y 6m	3	Natal Scorpio Apr, Jun 1941	2	3y 2m
Jodie Foster 19 Nov 1962	Pisces Mar 1974	1	Aquarius Jul 1976	1	2y 4m
Dustin Hoffman 8 Aug 1937	Capricorn Feb 1949	1	Aries Aug 1951	1	2y 6m
Bob Dylan 24 May 1941	Taurus May 1953	1	Taurus Jan 1953, Apr, Oct 1955	3	2y 6m
Julia Child 15 Aug 1912	Sagittarius Dec 1923	1	Gemini Jun, Sept 1927	2	3y 7m
Cher 20 May 1946	Libra Nov 1957	1	Cancer Jan 1961	1	3y 2m

Jupiter return Saturn opp	Jupiter return	Hits	Saturn opp	Hits	Time between 1st Jupiter return and last Saturn opp in adolescence
Elton John 25 Mar 1947	Scorpio Jan, May, Sept 1959	3	Leo Jan 1962	1	3y 0m
Olivia Newton-John 26 Sept 1948	Sagittarius Jan 1960	1	Virgo Apr 1964	1	4y 1m
Christopher Reeve 25 Sept 1952	Libra Jul, Nov 1964, Mar 1965	3	Libra Apr 1968	1	3y 8m
Annie Lennox 25 Dec 1954	Cancer Sept 1966, Jan, May 1967	3	Scorpio Jun, Nov, 1970 Mar 1971	3	4y 6m
Shirley Temple-Black 23 Apr 1928	Aries Jan 1940	1	Sagittarius Jul 1943	1	3y 6m
Sean Connery 25 Aug 1930	Cancer Aug 1942	1	Capricorn Aug 1944 Jan, Apr 1995	3	2y 8m
Joan Collins 23 May 1933	Taurus Sept 1944	1	Aquarius Aug 1947, Mar, May 1948	3	3y 8m
Keanu Reeves 2 Sep 1964	Taurus Jun 1976	1	Pisces Nov 1977, Jan, Jul 1978	3	2y 0m

Afterword

Adolescence is a state of change that everyone has to go through, but very few enjoy. Added to the uncertainty of when the changes will stop or start is the expectation that adolescents will somehow 'get through it' without any help or support. As a collective society, we expect adolescents to be troublesome, full of raging hormones and unstable emotions. Quite frankly, we often give them the idea we don't like them very much.

If we're lucky, as adults, all we have are memories of a few embarrassing moments no one else noticed or can recall. If unlucky, we are left with the notion we are unforgiven or emotionally damaged or we find ourselves in the continual process of trying to fix up where we went wrong. By understanding how we have matured, we can resolve our own past agonies and adjust our attitude towards our own adolescence.

When we understand ourselves, we can help our adolescents to understand and help themselves to find the pulse of their growth and development.

The celebrity examples presented here offer just some of the possibilities of the process of reaching our potential. Included in this book were also extreme examples of adolescents who didn't receive the help they needed at crucial times, and details of the consequences of leaving these vulnerable people to their own devices.

If we can understand the potential problems, we can be ready with the support that is needed. As concerned parents and teachers we can utilise our knowledge of the growth stage (Jupiter) to encourage students to take advantage of new opportunities and new situations, and the developing stage (Saturn) to refine and consolidate their newly learned skills. Not everyone will want to be a celebrity, of course, but most people want to make the most of their lives.

Appendix 1

Jupiter and Saturn in their
Signs by Calendar Year

*Where there is more than one sign, you need to look up your date of
birth under each section.*
Alternatively go to www.astro.com and enter your birth details.

Year	Jupiter	Saturn
1920	Leo or Virgo	Virgo
1921	Virgo	Virgo or Libra
1922	Libra or Scorpio	Libra
1923	Scorpio or Sagittarius	Libra or Scorpio
1924	Sagittarius or Capricorn	Scorpio or Libra
1925	Capricorn	Scorpio
1926	Capricorn or Aquarius	Scorpio or Sagittarius
1927	Aquarius, Pisces or Aries	Sagittarius
1928	Pisces, Aries or Taurus	Sagittarius
1929	Taurus or Gemini	Sagittarius or Capricorn
1930	Gemini or Cancer	Capricorn
1931	Cancer or Leo	Capricorn
1932	Leo or Virgo	Capricorn or Aquarius
1933	Virgo or Libra	Aquarius
1934	Libra or Scorpio	Aquarius
1935	Scorpio or Sagittarius	Aquarius or Pisces
1936	Sagittarius or Capricorn	Pisces
1937	Capricorn or Aquarius	Pisces or Aries
1938	Aquarius or Pisces	Pisces or Aries
1939	Pisces or Aries	Aries
1940	Aries or Taurus	Aries or Taurus
1941	Taurus of Gemini	Taurus
1942	Gemini or Cancer	Taurus or Gemini
1943	Cancer or Leo	Gemini

Year	Jupiter	Saturn
1944	Leo or Virgo	Gemini
1945	Virgo or Libra	Gemini or Cancer
1946	Libra or Scorpio	Cancer or Leo
1947	Scorpio or Sagittarius	Leo
1948	Sagittarius or Capricorn	Leo or Virgo
1949	Capricorn or Aquarius	Virgo or Leo
1950	Aquarius or Pisces	Virgo or Libra
1951	Pisces or Aries	Libra or Scorpio
1952	Aries or Taurus	Libra
1953	Taurus or Gemini	Libra or Scorpio
1954	Gemini or Cancer	Scorpio
1955	Cancer, Leo or Virgo	Scorpio
1956	Virgo or Leo or Libra	Scorpio or Sagittarius
1957	Libra or Scorpio	Sagittarius
1958	Libra or Scorpio	Sagittarius
1959	Scorpio or Sagittarius	Sagittarius or Capricorn
1960	Sagittarius or Capricorn	Capricorn
1961	Capricorn or Aquarius	Capricorn
1962	Aquarius or Pisces	Capricorn or Aquarius
1963	Pisces or Aries	Aquarius
1964	Aries or Taurus	Aquarius or Pisces
1965	Taurus or Gemini	Pisces
1966	Gemini or Cancer	Pisces
1967	Leo or Virgo	Pisces or Aries
1968	Virgo, Leo or Libra	Aries
1969	Libra, Virgo or Scorpio	Aries
1970	Scorpio or Libra	Taurus
1971	Scorpio or Sagittarius	Taurus or Gemini
1972	Sagittarius or Capricorn	Gemini
1973	Capricorn or Aquarius	Gemini or Cancer
1974	Aquarius or Pisces	Cancer or Gemini
1975	Pisces or Aries	Cancer or Leo
1976	Aries, Taurus or Gemini	Leo or Cancer
1977	Taurus, Gemini or Cancer	Leo or Virgo
1978	Gemini, Cancer or Leo	Virgo

Year	Jupiter	Saturn
1979	Leo, Cancer or Virgo	Virgo
1980	Virgo or Libra	Virgo or Libra
1981	Libra or Scorpio	Libra
1982	Scorpio or Sagittarius	Libra or Scorpio
1983	Sagittarius	Scorpio
1984	Sagittarius or Capricorn	Scorpio
1985	Capricorn or Aquarius	Scorpio or Sagittarius
1986	Aquarius or Pisces	Sagittarius
1987	Pisces or Aries	Sagittarius
1988	Aries, Taurus or Gemini	Sagittarius or Capricorn
1989	Taurus, Gemini or Cancer	Capricorn
1990	Cancer or Leo	Capricorn
1991	Leo or Virgo	Capricorn or Aquarius
1992	Virgo or Libra	Aquarius
1993	Libra or Scorpio	Aquarius
1994	Scorpio or Sagittarius	Aquarius or Pisces
1995	Sagittarius	Pisces
1996	Sagittarius or Capricorn	Pisces or Aries
1997	Capricorn or Aquarius	Aries
1998	Aquarius or Pisces	Aries
1999	Pisces, Aries or Taurus	Aries or Taurus
2000	Aries, Taurus or Gemini	Taurus or Gemini
2001	Gemini or Cancer	Taurus or Gemini
2002	Cancer or Leo	Gemini
2003	Leo or Virgo	Gemini or Cancer
2004	Virgo or Libra	Cancer
2005	Libra or Scorpio	Cancer or Leo
2006	Scorpio or Sagittarius	Leo
2007	Sagittarius or Capricorn	Leo or Virgo
2008	Capricorn	Virgo
2009	Capricorn or Aquarius	Virgo or Libra
2010	Aquarius, Pisces or Aries	Libra or Virgo
2011	Pisces, Aries or Taurus	Libra
2012	Taurus or Gemini	Libra or Scorpio
2013	Gemini or Cancer	Scorpio

Year	Jupiter	Saturn
2014	Cancer or Leo	Scorpio or Sagittarius
2015	Leo or Virgo	Sagittarius or Scorpio
2016	Virgo or Libra	Sagittarius or Capricorn
2017	Libra or Scorpio	Sagittarius or Capricorn
2018	Scorpio or Sagittarius	Capricorn
2019	Sagittarius or Capricorn	Capricorn
2020	Capricorn or Aquarius	Capricorn or Aquarius
2021	Aquarius or Pisces	Aquarius
2022	Pisces or Aries	Aquarius
2023	Aries or Taurus	Aquarius or Pisces
2024	Taurus or Gemini	Pisces or Aries

Appendix 2

A Millennium of
Jupiter/Saturn Conjunctions

Date	Element	Degree	Date of next conjunction nearest to the same degree
8 Nov 1007	Earth	13°Vir04' D	17 Jul 1802
7 Mar 1008		10°Vir22' R	
1 Jun 1008		08°Vir28' D	
20 Apr 1027	Fire	25°Ar25' D	19 Jun 1821
18 Nov 1047	Earth	05°Cap08' D	26 Jan 1842
19 Sept 1067	Earth	21°Vir25' D	21 Oct 1861
26 Feb 1087	Earth	03°Tau22' D	18 Apr 1881
9 Feb 1107	Earth	16°Cap27' D	28 Nov 1901
7 Aug 1127	Earth	29°Vir18' D	10 Sept 1921
4 Jun 1146	Earth	17°Tau30' D	8 Aug 1940
			20 Oct 1940
			15 Feb 1941
11 Dec 1166	Earth	21°Cap42' D	19 Feb 1961
8 Nov 1186	Air	12°Li03' D	31 Dec 1980
			4 Mar 1981
			24 Jul 1981
16 Apr 1206	Earth	25°Tau46' D	28 May 2000
5 Mar 1226	Air	02°Aq58' D	21 Dec 2020
21 Sept 1246	Air	19°Li07' D	31 Oct 2040
25 Jul 1265	Air	09°Ge41' D	7 Apr 2060
31 Dec 1285	Air	08°Aq01' D	15 Mar 2080
25 Dec 1305	Water	00°Sco49' D	18 Sept 2100
20 Apr 1306	Air	28°Li05' R	
19 Jul 1306	Air	26°Li00' D	
1 Jun 1325	Air	17°Ge52' D	15 Jul 2119
24 Mar 1345	Air	19°Aq01' D	14 Jan 2140

Date	Element	Degree	Date of next conjunction nearest to the same degree
25 Oct 1365	Water	07°Sco00' D	21 Dec 2159
9 Apr 1385	Air	25°Ge53' D	28 May 2179
16 Jan 1405	Air	23°Aq46' D	7 Apr 2199
14 Feb 1425	Water	17°Sco18' D	7 Apr 2060
18 Mar 1425		16°Sco32' R	
26 Aug 1425		12°Sco40' D	
14 Jul 1444	Water	08°Can57' D	
8 Apr 1464	Water	04°Pi35' D	
18 Nov 1484	Water	23°Sco10' D	
25 May 1504	Water	16°Can25' D	
31 Jan 1524	Water	09°Pi13' D	
18 Sept 1544	Water	28°Sco05' D	
25 Aug 1563	Water	29°Can10' D	
3 May 1583	Water	20°Pi10' D	
18 Dec 1603	Fire	08°Sag18' D	
16 Jul 1623	Fire	06°Leo36' D	
24 Feb 1643	Water	25°Pi06' D	
16 Oct 1663	Fire	12°Sag57'D	
24 Oct 1682	Fire	19°Leo08' D	
9 Feb 1683		16°Leo43' R	
18 May 1683		14°Leo30' D	
21 May 1702	Fire	06°Ar36' D	
5 Jan 1723	Fire	23°Sag19' D	
30 Aug 1742	Fire	27°Leo09' D	
18 Mar 1762	Fire	12°Ar21' D	
5 Nov 1782	Fire	28°Sag06' D	
17 Jul 1802	Earth	05°Vir07' D	
19 Jun 1821	Fire	24°Ar38' D	
26 Jan 1842	Earth	08°Cap54' D	
21 Oct 1861	Earth	18°Vir22' D	
18 Apr 1881	Earth	01°Tau35' D	
28 Nov 1901	Earth	13°Cap59' D	
10 Sept 1921	Earth	26°Vir35' D	

Date	Element	Degree	Date of next conjunction nearest to the same degree
8 Aug 1940	Earth	14°Tau26' D	
20 Oct 1940		12°Tau27' R	
15 Feb 1941		09°Tau07' D	
19 Feb 1961	Earth	25°Cap12' D	
31 Dec 1980	Air	09°Li29' D	
4 Mar 1981		08°Li06' R	
24 Jul 1981		04°Li56' D	
28 May 2000	Earth	22°Tau43' D	
21 Dec 2020	Air	00°Aq29' D	
31 Oct 2040	Air	17°Li55' D	
7 Apr 2060	Air	00°Ge46' D	
15 Mar 2080	Air	11°Aq52' D	
18 Sept 2100	Air	25°Li32' D	
15 Jul 2119	Air	14°Ge51' D	
14 Jan 2140	Air	17°Aq04' D	
21 Dec 2159	Water	07°Sco58' D	
28 May 2179	Air	23°Ge03' D	
7 Apr 2199	Air	28°Aq19' D	

Notes

1. 'Fergie: I was a lesbian.' *The Daily Mirror* www.mirror.co.uk/showbiz/ tm_headline=fergie--i-was-a-lesbian&method=full&objectid=18844637&siteid=89520-name_page.html. Retrieved April 2012.

2. Wilde, Jon. 'More than skin deep.' 8 November 2003. *The Guardian* http://film.guardian.co.uk/interview/interviewpages/0,6737,1080388,00.html. Retrieved 2 May 2008.

3. 'The 50 Most Generous Philanthropists.' *Business Week*. www.businessweek.com. Retrieved April 2012.

4. 'Pamela Anderson Biography.' Yahoo! Movies. http://movies.yahoo.com/movie/contributor/1800332320/bio. Retrieved 17 August 2010.

5. Mytnick, Colleen. 'Life According to Tom Hanks.' October 2009. *Cleveland Magazine*. www.clevelandmagazine.com. Retrieved 6 November 2010.

6. Rettenmund, Matthew. *Madonnica: The Woman & The Icon From A To Z*. Macmillan, 1995, p.45.

7. Ibid, p.45.

8. Walters, Barry 1 June 2006. 'Crucifixes, Leather and Hits'. *Rolling Stone*.

9. Grunt, Gary. 'Madonna's giant cross offensive.' 23 May 2006. http://news.bbc.co.uk/2/hi/entertainment/5006008.stm. Retrieved 28 May 2006.

10. 'Marilyn: The case for 'assisted suicide'. *Independent*, March 18 2007.

11. Hedin Benjamin (ed.), 2004, *Studio A: The Bob Dylan Reader*, p.259. Reproduced online by Joyce Carol Oates , 'Dylan at 60.' http://www.usfca.edu/~southerr/ondylan. html. Retrieved 29 September 2008.

12. 'The Pulitzer Prize Winners 2008: Special Citation.' Pulitzer. May 7, 2008. http://www.pulitzer.org/citation/2008,Special+Awards+and+Citations. Retrieved 6 September 2008.

13. Child, Julia. *My Life in France*, p.5. Duckworth Overlook, London, 2009.

14. Ibid p.18.

15. Ibid p.11.

16. Tobler, John (1992). *NME Rock 'N' Roll Years* (1st ed.). London: Reed International Books Ltd. p.391.

17. 'Rock Almanac: 30 June 2008.' spinner.com. http://www.history.com/this-day-in-history.do?action=Article&id=3403. Retrieved 16 March 2009.

18. Rogers, Thomas. 21 January 2009. 'Where have all the drag queens gone?' Salon. http://www.salon.com/mwt/feature/2009/01/31/drag/.Retrieved April 2012.

19. http://www.dailyrecord.co.uk/showbiz/celebrityinterviews/2011/07/18/old-age-just-gets-in-my-way-says-superstarsinger-cher-86908-23279092/ Retrieved April 2012.

20. Goodall, Nigel. *Elton John: The Visual Documentary*. Omnibus Press, London 1993.

21. 'Man of Steel.' *The Guardian*, September 17, 2002, accessed 14 October 2006.

22. Yule, Andrew, 'Neither Shaken Nor Stirred.' *Little, Brown Book Group*, London, 1992, p.21.

23. 'Mud & Glory.' April 2005. http://www.footballcentral.org/ sfa/associations/scottish-junior-football-association/junior_game/sean_connery.cfm. Retrieved 19 May 2008.

24. 'Terence Young: James Bond's Creator?' http://www.hmss.com/films/young.htm. Retrieved 29 September 2007.

25. 'Sean Connery', *Playboy* 1965-2011. http://seanconneryonline.com/art_playboy1165.htm. Retrieved 25 October 2011.

26. *Picture Post* magazine, 11 September 1954.

27. "For girls, puberty begins around 10 or 11 years of age and ends around age 16. Boys enter puberty later than girls – usually around 12 years of age – and it lasts until around age 16 or 17." 'Teenage Growth & Development: 11 to 14 Years'. pamf.org. http://www.pamf.org/teen/parents/health/growth-11-14.html. Retrieved April 2012.

28. Caspi, A., Lynam, D., MoYtt, T. E., & Silva, P. A. (1993). 'Unraveling girls' delinquency: biological, dispositional, and contextual contributions to adolescent misbehavior.' *Developmental Psychology*, Vol 32, pp. 631–635.

29. 'Pubertal maturation in female development.' *Paths through life*, Vol. 2. Stattin, Håkan; Magnusson, David; Hillsdale, NJ: Lawrence Erlbaum Associates, Inc. 1990.

30. Susman, EJ; Dorn, LD; Schiefelbein, VL. 'Puberty, sexuality, and health.' *Comprehensive Handbook of Psychology*. New York: Wiley; 2003.

Other Titles from The Wessex Astrologer
www.wessexastrologer.com

Martin Davis
Astrolocality Astrology: A Guide to What it is and How to Use it
From Here to There: An Astrologer's Guide to Astromapping

Wanda Sellar
The Consultation Chart
An Introduction to Medical Astrology
An Introduction to Decumbiture

Geoffrey Cornelius
The Moment of Astrology

Darrelyn Gunzburg
Life After Grief: An Astrological Guide to Dealing with Grief
AstroGraphology: The Hidden Link between your Horoscope and your Handwriting

Paul F. Newman
Declination: The Steps of the Sun
Luna: The Book of the Moon

Deborah Houlding
The Houses: Temples of the Sky

Dorian Geiseler Greenbaum
Temperament: Astrology's Forgotten Key

Howard Sasportas
The Gods of Change

Patricia L. Walsh
Understanding Karmic Complexes

M. Kelly Hunter
Living Lilith: the Four Dimensions of the Cosmic Feminine

Barbara Dunn
Horary Astrology Re-Examined

Deva Green
Evolutionary Astrology

Jeff Green
Pluto Volume 1: The Evolutionary Journey of the Soul
Pluto Volume 2: The Evolutionary Journey of the Soul Through Relationships
Essays on Evolutionary Astrology (ed. by Deva Green)

Dolores Ashcroft-Nowicki and Stephanie V. Norris
The Door Unlocked: An Astrological Insight into Initiation

Greg Bogart
Astrology and Meditation: The Fearless Contemplation of Change

Henry Seltzer
The Tenth Planet: Revelations from the Astrological Eris

Ray Grasse
Under a Sacred Sky: Essays on the Practice and Philosophy of Astrology

Martin Gansten
Primary Directions

Joseph Crane
Astrological Roots: The Hellenistic Legacy
Between Fortune and Providence

Bruce Scofield
Day-Signs: Native American Astrology from Ancient Mexico

Komilla Sutton
The Essentials of Vedic Astrology
The Lunar Nodes: Crisis and Redemption
Personal Panchanga: The Five Sources of Light
The Nakshatras: the Stars Beyond the Zodiac

Anthony Louis
The Art of Forecasting using Solar Returns

Petros Eleftheriadis
Horary Astrology: The Practical Way to Learn Your Fate

Oscar Hofman
Classical Medical Astrology

Bernadette Brady
Astrology, A Place in Chaos
Star and Planet Combinations

Richard Idemon
The Magic Thread
Through the Looking Glass

Nick Campion
The Book of World Horoscopes

Judy Hall
Patterns of the Past
Karmic Connections
Good Vibrations
The Soulmate Myth: A Dream Come True or Your Worst Nightmare?
The Book of Why: Understanding your Soul's Journey
Book of Psychic Development

Neil D. Paris
Surfing your Solar Cycles

Michele Finey
The Sacred Dance of Venus and Mars

David Hamblin
The Spirit of Numbers

Dennis Elwell
Cosmic Loom

Gillian Helfgott
The Insightful Turtle

Bob Makransky
Planetary Strength
Planetary Hours
Planetary Combination

ABOUT ALEX TRENOWETH

Since writing *Growing Pains*, Alex Trenoweth has travelled across the globe – from the UK to the US to South Africa, India, Australia and very soon, South America – lecturing on the topic of astrology and education. Her passion for teaching difficult adolescents, her sound research based on statistical analysis on pupil behaviour, a keen eye for observation as well as a deep love of astrology all contributed to her being voted 'Best International Astrologer of the Year 2015' by the Krishnamurti Institute of Astrology in Kolkata, India.

She may be in frequent demand at astrology conferences around the world, but she remains happiest in the classroom.

You can contact Alex through her website www.alextrenoweth.com

Lightning Source UK Ltd.
Milton Keynes UK
UKOW01f0440051117
312175UK00002B/56/P